Competitive
Interests

Competitive Interests

COMPETITION AND COMPROMISE
IN AMERICAN INTEREST
GROUP POLITICS

Thomas T. Holyoke

Georgetown University Press
Washington, DC

To Melanie,
for love and patience

Georgetown University Press, Washington, DC www.press.georgetown.edu

Library of Congress Cataloging-in-Publication Data

Holyoke, Thomas T.
    Competitive interests : competition and compromise in American interest group politics / Thomas T. Holyoke.
        p. cm. — (American governance and public policy series)
    Includes bibliographical references and index.
    ISBN 978-1-58901-779-5 (pbk. : alk. paper)
    1. Pressure groups—United States.   2. Lobbying—United States.   I. Title.
    JK1118.H56 2011
    324'.40973—dc22

                                                          2011004082

15 14 13 12 11   9 8 7 6 5 4 3 2
First printing

Printed in the United States of America

CONTENTS

ILLUSTRATIONS

Tables

ACKNOWLEDGMENTS

A DECADE has passed since I first started thinking about the ideas in this book. I was motivated to study interest group competition because as a graduate student I was reading literature that seemed not merely outdated but a little disconnected from reality as I thought I knew it. By the time I came to graduate school at the George Washington University, I had already worked for several organized interests as an assistant lobbyist and for the New York State Senate on the receiving end of a fair amount of lobbying, so I was sure that notions of subgovernments and iron triangles just could not be true. In other words, I was sure that competition was all-prevailing and great scholars such as Theodore Lowi were wrong. I wonder how many other dissertation projects have been founded in such hubris.

Countless individuals deserve credit for disabusing me of my naïve self-assurance and helping me better understand the important insights of those scholars who came before me. Without the time and insight they gave me I would never have learned to appreciate the considerable body of important work that has already been done in interest group scholarship, or been able to make what I hope is a decent contribution to that work. Linda Fowler, then at Syracuse University where I earned a master's degree, gets credit for convincing me to study interest groups in the first place (and for giving me my first insight into what it means to be a university professor and scholar). Steve Balla helped me develop my ideas from my very first year at the George Washington University and also pushed me to conduct independent research on lobbying that led to my first peer-reviewed publication while I was still taking courses. Chris Deering actually taught me interest group politics, helped me get my ideas for this project together, and of course, shepherded me through the dissertation process. Jeff Henig helped me explore state-level lobbying by charter schools, which led to a number of insights, publications, and most important, employment as a graduate student. I never took a class from Sarah Binder, but she was kind enough to comment on my chapter on interest groups and gridlock. Eric Lawrence and Hal Wolman get special thanks for setting my dissertation back by about half a year when they pointed out at a presentation that my original definition of "competition" made no sense at all. Finally, it was the late Lee Sigelman who offhandedly mentioned that all of these chapters could hang together as a book if I would just put some time into it. Five years later I hope I have proven him correct.

Whether they remember it or not, several others have given me tremendous advice over the years. Mike Heaney has been very encouraging and thoughtful in all of his comments over the years, especially during those summers when we both worked at the Centennial Center at the American Political Science Association (APSA). I also received a great deal of input and encouragement from Susan Webb Yackee, Marie Hojnacki, William Browne, Beth Leech, Bryan McQuide, and Marion Currinder. Frank Baumgartner gave kind encouragement after I was thoroughly beaten up by a conference discussant (on my paper ultimately published in the *American Journal of Political Science*). Thanks are also due to my fellow charter school research conspirators (and very good friends), Natalie Lacireno-Paquet and Heath Brown.

I owe debts I can never repay to several political "elites" whom I have worked for and with and who taught me a great deal about interest group politics, especially Brenda Neville, Nellie Santiago-Fernandez, Tom Schlessinger, Ralph Tabor, Eric Ciliberti, Jeri Marxman, Naomi Edelson, and Naomi Friedman. I am especially indebted to Scott Weiser of the Iowa Motor Truck Association who for three years taught me the politics, arts, and ethics of lobbying. I owe an equal debt to the many research assistants I have had over the years. Adam Schleich, Chet Riley, Ashlin Mattos, Caitlin Sawatsky, and Deborah Imbach have my undying gratitude (if too little compensation) for their work. So too do all of the students who have been in my Interest Group Politics course over the years. All of the lobbyists who generously gave their time (some gave it grudgingly, while others would just not stop talking) have my thanks. All of my colleagues at Hastings College and California State University, Fresno, have my thanks, especially Jeff Cummins who read and commented on parts of the papers leading to this work. I also want to thank Mark Somma who as associate dean paid for the copyediting of the chapter that initially went to various publishers. Thanks also to the dean of the Columbian College at the George Washington University and the Office of the Provost at California State University, Fresno, for funding this project, and to APSA's Centennial Center for giving me three summers worth of office space while I conducted follow-up research.

Finally, I would like to thank Don Jacobs and all of the staff at Georgetown University Press who were invaluable in publishing the final product.

Introduction

THE lobbyist had seen better years. His interest group, the Independent Insurance Agents of America (IIAA), was considered by many Washington insiders to be one of the great powerhouses of the capital city's lobbying community and he was used to getting his way. That was until now, for 1998 was looking more and more like it might be the worst year of his career. The issue was one of bread-and-butter significance to his members: Would banks and securities investment firms and brokers be permitted to sell insurance products in their own branch offices, thereby making independent agents obsolete? IIAA's historic position, unchanged since Congress first erected firewalls between these industries during the Great Depression with the Glass-Steagall Act, was an emphatic "no." For nearly seventy years insurance industry and agent groups had successfully kept their business safe from the hungry hounds of Manhattan's financial district. When bankers and brokers came to Capitol Hill to convince lawmakers that Glass-Steagall barriers were merely artifacts of an antiquated past now hindering twenty-first-century finance, the lobbyist would mobilize thousands of insurance agents to flood congressional offices with e-mail, letters, phone calls, and angry personal visits. Whatever sparks of interest members of Congress might have in aiding Wall Street was quickly squashed by IIAA's grassroots hammer.[1]

But 1998 was turning out to be different. With a strong economy, consumers were putting more of their savings into stocks rather than bank accounts, which made the bankers eager to find new lines of business to make up for their losses. As a result, the American Bankers Association, the Financial Services Roundtable, and the rest of the banking lobby were now pulling out all of the stops in their advocacy campaign. Multipurpose, one-stop-shop banks that sold investment and insurance products were now their issue du jour. And members of Congress were suddenly *listening* to them and *agreeing*, including House Banking Committee chair Jim Leach (R-IA). The defection of interest groups representing insurance corporations from the historical industry—agent alliance had helped bring about this frightening circumstance. Now the thoughtful, moderate, and political action committee (PAC)–averse

Iowa congressman was actually talking about repealing Glass-Steagall and giving banks and investment firms the regulatory flexibility necessary to create a new large and integrated financial industry.

Not that bankers and brokers were going to be allowed to jump in with both feet. No, Leach was striking a middle road with a compromise bill giving them only limited access to insurance markets. They could acquire insurance agencies as affiliates, but they could not directly employ their own agents or eliminate separate agencies entirely. For a lobbyist representing *independent* agents, Leach's "prudent compromise," as many lawmakers and lobbyists were calling it, meant a significant and unwelcome change in how they did business. Unfortunately, it also left him with little basis for saying "no" without appearing obstinate. Staging another insurance agent "lobby day" at the Capitol to press the electoral connection now would only create enemies. Lobbyists who persist in being stubborn in the face of consensus, he knew, soon find themselves marginalized, not only on this issue but on pretty much any other issue Congress might take up in the future affecting insurance agents. The proof of this came when Senate Banking Committee chair Alfonse D'Amato (R-NY) announced that insurance agents must compromise with the bankers or they would be cut out of any deal and Congress would enact legislation giving bankers and investors unbridled control over their business. His successor, Sen. Phil Gramm (R-TX), the following year was even less sympathetic to IIAA's pleas.

So the lobbyist threw in the towel and joined the banking, investing, and insurance corporation coalition, helping to turn Leach's bill into the landmark Gramm-Leach-Bliley Act of 1999. He knew the independent agents he represented would be angry about the compromise; they were, but the alternative would have been even worse. Combined, bankers, Wall Street investors, and insurance companies had the resources to outlast IIAA in a protracted fight. In the end there really was no choice but to accept the new bill. At least bankers and Wall Street firms were not getting everything they wanted. Members wanted the lobbyist to resist, but in the end pressure from Leach and Gramm, backed by the strength of the interest groups arrayed against IIAA, broke his political back.

This story does more than narrate the conclusion of a decade-long struggle between some of the most powerful organized interests in Washington from one lobbyist's point of view; it provides an example of the type of interest group politics that I believe has become increasingly common in the United States. Consider several features of the story. First, this conflict between industry groups was born out of competition over what was in the best interests of each organization's members. The banking and investing industries needed new markets to exploit, and insurance agents needed to defend their business from being swallowed by new all-purpose financial behemoths such as Citibank, Chase, and J. P. Morgan. What benefited one set of interests harmed another, forcing them to compete in an effort to shape public policy to their advantage.

Second, the interests of these groups' members had not always been competing. Since Glass-Steagall was enacted in the 1930s, these industries had managed to co-exist. Insurance was regulated by the states, whereas banking and investing were regulated primarily at the federal level. This jurisdictional split made it possible for insurance agents to go about their business without intruding on the market territory of bankers and investors. In other words, for decades their interests were not competing. Shrinking market opportunities in banking, however, and the virtual usurpation of insurance regulation by the federal government in the Riegle-Neal Interstate Deregulation Act of 1994 provided enough pressures and incentives for bankers and investors to want to push into the insurance business as they strove to create new, all-purpose superbanks. Now the interests of one set of groups were likely to harm another; now they were competing.

Third, this competition was not between the types of interest groups most of us think of as political enemies, that is, not the "good government" public interest group versus the big business group. Instead this conflict was among what political scientists call business and trade groups, or simply "economic" groups, because they represent market-driven businesses. These interest groups were fighting, not over some notion of the public good but over whose members were going to dominate the banking and insurance industries in the twenty-first century. Citizen's groups lobbying for regulation in the public interest were involved in the financial modernization wars of the 1990s, mostly attempting to apply Community Reinvestment Act rules (requiring investment in low-income neighborhoods) to whatever new financial entities emerged, but the truly titanic struggles were between economic interests. It was bankers and investors versus insurance agents, with opportunistic insurance companies supporting first one side and then the other.

Yet this story was also about political compromise, though under duress in the case of the insurance agent lobbyist. Group coalitions are common in modern politics, but coalitions like the one described here are based on compromises that require participants to give up something their members want in order to achieve other goals, in this case agents giving up their independence from bankers in return for the survival of their profession. But compromises are not always equal, and certainly in this case the agent lobbyist gave up a great deal. Gaining something through compromise was simply better than fighting because conflict was not likely to yield anything but ill will from legislators, wasted resources, and most likely, a serious loss of prestige.

Finally, this story was also about the many pressures influencing the choices modern lobbyists make. Members of organized interest groups employing lobbyists, be they members in the traditional sense or patron organizations funding the group, may desire one policy outcome, whereas a majority of legislators and the interest groups backing them may want something else. Lobbyists for interest groups must balance these pressures by deciding who is more important to please at that particular moment. For the IIAA lobbyist it became more important to accept the compromises offered by Leach, even if it meant risking the independence of his members and their loyalty to his organization. At least the banking and insurance industries did not get everything they wanted either.

This story should not seem unusual to any regular observer of American politics, so one might conclude that any study of interest group politics that does not in some way embrace competition has made a fatal mistake from the get-go. It is therefore a little surprising that group theory since the late 1960s has done just that, actually displacing an older theory that saw interest group competition as the governing dynamic of the political process. How scholarship went from one to the other, and has now very slowly started to swing back toward a more competitive view of group politics, is a story worth telling and a good place to start.

———■———

In chapter 1 I trace the history of interest group theory as it relates to competition, or the lack thereof, as well as recently observed changes in group politics suggesting that it is time to rethink prevailing theory. Chapter 2 embraces this challenge by combining the two core literatures in interest group research, how groups form by overcoming barriers to collective action and how lobbyists gain access to lawmakers to build a new model of lobbyist decision making in a competitive environment. Chapter 3 presents my research design: how I collected data by interviewing lobbyists working on six issues, and how I create some of the key measures used later in the book. In chapter 4 I use a multivariate model to empirically test hypotheses regarding three different pressures on lobbyists and how they make strategic decisions in a competitive environment.

The remaining chapters explore the implications of this "competitive model." Chapter 5 explores coalition formation by lobbyists under competitive pressures from other groups, as well as pressure from legislators and each lobbyist's group members. The next two chapters move into the realms of legislative and public policy studies. Chapter 6 focuses on how congressional committee chairs may use hearings to suppress group competition in support of their own agendas and how the level of group competition and conflict sometimes changes over the life of a bill. Chapter 7 completes this line of inquiry by examining whether conflict between competing groups contributes to gridlock, both within Congress and between Congress and the president. Finally, chapter 8 concludes the book by exploring the role that "neopluralism," a political theory based on competition between interest groups, plays in a democratic society.

Note

1. This narrative came from interviews I conducted with lobbyists in 2001 working on the Gramm-Leach-Bliley Act.

PART I

Causes of Interest Group Competition

CHAPTER 1

∎

Competition and Interest Group Politics

Aʀɢᴜɪɴɢ that Americans are competitive is hardly a great, new insight. Perhaps because we want to believe that free market competition leads to financial success or just because we live in a society with limited resources and opportunities, we seem to be constantly competing. We compete in sports to see who is physically superior so we can cover the winner in glory and medals while we send all other participants home tired and despondent. We compete in relationships, striving with others for recognition from parents, friends, bosses, and potential mates. When we cannot resolve our differences informally, we compete in court, forcing losing parties to transfer valued assets, usually money, to winners while gaining nothing in return. Competition means risking effort, resources, and even self-esteem in a struggle to achieve goals desired by others but not easily shared, even if we are willing to share. If there is a winner, then there must be at least one loser who may have lost more than what the goal was even worth by choosing to compete.

It comes then as no surprise that our politics, which determine who has the right to make public law and divvy up public resources, is competitive. The party that wins a majority of seats in Congress gets to govern; the losing party gets the back benches. A presidential candidate wins the general election and gets to set agendas; the other would-be leaders suffer ignominious defeat. Pro-life advocates will either ultimately succeed in overturning *Roe v. Wade* or pro-choice proponents will maintain the status quo. Journalists emphasize winners and losers when they write about politics, whether in tax reform legislation (Birnbaum and Murray 1986), business deregulation (Birnbaum 1992), or campaign finance reform (Drew 1999). Even many scholars portray politics as competitive, as exemplified in Harold Lasswell's (1936) famous book *Politics: Who Gets What, When, How.*

The Constitution's authors appear to have believed American politics would be competitive. Why else would checks and balances limiting political power have such a prominent role in their constitutional philosophy? Societies, James Madison argued, naturally subdivide into factions of citizens bound by common needs, beliefs, or desires, which he called "factions" and "interests." Consequently, he argued, the shared interest of one faction was likely to infringe on those of others, making it impossible for government to satisfy all factions simultaneously; thus he concluded in *Federalist No. 10* that group competition was both threatening and inevitable. So, were he alive today, Madison might be surprised to learn that for decades, scholars have largely rejected the idea that social groups regularly compete for power and influence in American politics. Social factions may have competing interests in the abstract, prevailing theory holds (after overthrowing an older tradition that assumed Madison was right), but legislators and lobbyists found it to their advantage to quietly partition power and political territory among themselves rather than openly compete. Understanding how this theory came to be and why it is now time bound is essential to make the case that group competition is alive and well today and deserves to be studied. It is, I believe, essential for identifying a new theoretical step to take, one that synthesizes two literatures that have come to dominate the study of advocacy and will allow us to better understand the modern, often competitive, world of interest group politics.

From Competitive Pluralism to Interest Group Balkanization

The intellectual history of interest group scholarship is well documented and does not need to be repeated here beyond what is pertinent to my argument (see Baumgartner and Leech 1998; McFarland 2004 for good histories). Nonetheless, I begin where most histories of group politics start, with Arthur Bentley.

Pluralism and Its Critics

An early precursor of the Behavioral Revolution and the scientific study of politics, Bentley (1908), the intellectual partner of John Dewey, argued that politics was fundamentally about competition between groups of individuals bound by common experiences, desires, and beliefs.[1] Indeed, Bentley argued that groups are the basic units of society, so much so that the behavior of individuals cannot be understood outside of their group contexts; their wants and desires are defined by the group's collective identity, or its "interest." Large nations like the United States contain so many groups, drawn from different ethnic backgrounds and walks of life, that it is nearly impossible for clear and enduring majorities to emerge and provide consensus on the rules of society and the use of public resources. Sounding like Madison, Bentley argued that what we have instead are pluralities of group interests, often with beliefs and desires so different from each other that demands articulated by one group are likely to be perceived as threatening to the interests of others. Using political advocacy to embody these interests in public policy transforms this social competition into political competition.

Bentley's work was largely ignored in his own time, but forty years later elements of his belief in politics as competition among a plurality of groups were resurrected as the basis of an ambitious theory of politics and government. For pluralist scholars such as Earl Latham (1952) and especially David Truman (1951), competing social interests were the explicit cause of the mobilization of political interest groups. When members of one faction perceive those of another to be advocating for policy outcomes that threaten their interests, they organize and employ lobbyists to push back against these encroachments. This lobbying, in turn, prods other social groups to organize, continuing a wave of mobilizations that Truman labeled "Disturbance Theory." Compromise between these competing interests leading to new law and a division of public resources simply reflected a balance of power with policy favoring the stronger. For pluralists this mobilization and competition was the engine driving American politics. Indeed, it was more than just a theory about how American politics operated; it became a normative blueprint for how the government and political system ought to function (Dahl 1956). Thus, a nearly full-blown paradigm shift occurred in political theory when critics of pluralism managed to knock out its foundations and reverse its conclusions. Suddenly, prevailing theory held that no meaningful interest group competition took place in American politics at all.

Not that all critics of pluralism, even of Robert Dahl's (1961) less grandiose version of it, directly challenged its assumption that American society is a plurality of social groups with competing interests. Theodore Lowi (1969), E. E. Schattschneider (1960), and even C. Wright Mills (1956) were more or less willing to accept Bentley's and even Madison's view of society as composed of competing interests; they simply doubted that competition was manifesting as actual political conflict. Competition might exist in the abstract, but due to a combination of political pressure and human obfuscation it was not stimulating widespread mobilization and conflict because not all groups perceived their interests to be threatened. The reason, Schattschneider (1960) argued, was that elites who benefit from serving the interests of one group at the expense of another could, and very often did, frame issues and the policies addressing them as unthreatening or even benevolent. A policy status quo favoring privileged groups could be perpetuated and members of affected groups kept quiescent because the latter were left unaware that their interests were being harmed when lawmakers served the former's demands (Bachrach and Baratz 1962). Even if they did realize the threat, Mancur Olson (1965) demonstrated that we still cannot assume that members of the affected factions will mobilize to actually compete in the political arena. Rational self-interest may prevent individuals from contributing to a potentially mobilized group's actual organization.

These arguments became part of a larger literature on interest group balkanization and policy stasis that emerged in the late 1960s and to a considerable extent holds sway today. The core assumption is that political institutions, Congress in particular, have been intentionally designed in a decentralized fashion with multiple power centers because such a structure more readily allows elites to quietly aim benefits at constituencies key to their political survival without appearing to threaten the interests of others (Lowi 1972). After revolting against House Speaker Joseph Cannon in 1910, committees in Congress gained considerable autonomy from party leaders and the power to dictate policy outcomes within well-defined domains (or jurisdictions) of lawmaking, such as agriculture, defense, and transportation (Deering and Smith 1997, 30). Norms of self-selection and property rights made it possible for legislators to win and retain seats on committees with jurisdiction over policies crucial to interests in their home districts and states, interests so politically mobilized that appeasing them was crucial to their own reelection.

Most of these mobilized interests were, broadly speaking, economic in that they sought financial support and regulatory protection for their members. Commodities growers desired price supports to ensure profits, highway and defense contractors lobbied for project funds, and manufacturers wanted regulation to stymie domestic and foreign competitors (Stigler 1971, 1972; Peltzman 1976). Groups with similar demands only had to lobby a single committee with jurisdiction over their issues. Fortunately for them, committee legislators could afford to provide everyone benefits because budgets and discretionary spending were growing from the 1950s through the 1970s; deficit spending made more money available even when these surpluses proved inadequate (Peterson 1992).

John Mark Hansen (1991), for example, describes how pro-farm state legislators made careers for themselves by serving agriculture constituencies and their interest groups in the House and Senate Agriculture and Appropriations committees. Lobbyists for farm special interests were given access to the policymaking process by these legislators because they had a mutual interest in keeping benefits flowing to group members. Legislators needed to know how best to serve these crucial electoral constituencies, and lobbyists were in positions to provide such information and to help members of Congress work the system to make it happen. Lobbyists would then trumpet their committee ally's accomplishments in the home district or state and raise money for their "friend's" reelection. Building and maintaining mutually beneficial relationships was how lobbyists normally did business, so it is little wonder that in his study of interest groups during the committee government era, Lester Milbrath (1963) saw lobbyists as little more than benevolent aides to legislators, not as corrupting parasites. To retain and expand their influence, lobbyists simply needed to help their friends stay in office. All their friends had to do was keep down or co-opt potentially competing interests.

Boldly claiming that serving mobilized interests benefited everyone (it was "patriotic" or "pro-jobs") kept other, latent interests from seeing any harm done to them. New interests that did manage to mobilize did not demand that benefits be taken away from those already established; they just wanted their own piece of the action. Legislators thus "bought off" these new claimants by giving them a slice of the public pie, which of course gave these interests an incentive to also support the status quo (Davidson 1981).[2] Political fallout from the greater deficits all of this buying-off produced were small because the costs of funding these policies fell on the public in the form of taxes and debt, diffuse enough sources of revenue to prevent most people from realizing that there was any cost for helping these well-heeled special interests (McCool 1990). Even if some did realize it, the highly decentralized nature of Congress made assigning blame or enacting reform difficult (Dodd 1977). The norm of reciprocity ensured that each committee's bill parceling out benefits went unamended on the floor, logrolling and back-scratching being the order of the day, and autonomy made it easy for committees to bottle up bills threatening the status quo (Shepsle 1979).

An Analytical View of Interest Groups and Subgovernments

At this point it might be useful to develop a more analytical view of lawmaking in a world of interest groups balkanized in policy domains partly because it helps set up the competitive model in the next chapter. Formal theories tend to see legislation as the manifestation of choices to address issue questions on the government's decision agenda at particular points on continua of theoretically infinite possible policy outcomes (e.g., Downs 1957; Hinich and Munger 1997). An outcome dimension represents some degree of government spending or level of regulation on the behavior of individuals or organizations, with an actual policy serving or harming an interest group located at one (and only one) position. Points on the left-hand, or liberal, side represent greater levels of spending or protectionist regulation than those on the right-hand side. Lacking counteractive lobbying from competing groups or other countervailing forces, legislators are only limited in how much they can provide, or how far left or right on the continuum a policy is, by the size of the public pie and perhaps some sense of fiscal and social responsibility.

Figure 1.1 shows what a policy subsystem might look like. Around a committee of three legislators shown in the upper part of the figure are three "client" interest groups, each connected to their patron legislator who provides them with policy benefits. The policy provided to each group is marked on a dimension unique to that group because only that group's members care about the issue: Only cane growers in Florida care about their level of sugar subsidy, only dairy farmers care about the fixed price of milk, only midwestern corn growers care about ethanol subsidies—though all are contained in the agriculture policy domain. As long as these groups dutifully repay their patron legislator's largess with electoral votes and campaign contributions, the status quo level of benefits will remain and perhaps even increase incrementally over time. As the lower portion of the figure demonstrates for group G_3 and legislator L_3, legislators establish administrative agencies within the executive branch in order to deliver the benefits to the client group. Agency heads are rewarded with large budgets and little oversight when they ensure that client group members receive their benefits, which provides them with an incentive to support the status quo as well. Such mutually beneficial relationships for all three groups in figure 1.1 is what Douglass Cater (1964) termed a "subgovernment," though "iron triangle" has become the more popularized term.

A unique policy dimension for each group means that the interests of groups enfranchised by committee legislators do not overlap.[3] The issue dimension for one group in figure 1.1 is isolated from the others, or as formal theorists put it, preferences are "separable." Legislators and lobbyists for these groups have defined the issues to justify the status quo ("protecting the American family farmer" or "what is good for business is good for America") and to suppress the perception that benefits to one group are coming at the expense of others, so every group in the subgovernment

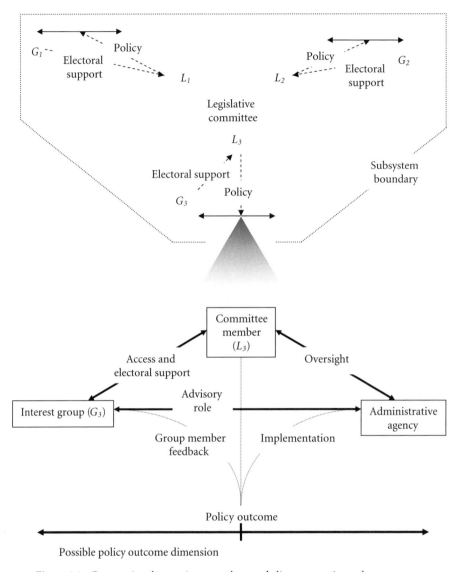

Figure 1.1. Congressional committee members and client groups in a subgovernment

gets policy that satisfies member interests without hurting each other. The subsystem is static because the policies rarely ever change. Unmobilized factions are left oblivious to the harm done to them and therefore remain latent rather than strive to influence where legislators choose to enact policy on a contested policy dimension. Interest group conflict does not exist because there does not appear to be any threat to defend against.

Growth, Change, and Competition in
Interest Group Politics

Although accepted by many scholars even today, perhaps because it appeals to their skeptical nature more than the pluralist's balance-of-power view, actually little systematic evidence exists to support the theory that such exclusive subgovernments are current political realities. Indeed, some doubt has been expressed as to whether they ever existed (Clemens 1997; Tichenor and Harris 2002). Much of what has been written by Bernstein (1955), Cater (1964), McConnell (1966), and Lowi (1969) relies on case studies of policymaking in one or a few domains in the 1950s and 1960s and, I argue, is time bound because the interest group community, the lawmaking environment, and Congress's method of operation have all changed significantly. If subgovernments characterize group politics and policymaking today, then three things should be true. First, the number of groups active in American politics must be small enough to be accommodated in the discrete policy domains described previously. Second, their interests should not be overlapping (and thus noncompetitive). Third, Congress must still be highly decentralized and driven by its committee system. All of these suppositions are highly suspect.

An "Exploding" Interest Group Community

Accurate data on the size and diversity of the American interest group community has always been hard to come by because a comprehensive registry of groups lobbying all institutions of the US government does not exist. Regarding the late-nineteenth-century period, we are largely left with a picture of a small cadre of well-heeled lobbyists for large new industries, such as railroads and oil companies, essentially bribing members of Congress (Herring 1929; Thompson 1986). The first real attempt at systematically sketching the contours of this community was done in the early twentieth century by Pendleton Herring (1929), who identified over five hundred lobbying organizations based in Washington, DC. Although small by today's standards, Herring thought it to be surprisingly large and diverse, replacing the "fat-cats" of the previous generation with highly sophisticated and legal lobbying techniques. The number does not appear to have changed much over the next forty years; Lester Milbrath (1963) pegged the number in 1960 at only 614. By 1981, however, Jack Walker (1983) counted 1,326 such groups in the nation's capital, suggesting that in the late 1960s and 1970s a significant burst of group formation occurred. Walker's finding was expanded upon by Kay Lehmann Schlozman and John Tierney (1986), who used the highly inclusive *Washington Representatives* directory to identify 6,601 organized interest groups.[4] But what is most compelling about Walker's findings is that the group community appeared to be still growing and doing so quite rapidly as the reach of government authority continues to grow (Leech et al. 2005).[5]

The precise moment when this interest group "explosion," as David Knoke (1986) calls it, occurred is hard to pin down, but the number of groups now active on the national political landscape is enormous. Mark Petracca (1992) found that the 1991

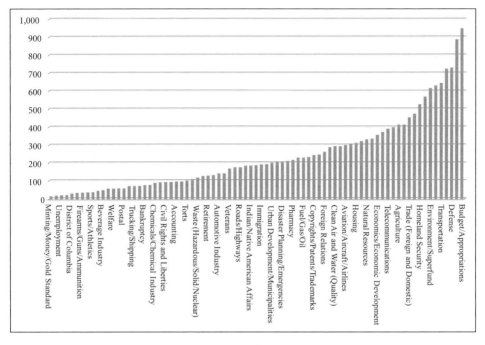

Figure 1.2. Number of interest groups per policy domain in 2009

Washington Representatives listed approximately 14,500 organizations, nearly four times as many as were listed in 1977. The directory's 2009 edition lists nearly 20,000 advocacy organizations. New groups not only mean new interests being articulated in existing policy domains but interests pushing for the recognition of entirely new domains as well. The congestion in these domains is far from evenly distributed, of course. *Washington Representatives* lists the number of groups that self-identify as lobbying on a variety of issues, which I graph in figure 1.2, from the domain with the least number of groups to the largest. Although many groups are counted in more than one policy domain, it is clear that tremendous variation exists, ranging from 23 groups lobbying on religious issues to 889 on health care issues.

New Interests, New Voices

This explosion in the number of advocacy organizations in Washington, DC, becomes more poignant when we consider whose interests these new groups represent. That they merely provide more representation for social factions already mobilized is unlikely. As James Q. Wilson (1973) argued, groups are much less likely to attract large memberships and thus command significant resources if they are simply duplicates of existing groups (Gray and Lowery 1997). Potential members whose interests lie in agriculture policy, for example, are unlikely to be attracted to a second American Farm Bureau Federation; if they were, then perhaps organizations such as the Grange might not have folded.[6] If the collective interests of a social group involved in agriculture differ significantly from those of most Farm Bureau members, they are much more likely to join or create their own organization, for example, Cesar Chavez's United Farm Workers.[7] Sometimes these newly mobilized interests push new issues and thus establish new policy domains, such as public housing and social welfare in the 1960s. In other cases they advocate new policies concerning existing issues, leading to the high level of group density in some of the policy domains in figure 1.2. Because the demands of these newcomers should differ from those of older groups (otherwise there would be no reason for them to form), they are now more likely to be seen as threatening the interests of others. Greater domain density suggests more competition between mobilized interests.

Many of the interests represented by these new groups are not even economic but involve issues of social welfare. Case studies by Andrew McFarland (1984) and Lawrence Rothenberg (1992) on Common Cause, a prominent example of these new public interest and citizen's groups, show the stark differences between them and the older business-oriented groups in terms of interests and agendas. As Jeff Berry (1999) explains it, after entering the post–World War II era, or the "post-material" era as he calls it, American society became wealthy enough to turn its attention to the less fortunate. Members were drawn to these groups by a personal desire to create policy that benefits society as a whole rather than receive select material benefits only for themselves. Of course, advocating common interests in protecting consumers or the environment often means regulating the activities of many businesses and professions, potentially harming the members of economic interests.

Not that all of these cause-oriented groups are new. The United Negro Foundation, the American Red Cross, and the American Audubon Society have been around for nearly a century. Peter Odegard (1928) studied the advocacy of the Anti-Saloon League for prohibition at the beginning of the twentieth century, and Herring (1929) and Milbrath (1963) found that many of these groups were active in the early twentieth century. What Walker found, though, is that they constituted the bulk of the increase in the group universe since the late 1960s. Data presented by Baumgartner and Leech (1998, 103) shows that the number of social welfare groups grew from 241 in 1959 to 1,938 by 1995, a rate of growth nearly four times that of business and trade associations.

Some citizen's groups were deliberately established to compete. Their "patrons" and "entrepreneurs," meaning the would-be political elites whom Walker argued were mobilizing these new social interests, such as Ralph Nader and John Gardner, specifically wanted to use advocacy to overthrow status quos and change policy. Some wanted to redirect public resources to extend governmental social safety nets to the less fortunate through welfare payments, public housing, and college financial aid. Others desired to break the political influence of economic interests. What they largely shared was a strategy of working to change the definitions supporting policy status quos, such as the idea that what was good for American business was good for America, which they felt was merely suppressing political competition. They were not simply seeking a portion of the public pie in a world where all claims could be accommodated—what they called politics as usual. They were injecting competition into politics, expressing demands they believed were in the best interests of the entire public and that could only be met by dismantling policies benefiting older, usually economic, interests. This statement by Common Cause founder John Gardner illustrates this point: "Common Cause would be a 'people's lobby' to combat the undue power of special interests. Common Cause would be 'pro-politics;' it would not shy away from using the experience of Washington insiders to apply 'pressure' for the public interest. Common Cause would be an action organization, not an 'education' organization. Lobbying would be its main goal, not the political education of its members" (Gardner in McFarland 1984, 7).

While many of these groups were successful in attracting members, others, public interest law firms such as the National Women's Law Center, had no members at all, but sustained themselves with donations from individuals and philanthropic organizations. Indeed, as Berry (1999) and Walker (1983) both found, external philanthropy, or "patrons," were responsible for many of these new groups. Organizations such as the Ford Foundation supported their desire to inject competition into the policymaking process: "A central assumption of our democratic society is that the general interest or the common good will emerge out of the conflict of special interests. The public interest law firm seeks to improve this process by giving better representation to certain interests" (Ford Foundation in Berry 1999, 26). Can so many groups and the interests they represent be integrated into noncompetitive policymaking subgovernments?

Centralizing Power and Tightening Budgets

While interest groups multiplied, Congress has, in a sense, contracted. In the late 1960s and early 1970s, junior members of Congress felt that the tight grip chairs held over committee legislation prevented them from being able to fully serve interests key to their own reelection coalitions. Like their seniors, they were trying to mobilize groups of constituents but found that the demands of these groups were not always welcomed by the old guard committee chairs. The interests mobilized by young New England Democrats, for instance, were anathema to more senior southern Democrats who still controlled committees (Davidson 1981). By 1975, reforms such as those made by the Hansen Committee had clipped the wings of these autocratic chairs and devolved more power to subcommittees and individual members, especially in the House of Representatives (Deering and Smith 1997, 38). The success of these Young Turks helped stimulate the new wave of mobilizations in the 1960s and 1970s as dispersion of power resulted in more access points in the government superstructure for more organized interests. The empowerment of young liberal Democrats on committees gave new citizen's groups friends in Congress and thus opportunities for access and influence (Meyer 2004).[8]

Yet two trends have slowed this expansion of power and opportunity to accommodate new interests. First is that discretionary budgets began to shrink in the 1970s. As Paul Peterson (1992) argues, Republican calls for fiscal discipline in the face of runaway deficits, first sounded by Barry Goldwater and Richard Nixon and dramatically amplified by Ronald Reagan in the 1980s, made it difficult for legislators to supply virtually endless financial benefits to an ever-increasing number of interest group claimants, no matter how crucial they were to reelection. Tax reduction in 1981, growing military expenditures, the Gramm-Rudman-Hollings spending caps, and Reagan's push to "de-fund the left" and "starve the government" all contributed to a general clampdown on federal largess. Discretionary spending, where group earmarks were often placed, fell from 66 percent in 1965 to 29 percent in 2006.[9] Even as the number of groups that legislators could serve expanded, the spigots necessary for serving many of them were being turned off.

The other change was the Republican takeover of the Congress in the 1994 elections. Again, the decentralized system of policymaking essential for quietly serving interest groups was based on norms of seniority, committee self-selection, property rights, and reciprocity (logrolling), and these norms were weakened by Speaker Newt Gingrich (R-GA) and his allies when Republicans became the majority party. Ideologically driven, they sought to centralize power in the hands of party leaders, using party loyalty more than seniority to elect committee chairs (Deering and Smith 1997, 186). Party leaders also exercised greater control over the fate of legislation, picking winners and losers based on the congruence of group member interests with conservative policy priorities (Deering and Smith 1997, 188).[10] All of this significantly decreased the number of lawmaking venues open to lobbyists. Long-lasting, mutually beneficial relationships with committee legislators lost value; lobbyists found that what really counted were connections to congressional leaders, especially House Majority Leader Tom DeLay (R-TX).

Whether or not these changes slowed the rate of new-group formation, the question remains: can the interests of the 20,000-plus diverse groups we have now be quietly accommodated by a centralized Congress with limited financial resources? How many new groups can enter a policy domain around a legislative committee, as shown in figure 1.1, before fulfilling every claim becomes impossible? Is it not more likely that as more groups mobilize and become active in domains centered on a relatively fixed and less independent set of committees, more citizens will feel that their interests clash with the interests of other groups and compete to defend themselves?

Changing Tactics

A hint that group politics and policymaking is changing appears in an article by Hugh Heclo (1978). He argues that the group explosion in the 1960s that resulted in the greater diversity of mobilized interests has largely torn most subgovernments apart. No longer is it possible for political institutions to accommodate every interest without regard for the impact of such policies on other interests. In their place, he argues, we now have policy domains populated by large and loosely structured networks of ideologically diverse advocates pursuing numerous interests, all competing to place their issues on the limited agendas of legislators. Perhaps the most visible consequence of this greater overlap of interests and interaction of groups is their growing propensity to form lobbying coalitions behind bills. As Robert Salisbury

(1990) points out, group coalitions have increasingly become the norm in this highly congested political world, and new policy is unlikely to be enacted without the broad consensus they appear to represent.

Salisbury's claim is substantiated by a burst of coalition studies (e.g., Hojnacki 1997, 1998; Hula 1999; Heaney 2004) that hint at the idea that the organizations comprising coalitions are acting on behalf of different, and thus potentially competing, interests. Granted, sometimes groups that are otherwise indifferent to each other may find that their interests can all be satisfied by omnibus bills and they may form coalitions. But when coalition partners' interests do overlap, these competitors are likely striking deals that give everyone something while requiring most everyone to make sacrifices (if not equally) in order to put aside conflict and pass legislation, as described in the introduction for the insurance agent lobbyist. Forming coalitions is therefore a strategy for resolving competitive difference, and their growing prevalence is more evidence that many groups have intersecting interests.

Of course some competing groups might prefer conflict to compromise, but what scholarship there is regarding the prevalence of group conflict is decidedly mixed. Austen-Smith and Wright (1994), Nownes (2000), Holyoke (2003), and Solowiej and Collins (2009) find that lobbyists often expect conflict and this expectation can influence their choice of tactics, whereas Baumgartner and Leech (1996), Hojnacki and Kimball (1998), Ando (2003), Lowery et al. (2005), and McKay and Yackee (2007) find little evidence of conflict. Much of this confusion may actually be attributable to the lack of a clear and consistent definition of "competition" and "conflict." Lack of a theoretically grounded definition has led some to simply assume that competition and conflict exist whenever groups offering collective benefits to citizens (open-membership, cause-oriented citizen's groups) lobby the same issues as groups offering benefits only to their members (closed-membership, professional and trade associations) and thus miss it entirely because they ignored the possibility that they might exist within these two categories.

Drawing conclusions regarding any phenomenon, such as interest group competition, based on simple typologies is perilous. Interest groups are increasingly forced to confront other interests that are not easily broken down by this binary typology, a fact made evident in the policy-domain-mapping studies of John Heinz and colleagues. Looking at four domains, Heinz et al. (1993) found large numbers of lobbyists representing varied interests who said they anticipated opposition from competitors as they advanced their preferred policies. Neither were the differences in "sides" clearly drawn between citizen's and economic groups, nor in any other way, except in the labor policy domain (Nownes 2000; Holyoke 2003). Just as significantly, Andrew McFarland (1993) found that citizen's groups were forming coalitions with economic groups in his study of the National Coal Policy Experiment. The causes and consequences of group competition simply cannot be reduced to a typology because such classification cannot account for the constraints and incentives motivating organized interests and their lobbyists. A theory of interest group competition must dig deeper; at the very least it must start with a clear definition of competition that can explain both conflict and compromise in coalitions.

Studying Interest Group Competition and
Its Consequences

It is not possible to easily transform the subgovernment depicted in figure 1.1 into an equivalent diagram of an issue network (but see Heaney 2006). But we know now that the last half century of change in American politics has made it very unlikely that a perception of no harm to other interests can be sustained as groups seek to satisfy their members' interests, especially when some citizen's groups are deliberately drawing attention to the harm. Overlapping, and therefore competing, interests mean many groups are now concerned with the same policy outcome dimension used in the lower part of figure 1.1 rather than having their own, unique continuum of possible outcomes. More interests would now be seeking access to, and influence with, the same three legislators in figure 1.1 to support their positions on the same outcome dimension, creating a web of crisscrossing dashed lines from groups to legislators. If greater financial support for cane growers in rural Florida means less money for public housing in Miami because of tight budgets, then groups that advocate for these interests prefer different outcomes on the same dimension. More money for one, a position on the left of the issue dimension, means less for the other interest. Both are interested in the same issue, but if the three lawmakers serve one, they hurt the other, and both will compete to convince legislators to favor them at the other's expense.

This example then provides us with a description of interest group competition. What one group desires is perceived to come at the expense of others, so that on the same issue question (How much support should government provide sugar cane growers?) competing desires take the form of two different preferences for policy outcomes. The result may lead to conflict, where lobbyists try to convince legislators to support only their preferred outcome. They might also negotiate a middle point and form a coalition to lobby together for a compromise policy. Perhaps the legislators will strike a deal and pressure the lobbyists to accept it, or perhaps competition will only lead to conflict and no position will be enacted.

What makes this process so interesting is that the government's final policy position on an outcome continuum need not reflect the preferred positions of any interest group. Lawmakers may pick positions between their preferred positions or perhaps outside the interval of these positions. This raises a number of interesting questions. How strong must a group be to pull the outcome closer to its position? What does it mean when coalitions form on specific issues, represented by a single-outcome dimension, and participation requires lobbyists to set aside differences and cooperate? Are these lobbyists now advocating positions different from those desired by their members? How strong an incentive or threat is needed to keep lobbyists strictly faithful to the positions favored by their members? How far can they be pushed and what happens when the issue is supremely important to group members? When do lobbyists have the freedom to form an ideologically broad coalition of strange bedfellows?

Higher levels of analysis present more questions. Does the inability of groups to form broad coalitions supporting compromise positions mean that legislation is less likely to pass? Does group competition contribute to gridlock? If so, then group competition becomes extremely important for understanding not only the policy-making process but whose interests are being served and how well lobbyists actually represent the factions of society—their constituents as it were—that they are employed to represent. These are some of the important normative implications for those interested in representation in our pluralist society. A model using the assumptions laid out in this chapter should shine light on such crucial questions. I devote the remaining pages of this book to the model, the tests of it, and its consequences for public policymaking in a democratic society.

Notes

1. I am indebted to Salisbury's 2000 paper on Bentley for this insight and for pointing me toward Peter Odegard's introduction to the 1967 Belknap edition of Bentley's book.

2. A different critical assault on pluralism came from Murray Edelman (1964) and William Domhoff (1967, 1978). Instead of a highly decentralized system with multiple power centers, they argue that American politics was controlled by a monolithic cadre of elites made up of politicians, important businessmen, and high-ranking military leaders. Competing interests might exist, but they fought on the margins of the military-industrial complex.

3. In this sense the policy outcome dimension is a heuristic constructed by lobbyists and lawmakers to give the impression that policy benefits serve only a single interest.

4. In all fairness, Walker, using the less-inclusive *Washington Information Directory*, limited his study to only those groups that had memberships and were based in Washington, DC, supplemented with groups found in congressional testimony, the *Encyclopedia of Associations*, and *New York Times Index*. These directories are more restrictive in their inclusion than publications such as *Washington Representatives*. This directory's inclusion criteria captures "institutions," or entities without members such as corporations and foundations that, as Salisbury (1984) finds, are a large part of the national lobbying community.

5. Walker used the date of organizational birth to show the rate at which new groups appeared.

6. As Browne (2001) notes, the Farm Bureau represented many of the same people and thus lobbied for many of the same interests as the Grange but was seen as doing a better job at it.

7. Smaller, more interest-specific organizations do form. For example, in addition to the Farm Bureau there are many commodities groups like American Corn Growers Association and National Cotton Council. Indeed, many economic interests are subdivided. Banking has broad, peak organizations such as American Bankers Association along with the small-bank-specific Independent Bankers Association and the savings industry's America's Community Bankers. Neither of these smaller groups are affiliated with ABA and have often fought it.

8. From the 80th Congress in 1947 to the 105th in 1997, the mean Common Space score for Democrats, House and Senate, shifted from a moderate −.18 to a more liberal −.32 (Poole and Rosenthal 1997).

9. From the US Office of Management and Budget, in *Vital Statistics in American Politics, 2005–2006* (Stanley and Niemi 2010).

10. From the 80th Congress to the 105th, the difference between the two parties' mean Common Space scores grew from .49 to .69. At the same time, the percentage of legislators considered moderates, with scores between −.20 and .20, fell from 37 percent in 1947 to 13 percent in 1997.

CHAPTER 2

The Competitive Model

IF competition is so important a characteristic of modern interest group politics, then we need to understand its causes and consequences. This requires a theory of competitive lobbying that can be a foundation for building a model of how lobbyists make decisions in a competitive environment. Moreover, if this theory is to seriously advance interest group research, it must embrace the two major literatures comprising the bulk of interest group scholarship. The first is about a group's internal politics, that is, why individuals choose to join, why they stay, and how they relate to the elites running it. The second regards how the group's lobbyist reacts to the political environment, namely, how the lobbyist gains access and influence with lawmakers by providing valuable information and resources.

These literatures have largely been developed in isolation from each other, as if how and why groups form has little to do with how their lobbyists go about the business of advocacy. This standpoint makes sense if we accept Olson's (1965) view of lobbying as a "by-product" of select material incentive-based member recruitment, but we know that many people join groups because they feel passionately about politics and want to be involved. Very often their passion helps lobbyists gain access to legislators because it is easy to show elected officials that there are people ready and willing to reward them with votes if group member policy demands are met, but lobbyists may also find that politically passionate members can make it extremely difficult to engage in the give-and-take of bargaining that is so essential for achieving policy goals in legislative politics. This connection has not often been recognized, but I argue that it is essential for understanding lobbying in any policy domain characterized by group competition. In this chapter I discuss these two literatures, organizational maintenance and legislative advocacy, and show how both are crucial pieces of a model of lobbying because of the tension competition from other interest groups generates between maintenance and advocacy. I then present the competitive model, deduce several testable hypotheses from it, and briefly discuss some of its consequences at higher levels of analysis.

Starting Points

As I argue in chapter 1, group competition exists when the collective interests of two or more memberships are perceived to intersect so that one cannot be served without harming the others. This definition describes a state of affairs rather than a choice. What is a choice and can therefore be modeled is whether a lobbyist decides to advocate for a position that leaves competitors with no option but conflict or for one that opens the door to compromise. Perhaps nothing illustrates this choice better than joining interest group coalitions because, assuming that no two groups can represent the exact same social interests, joining one often means compromising member interests in order to speak with one voice. Asking why lobbyists would go against members' wishes in this way provides a framework for studying competitive lobbying.

The Actors

Robert Salisbury (1969), in his seminal paper on the exchange theory of group mobilization, makes an important, if often overlooked, analytical distinction. It is the lobbyist, he argues, who takes the time and expends the resources necessary to organize an interest group. It is no great additional step, then, to also say that it is the lobbyist who decides how best to represent the interests of members before government and which strategies and tactics are best for advancing those interests. Lobbyists, in other words, are individuals separate from those they represent, and this separation opens up the possibility that they may not always have the same motivations and goals as their members. Lobbyists probably share their members' political ideologies and policy preferences, but their primary motivation for starting interest groups, as Salisbury sees it, are different. For members the group is about representation in the political process and selective benefits; for lobbyists it is about employment and careers. It is important for lobbyists to please group members because their employment depends upon the members' contributions, but this relationship does not mean lobbyists' actions are simply the manifestations of member preferences. Lobbyists are their own animals, and they first and foremost seek to advance their own careers. Thus Salisbury's distinction leaves open the possibility that there are other pressures on lobbyists that might be at odds with the desires of group members. In Ainsworth and Sened's (1993) view, it is this potential for conflict between different audiences that allows us to explain how lobbyists make strategic decisions.

The Policy Outcome Space

Actors require something to make choices about, something that gives context and meaning to their behavior. For lobbyists this "something" is provided by the issues on which they advocate and the policy solutions they advocate for (or against). An "issue," as Kingdon (1984, 3) describes it, is an attempt by government to address some problem that has been deemed legitimate for action by institutional gatekeepers. How should government address a perceived public problem? Doubtless a great

THE COMPETITIVE MODEL ■ 23

deal of lobbying has already occurred just to get an issue question onto the government's decision agenda, but my concern in this chapter is how they are resolved as lobbyists push for particular policy solutions. Following in the tradition of classical spatial theory as laid down by Downs (1957) and subsequently developed by a generation of political scientists (see Hinich and Munger 1997), I assume that how issues might be resolved is represented by a unidimensional continuum of potential policy solutions (as Baumgartner et al. [2009] note, discourse tends to reduce issues to a unidimensional continuum of outcomes). Positions on the left are more liberal solutions, spending more public resources or imposing more restrictive regulations; those on the right are increasingly conservative in that they represent less spending and less regulation. A lobbyist can only advocate for one of these positions at a given point in time, but it need not be the one ideally preferred by the members they represent.

The Advocacy Choice

Every lobbyist for a group seeking to influence a policy must choose a position on the policy outcome continuum to support. They can choose a position that reflects their members' collective interest, or they can offer olive branches to lobbyists for competing groups and the legislators backing them by supporting positions closer to those the competitors' members prefer. Either choice comes with risks. If they choose to support any position different from those chosen by their competitors, they will have to fight for it against those competitors. If they join a coalition supporting a joint position that is not the one preferred by their members they may jeopardize member support. Just how lobbyists balance these pressures on contentious issues is the main result of the model I lay out later in this chapter. How coalitions can form from the collective position choices of competing lobbyists is taken up in chapter 5. The point to remember now is that each lobbyist's strategy is to choose a position on the outcome continuum that best balances the conflicting pressures they are under. Whether they end up fighting or cooperating with some or all of their competitors is a consequence of these strategic choices. The choice is thus not between cooperation and conflict per se, but which position, out of a theoretically infinite number of possible positions on the outcome, to support. Not to say that cooperation and coalition building are mere by-products, for as I will show, the value lobbyists place on different positions depends very much on who else might support that same position and who will not.

Theoretical Underpinnings

Formal, and often informal, theories of behavior in the social sciences often begin with two assumptions. First, large-scale events, like revolutions, policymaking, and elections, are the outcomes of the collective choices of individuals and are therefore driven by the motivations of individuals. Second, the choices resulting from these individual motivations are shaped by contextual incentives and constraints (carrots and sticks). Indeed, this interaction of goal-directed behavior modified by context that underpins rational choice theories (Plott [1991] calls it the fundamental equation) has found its way into alternative theories of choice as well (Jones 2001). I stay with a more formalized approach in this chapter because lobbyists, like many elites, attempt to achieve their goals in environmental and institutional contexts that shape their decisions. Their goal is to realize as much of their members' interests in public policy as possible. Environmental and institutional incentives and constraints determine what is possible and are described in the two primary interest group literatures.

Collective Action and Organizational Maintenance

Although lobbyists are separate from those they represent, members are far from irrelevant. Without them, resources, organizational backing, and employment would be lacking. To represent members' interests is a political organization's reason for existing, and the composition and breadth of its membership goes a long way towards structuring its identity and the lobbyist's legitimacy in the eyes of lawmakers (Wilson 1973; but see Heaney 2004). They are the walking spokespersons for their members' collective desires. And lobbyists, Luttbeg and Zeigler (1966) find in their study of the National Education Association, often do see themselves as faithful agents representing their collective group member principal. So, how lobbyists want to see an issue resolved with policy, the position they choose to support on the outcome continuum, is defined to a considerable extent by how their members want to see it resolved.[1] Members who are not satisfied with the position their lobbyist and therefore their interest group stake out on an issue will, as Hirschman (1970) puts it, attempt to use "voice" to change the organization from within (probably by trying to fire the lobbyist) or "exit" the group entirely. The loss of members costs the lobbyist financial resources and detracts from the group's legitimacy (Wilson 1973). It costs the lobbyist political muscle, harms career prospects, and probably threatens his or her current job.

To determine what position a faithful lobbyist will choose on an issue would be easy if all group members had the same preference for policy outcomes, but they often do not. Instead, lobbyists face distributions of member preferences and variation in how intensely members feel about issues. How similar and how intense member preferences are may break down by the types of incentives groups use to convince them to join, Sabatier (1992) argues. Individuals deeply concerned about how a policy affects them are arguably more likely to join groups offering purposive incentives (opportunities for meaningful political participation) such as citizen's groups, but because they feel passionately about policy, they are also less likely to want to be part of a membership that includes a significant diversity of opinion. Greater intensity of feeling on the part of members is likely to be inversely related to the range of their policy preferences.

Of course, even when preferences are fairly similar within a group, intense feelings may still make it hard for members to agree on a position. A recent example is the Audubon Society of Arizona, which nearly fell apart after an internal fight over whether to support a land swap between the federal government and a mining company (Dougherty 2009). Alternatively, groups that primarily offer select material incentives may be less likely to attract members with similar preferences simply because advocacy is incidental to membership. Still, whatever the incentive, when members are relatively united regarding the position they want their organization to take and feel strongly about it, their lobbyist risks much by failing to do so. For them the position to take is clear.

To illustrate this point, I give an example that will run throughout this chapter. Say the issue under debate is the level of government subsidy for the wholesale price of fresh milk, an issue I examine more closely later in this book. The issue emerged on the government's agenda in the 1990s, and different proposals have been advocated to answer the question of what subsidy level, if any, government ought to provide. Members of the interest group Consumer Federation of America (CFA) are likely to be left leaning overall; they generally would like to see the state subsidize milk production because it helps keep the retail price of fresh milk low and thus more affordable for poorer consumers. Not everyone in CFA may agree on just how high the subsidy should be or how low the retail price should go, but they still cluster on the liberal end of the milk-pricing outcome space even if they are widely distributed over that portion of the space.

Assuming that the individual policy preferences of members are normally distributed over the policy outcome space makes it possible to identify both CFA's collective "ideal" preference position as well as the freedom its lobbyist has to deviate from it. Although larger standard deviations mean less member unity, the optimal position for CFA's lobbyist to take is always (all things being equal) at the mean. CFA member preferences, however, may not only vary by spatial position but also by the intensity with which they are held. They may feel that this issue is a crucial one and that no compromises leading to higher milk prices are acceptable. Members so motivated are more likely to take the time to follow their lobbyist's choices and protest when any deviations from their (the members') preferred position, or at least the group's ideal position, occurs.[2] This combination of the range of member preferences and the collective intensity of members for their preferred outcomes defines what I consider to be the CFA lobbyist's payoff curve over the milk-pricing issue.

In figure 2.1 I sketch three possible scenarios. In Member Curve 1, CFA members are divided over how they would like to see the issue resolved with policy, though by and large they do not care intensely about what position their lobbyist advocates. Their lobbyist has broad discretion, or wiggle room, to push positions other than the mean, that is, other than the group's collective ideal on milk pricing. The situation is altered in Member Curve 2. Whether members feel more intensely about the issue or they are more unified in their collective preferences, the lobbyist's wiggle room is narrower. CFA's lobbyist is most constrained in Member Curve 3 where members are largely unified and care a great deal about what their advocate does. Any choice to support a position other than the mean, any deviation, costs the lobbyist and the federation dearly in member support.

Information-Based Advocacy

So, if lobbyists risk their organization's strength and reputation when they support positions other than the collective mean, why would they ever choose to do it? Or, in the context of coalition formation, if competition exists when there is a difference

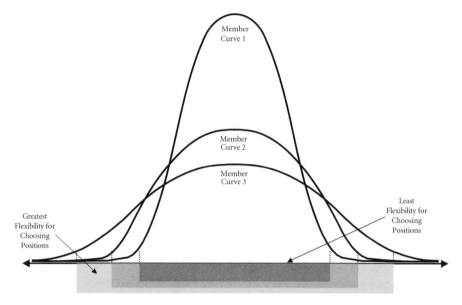

Figure 2.1. Possible distributions of group member preferences and intensity

between the positions collectively preferred by the members of two or more groups, and a coalition can only support one position on an issue, why would any lobbyist ever choose to join one? Where is the logic in risking organizational support, resources, and prestige by making compromises just to gain the support of other interest group lobbyists? And yet Kevin Hula (1999) shows us that lobbyists join coalitions all of the time, so they must hope to gain something even more valuable in return. But what benefit could justify a strategy of compromising member interests? The answer is simple: lobbyists support alternative positions to gain more support from legislators. Only legislators can formally decide which position on the outcome space will become law and lobbyists cannot gain anything for their members without their aid. As I show in chapter 5, group coalition positions are often chosen precisely because all of the lobbyists involved believe that it stands the best chance of gaining the most congressional support.

Political scientists have developed a hefty literature on the lobbyist–legislator relationship.[3] Because of distinctly different intellectual starting points, the literature divides into two camps, but I believe they have now evolved toward each other and largely lead toward the same conclusion. One has its origins in Olson's (1965) theory of select incentives. People or businesses join organized interests because they desire to gain something they could not get otherwise. Often the benefits they seek, such as financial subsidies and protectionist regulation, can only be provided by the state, so lobbying is necessary. This strand of theory has been embraced by economists, who conceive of lobbying as "rent seeking," that is, privileged corporations want government policy that gives them a significant edge over their rivals (Stigler 1971;

Peltzman 1976; Grossman and Helpman 2001). It is the lobbyist's job to procure this rent. Legislators want to provide rents because, in exchange, they receive campaign contributions and votes that support their primary goal of reelection when the beneficiaries are part of their electoral constituency (Mayhew 1974). However, Ainsworth and Sened (1993) argue that legislators are not always sure to whom they ought to provide this largess. Successful lobbyists bridge this information gap by letting the right legislators know that a constituency, who happen to be the lobbyist's members, exists who will reward these elected officials with money and votes in return for favorable policy. Legislators, members, and, of course, lobbyists all benefit when legislators grant these lobbyists access.

The other theory is grounded even more firmly in the notion of lobbyists as information providers. It begins with Lester Milbrath (1963), who argues that lobbyists gain influence by helping ideologically sympathetic legislators achieve their goals. The presumption is that lobbyists offer their services to, and essentially become adjuncts to the staff of, legislators who not only desire reelection but wish to influence policy and gain higher office as well (Fenno 1973; Dodd 1977). Based on Kingdon (1973) and Clausen (1973) and developed by Austen-Smith and Wright (1992), Austen-Smith (1993), Wright (1996), and Lohmann (2003), the theory holds that legislators do not so much lack information as they have an overabundance of it. They must develop trustworthy lines of communication that cut through the cacophony of petitioners to help them find what is most useful for achieving their goals. Lobbyists able to provide information regarding constituent preferences, the desires of financial contributors, the wants of other political actors, the ways in which bureaucrats implement policy, and so on and do so reliably on a regular basis are granted access and become part of the legislator's policy and career advancement "enterprise" (Ainsworth 1997, 518; Hall and Deardorff 2006).

What both theories assume is a congruency of ideological beliefs, not merely on specific issues but very often in general dispositions. Over time, lobbyists build solid and lasting relationships between legislators and their group members that can define entire careers. Sen. Edward Kennedy's (D-MA) connection to organized labor and Rep. Tom DeLay's (R-TX) to the Christian Coalition are examples. When it comes to a specific issue important to group members, legislators will support positions similar to those that members desire for two reasons: First, those positions are the ones most likely to satisfy member demands and assure reelection, and second, these members are also mobilized voters. All lobbyists have to do is accurately report the desires of these constituencies and suggest ways in which legislators might keep them satisfied with policy. So, the empirical observation of Kollman (1997), Hojnacki and Kimball (1998), and Leech and Baumgartner (1998) that lobbyists target their "friends" on legislative committees, where most policy is formed, is true because both are trying to serve the same organized and vocal constituencies.

The crucial caveat to this otherwise robust theory is that legislators, like lobbyists, frequently must take positions on issues at odds with their constituents' desires, including those in organized interests, because of the demands of the institution in which they serve (Shepsle and Weingast 1994). Majority rule alone requires legislators to make compromises just to pass bills, especially with the erosion of the logrolling (mutual back-scratching) norm (Deering and Smith 1997, 50). Another reason is that legislators themselves often want to please larger audiences. House members must position themselves carefully on issues key to larger constituencies if they want to run for senate or a governorship, just as senators and governors must when running for president. Winning election to committee chair or party leader positions also tends to require legislators to put the needs of others ahead of their own constituents. Still another reason has to do with the centralization of power since the Republican takeover in 1995 and the nationalization of many issues. Greater media scrutiny of Congress and more intense competition between the two major parties have pushed party leaders to stake out national positions on issues that have traditionally been parochial or the province of a few committee legislators (Deering and Smith 1997, chapter 2). Leaders now frequently pressure rank-and-file members to adhere to party positions potentially at odds with their constituent preferences, the so-called "party effect" (Binder, Lawrence, and Maltzman 1999, 816), something I explore further in chapter 6.

What do these institutional and party pressures mean for lobbyists? The diminishing autonomy of their congressional allies makes it harder for lobbyists to obtain benefits for their mutual constituents. As much as the growth in the sheer number of groups, this centralization of power in Congress has severely eroded the subgovernments that made it possible for lobbyists to form tight, mutually profitable relationships with committee legislators and develop legislation that did not substantially compromise group member interests. Moreover, the increase in the number of groups has created a difficult problem of supply and demand. Not everyone gets to be a Jack Abramoff or Gerry Cassidy with close ties to the Republican and Democratic leaderships. The advocate who violates the expectations of the legislator–lobbyist exchange relationship by pressuring legislators to stay true to constituent, and therefore group member, preferences in the face of pressure from the leadership risks his or her access. The many lobbyists clamoring for attention make it easy (or at least easier) for legislators to make up information loss with another source more willing to be a "team player."

In other words, in many and perhaps most information-based relationships, a subtle power struggle takes place, and lobbyists are increasingly finding themselves on the weaker end. Fearing the loss of access, so crucial to a successful career, he or she may end up helping legislators advance or defend positions not always in harmony with group member preferences. The CFA lobbyist might have to support lower milk subsidies, a position in the right-hand tail of one of the distributions in figure 2.1. Refusing to do so might mean exile from legislators' inner circles, removal from their enterprises, and significant career damage because they have lost a relationship from their portfolios. Even the most powerful Washington super-lobbyists are subject to such pressures, as was seen when lobbyists for the mighty AARP (formerly known as the American Association of Retired Persons) bowed to pressure from the Bush administration and the Republican leadership in 2003 to support a Medicare reform package their members disliked. When lobbyists take more extreme positions relative to the positions their legislator friends are supporting, failure in their advocacy and subsequent exclusion from the table where the agenda is set are almost guaranteed. In other words, faithfully representing their members' interests can put lobbyists' careers at risk.

Strategically Choosing Positions

The concept of lobbyists as actors trying to please two masters with potentially different policy preferences provides a foundation for sketching a model of strategic lobbying, or strategic position taking, which I do by expanding the dairy-pricing example, although I do not yet give CFA a competitor. Although the federation's lobbyist is conceivably subject to pressure from all group members, when it comes to legislators the information theory of access suggests that only legislators with whom the lobbyist has built exchange relationships can pressure him or her. Stage one of laying out the competitive model therefore involves identifying who these legislators are; I call this subset of the legislature the CFA lobbyist's "access set."

The identification of this subset is relatively simple to do with some basic math and a few assumptions, such as the existence of the small, twenty-one-member unicameral legislature arranged on the liberal–conservative ideological continuum depicted in figure 2.2A. This continuum is general in that it represents legislators' general ideological dispositions, what are often measured with DW-Nominate scores based on roll-call votes, not their preferences for specific policy on the milk-pricing issue. Which legislators the lobbyist builds relationships with is shaped by three constraints. As Wright (1996) argues, for lobbyists to gather information from group members regarding their interests and then use that information to convince legislators it is in their interests to serve those members with policy, is costly. Thus the first constraint is R, the resources CFA derives from members and patrons to invest year after year in building and maintaining political relationships.

The other two constraints capture the reluctance legislators may have to grant access, perhaps because they do not entirely trust CFA and need to be convinced that the information their lobbyist provides and any efforts they are being asked to make on CFA's behalf really are in their own best interests. One is the sheer ideological distance on the continuum between CFA's ideological position, which I set at 3, and legislator k's general ideological position, $|CFA - L_k|$. The other is how intensely a legislator is committed to his or her position versus CFA prior to lobbying (or how distrustful he or she is of CFA), symbolized as I_k.

Nuances of relationship building are lost by boiling it down to something akin to a financial transaction, but it leads to a nice, intuitive result. If the cost of building a relationship with a legislator is $C_k = I_k(|CFA - L_k|)$, then presumably the lobbyist will continue building them until resources are exhausted, that is, when the sum of the per-legislator cost, C, equals R. Assuming the lobbyist wants to establish as many relationships as possible, then given the $C = R$ restriction, it is easy to determine who will be brought into CFA's access set (its portfolio) because relationships will be established with the "cheapest" legislators first. Those legislators will have ideological

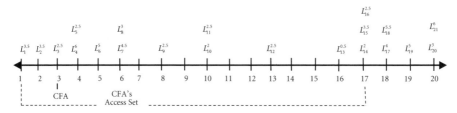

Figure 2.2A. General ideological distribution of legislators and the CFA lobbyist's access set

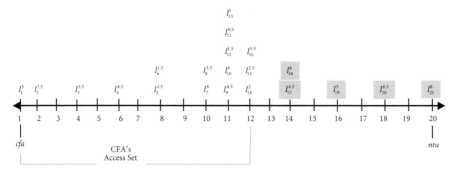

Figure 2.2B Distribution of legislator preferences on milk pricing

positions in figure 2.2A that are closest to *CFA* and will not feel as intensely about their positions (low values of *I*).[4]

If the federation provides its lobbyist with 250 units of resources, $R = 250$, and given legislators' ideological positions and intensity scores (the superscripts) in figure 2.2A, the combination of legislators within the area marked "access set" is the largest combination of lawmakers whom the lobbyist can afford to build relationships with. Of total resources, 239 is spent here, so the set's value to the lobbyist is $V = 239$ (this will be important later). This result is intuitive because keeping costs as low as possible means the lobbyist targets legislators with preferences closer to the federation's members. Lobbyists are lobbying ideological friends, but those lobbying for wealthier groups are able to gain more influence.

Legislators in CFA's access set in figure 2.2A, L_1 through L_{16}, are also the only legislators its lobbyist needs to worry about as he or she chooses a position to actually advocate on issues such as milk pricing, which is the second stage of my model-building enterprise. The continuum in figure 2.2B is similar to figure 2.2A except that it now represents possible policies that answer the issue question of how large a subsidy the government should provide rather than general ideological dispositions (I distinguish this issue scenario with lowercase letters). How legislators are distributed on this space is different from their general ideological positions because issue positions may be influenced by their need to pursue reelection goals or advancement to higher office. They may also reflect compromises as committee chairs and party leaders assemble majorities. These issue positions are also chosen by legislators prior to any lobbying on the issue by CFA (or any other group), an artificial separation in the timing of advocacy, but one that highlights the challenge before the CFA lobbyist.

CFA's members generally prefer a substantial subsidy so that low-income families and single mothers can afford fresh milk, so I assign the group's collective position in figure 2.2B, *cfa*, to be 1. The lobbyist's problem is that legislators in CFA's access set, those he or she has influence with, are supporting positions different from what CFA members ideally prefer. This lack of position congruence between *cfa* and l_2 through l_{16} puts the lobbyist between a group maintenance rock and a political hard place because both audiences expect the lobbyist to support them. He or she must strive to convince legislators, and only those legislators in CFA's access set, to support a position other than those they initially chose in figure 2.2B.

The Choice

To keep this panel simple, I portray the CFA lobbyist's efforts to build support for a milk-pricing position as being similar to building exchange relationships. Again, he or she has finite resources to use to persuade legislators to support positions more favorable to the interest group on the policy outcome space. Again, the total cost of persuasion, c, cannot exceed resources, r, available for lobbying this issue, and again these resources must be stretched as far as possible. Thus the lobbyist must also consider changing positions, even as he or she tries to persuade legislators l_1 through l_{16} to change theirs. Indeed, how lobbyists select positions is the competitive model's main prediction. The lobbyist's task is to find the position he or she anticipates will receive the most support from legislators in CFA's access set and from group members.

In figure 2.2B I again list the intensity, i_k, of each legislator's preference for his or her *ex ante* (pre-lobbying) position on milk pricing as superscripts. The cost of successfully persuading each legislator on this issue is $c_k = i_k(|g_{cfa} - l_k|)$, with g_{cfa} a position the lobbyist is thinking about supporting, not necessarily the one CFA members collectively prefer (*cfa* = 1). A legislator can be persuaded to support g_{cfa} if the cost of doing so, c_k, is less than r, and then the lobbyist can use what resources remain to persuade the next one until resources are exhausted. But $|g_{cfa} - l_k|$ changes from position to position, so how many legislators can be persuaded also varies from position to position. What influences the lobbyist's position choice, however, is the number of legislators in CFA's access set that he or she anticipates will not be persuaded. These legislators expect the federation's lobbyist to help them achieve their goals. If the lobbyist fails to convince them that it is in their interests to support g_{cfa} instead, the persuasion attempt will be seen as a breach of the exchange relationship contract. Unpersuaded legislators will react angrily by restricting the lobbyist's access, perhaps cutting him or her out entirely.

An unpersuaded legislator's anger diminishes the relationship's value to the lobbyist, where value v_i is the cost to establish it originally and include the legislator in his or her access set as laid out in figure 2.2A with $R = 250$. If, from position 1 in figure 2.2B, a lobbyist can persuade l_1 through l_{16} to support that position, then no loss occurs in the total value of these relationships at all ($V = 239$). If the lobbyist does not have enough resources to persuade them all, the degree of expected punishment from those, and only those, who are unpersuaded reduces the total value of these relationships by the distance on the continuum between g_{cfa} and l_k and the intensity (i_k) of the legislator's preference in figure 2.2B. The equation

$$v_k = c_k \left[1 - \left(\frac{i_k(|g_{cfa} - l_k|)}{c_k} \right) \right]$$

calculates the new, diminished value of a relationship with an unpersuaded legislator, where c_k is the cost of having established it originally.

For example, if the CFA lobbyist's resources for the milk-pricing campaign are $r = 210$ and he or she wants to lobby for position *cfa* in figure 2.2B, then I can calculate how many legislators l_1 through l_{16} he or she can expect to persuade given the spatial distance between their ex ante positions and position 1, multiplied by how intensely legislators feel about their initial positions. At *cfa* the lobbyist has enough resources to convince everybody in his or her access set except l_7, l_9, l_{10}, and l_{16} because those four legislators either prefer positions too far from position 1 or feel too intensely about them, or both. If the lobbyist actually chooses position 1 (*cfa*), then those relationships are harmed, their reduced value to the lobbyist calculated using the above equation, and now the value of all sixteen add up to only $V_1 = 164$.[5] If the lobbyist instead advocates for position 5, he or she could persuade everyone except l_{11} and l_{16}, and $V_7 = 190$. Calculating the total relationship value for every position creates the Legislator Support curve in figure 2.3A. At positions 8 through 11, every legislator in CFA's access set will be persuaded ($V = 239$), which is unsurprising since 11 already had the most support prior to lobbying. This approach not only captures the ability of lobbyists to persuade legislators but also shows the pressure they themselves are under by incorporating the possibility of retribution from angry lawmakers (loss of valuable relationships) into their strategies.

Yet if position 1 in figure 2.2B is the federation's group member ideal, then the lobbyist, as Hirschman (1970) reminds us, may also be punished by members if he or she supports any position other than 1. Because *cfa* is the mean of the distribution of member policy preferences, the lobbyist will anger more and more members by advocating positions on the outcome space further from *cfa*, multiplied by m, which captures how intensely members collectively prefer *cfa*. At *cfa* this is 0, but their anger increases as $|cfa - g_{cfa}|$ and m increase. If $m = 5$, and CFA has 250 members, and members punish the unfaithful lobbyist by abandoning the group, then I calculate the loss in member support by subtracting the product of $m(|cfa - g_{cfa}|)$ from 250. I graph the resulting loss rate in member support over all positions as the solid, black line in figure 2.3A.

Keep in mind that the CFA lobbyist is not just trying to advocate for the interests of group members or legislators. He or she is trying to balance these conflicting pressures, trying to anticipate which position will keep both as satisfied as possible.

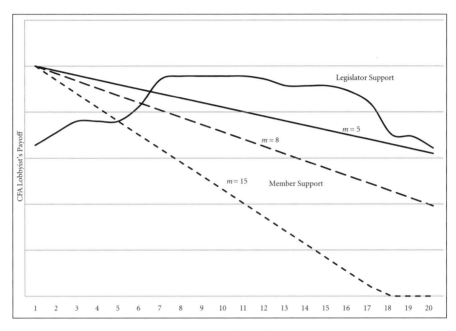

Figure 2.3A. Legislator and member support curves

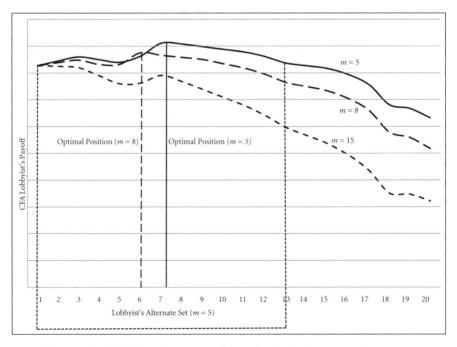

Figure 2.3B. CFA lobbyist's joint payoff at varying levels of group member support

I identify this balancing by combining the Member Support and Legislator Support curves into a single black Joint Payoff Curve graphed in figure 2.3B, which reveals several things. First, the optimal position where the federation's lobbyist anticipates jointly maximizing support (or minimizing punishment) from both audiences is not *cfa* nor positions 8 through 11, but 7. He or she anticipates that position 7 will garner the most support (or the least punishment) simultaneously from group members and legislative allies. It will not fully satisfy either set but as the best choice that the lobbyist can expect to make under conflicting pressures it is the logical position to choose. Second, the small-dash lines mark a range of positions under the curve that also provide the lobbyist greater joint support than *cfa*, what I call the "alternate set" (which will be important in chapter 5).

Finally, the distance between *cfa* and this optimal position changes if group members feel more strongly about *cfa*. If I increase the group's collective preference intensity to $m = 8$, the new line in figure 2.3A and new curve in figure 2.3B shift the lobbyist's optimal position from 7 to 6 in figure 2.3B, closer to *cfa*. A more extreme case is $m = 15$, where members care very intensely about their preferences, often the case in groups primarily composed of citizens who respond to purposive incentives, such as Consumer Federation of America. Now legislator support cannot compensate at all for losing members, and the lobbyist's optimal position is *cfa*. Of course this loss would be counterbalanced if legislators cared more about their positions (greater values of i_k). Or it could happen as the result of interest group competition.

The Indirect Effect of Competitive Lobbying

Now I am ready to introduce a competing interest group. The main effect of a competitor on the CFA lobbyist is indirect, which is why I began developing the model without one. The National Taxpayers Union (NTU) is a conservative organization that opposes government regulation of markets generally and of dairy pricing in particular. As with CFA, I identify NTU's access set (the group's general ideological position is set at 18, $R = 250$) and display it along with CFA's in figure 2.4. Legislators that fall into both sets have relationships with both lobbyists; thus they create a "contested set," which is the key to understanding competitive lobbying. Similar to the outcome space in figure 2.2B, I assign NTU's member ideal position on milk pricing to be 20, no subsidy at all, which given the definition in chapter 1, means it is competing with CFA.

Like its competitor, NTU's lobbyist uses organizational resources to persuade legislators to support a position jointly minimizing punishment, both from them and from their own group members. NTU's allies in the contested set, however, are also being lobbied by CFA. Yet NTU's very presence changes the pressures driving the CFA lobbyist's choice. To successfully lobby contested legislators, in this case l_3, l_5, l_8–l_{16}, the CFA advocate must persuade them not only to change their initial outcome preferences but also to reject counterpersuasion by NTU. This new challenge drives up the cost of lobbying each, but only each, contested legislator by the distance between the positions of the two lobbyists, $|g_{cfa} - g_{ntu}|$, so that both will have to

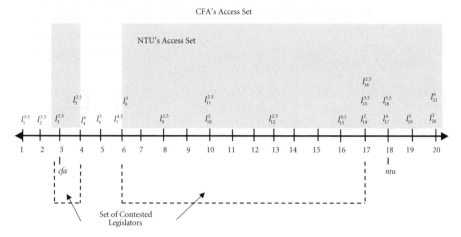

Figure 2.4. Ideological distribution of legislators and interest group lobbyists' access sets

spend more on advocacy. For CFA's lobbyist, the portion of this distance from $|g_{cfa} - l_k|$ is part of the cost of persuasion without a competitor; the remaining $|l_k - g_{ntu}|$ is the additional cost of countering NTU's advocacy.

The result of this competition is that both lobbyists are likely to persuade fewer legislators. To make matters worse for the CFA lobbyist, not only are more legislators likely to remain unconvinced and punish accordingly, but some allies may end up being persuaded to support NTU at position 20, which drives up the potential penalty incurred by the CFA lobbyist for failing to be persuasive. Lost legislators will have been convinced that it is in their best interests to support position ntu and will want CFA to do the same. They may not really end up supporting ntu, but the CFA lobbyist can only anticipate possible outcomes. I assume that he or she anticipates the worst-case scenario, that is, every unpersuaded legislator in the contested set will be persuaded by NTU. This more severe loss of support is captured by replacing part of the previously given equation, $|g_{cfa} - l_k|$, with the following:

$$v_k = c_k \left[1 - \left(\frac{i_k \left(|g_{cfa} - g_{ntu}| \right)}{c_k} \right) \right]$$

Thus the result of competition from the CFA lobbyist's point of view is an increase in the potential loss of support from the very legislative allies he or she had spent time and resources building relationships with and was counting on for help. Of course, NTU's lobbyist has the same problem with persuading legislators because of competition from CFA.

This competitive effect is seen in figure 2.5, where I graph the noncompetitive Joint Payoff Curve from figure 2.3B ($m = 5$) in solid black along with a new combined curve for CFA incorporating the additional loss of legislator support to NTU ($ntu = 20$) in

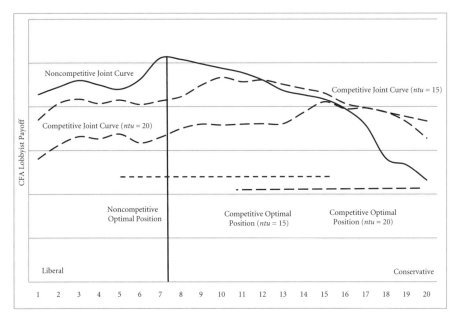

Figure 2.5. Noncompetitive and competitive payoff curves for CFA (indirect competitive effect)

a large-dashed curve. The change is striking. By taking the field, NTU's lobbyist forces CFA's lobbyist to anticipate a more costly campaign because persuading allies is now harder and punishment may be worse from CFA's allies that NTU manages to bring into its fold. By lobbying for a position further from *cfa*, NTU creates a gap between the payoff CFA's lobbyist would have received absent competition and what he or she is now likely to receive. And with more legislators now inclined to support positions on the right side of the continuum, the CFA lobbyist must also consider supporting positions further right in order to gain enough legislator support to balance the now increasing loss of members. The new optimal position is now at 15. This difference between the curves and between the noncompetitive and competitive optimal positions is the "indirect competitive effect."

Three other results are worth pointing out as well. First, figure 2.5 shows that the competitive curve has a somewhat gentler slope on the conservative side of the outcome space than on the liberal side where CFA members prefer their lobbyist take a stand. This difference in slope occurs because CFA's lobbyist must commit more resources to keep the support of fewer allies, which is cheaper for the interest group at positions further from *cfa* than would be the case if there was no competition from NTU. Unfortunately (for the lobbyist), introducing a competitor group does not change how CFA's members feel about the issue. They will continue to desert CFA at the same rate, but legislators will provide less compensation for positions closer to *cfa*. A wily lobbyist might convince members that flexibility is wise (see chapter 8), but highly ideological members may not be inclined to tolerate any compromise.

Second, this effect is indirect because it is felt by the lobbyist only through the increased difficulty in successfully lobbying some legislators, not a direct payoff loss equivalent to the resources wielded by the competitor (see chapter 5). It is similar to Austen-Smith and Wright's (1992) counteractive lobbying model because both competitors are trying to convince legislators to support them at different positions. My model is different, though, because here lobbyists are also changing their positions as they search for ones that maximize support from both audiences in a competitive context.

Third, the NTU lobbyist's noticeable influence on the CFA lobbyist's choices does not mean that the battle is only about whether to support position *ntu* (no milk subsidy at all). The National Taxpayers Union's lobbyist is also trying to determine which position leftward of *ntu* to support because he or she is under pressure from legislators and therefore indirectly from CFA. The battle is over the degree of subsidy because competitive forces are pulling both lobbyists away from what their members ideally prefer, toward the center of the policy outcome space. As the small-dashed curve in figure 2.5 shows, by taking a position leftward of *ntu* (position 15), NTU's lobbyist reduces $|g_{cfa} - g_{ntu}|$, which is the cost both pay to persuade each contested legislator. Consequently, the more NTU's lobbyist moves toward the center, the less incentive the CFA competitor has to consider positions so far to the right because his or her legislator support curve is now declining somewhat less precipitously. It shows that lobbyists for competing groups are indirectly dependent on each other, each trying to anticipate what position the other will support.

What position will finally emerge from this process of gradual adjustment, and might it provide common ground for CFA and NTU to form a milk-pricing coalition supporting the same position? I take up these questions in chapter 5; it is enough to say that it depends on the advocacy resources each can draw on, how intensely their members feel about the issue and how unified they are, and the distribution of legislators. In other words, these three factors are the basic variables of the competitive model and will form the basis of the statistical model I test in chapter 4. As these factors change, choices of positions change, and competing lobbyists may potentially move closer together or further apart. This movement is not only the indirect competitive effect at work, it is the main result of competitive lobbying.

Recapitulation

Both lobbyists, considered to be competing because the interests of their members on an issue are not aligned, select their positions by balancing conflicting constraints. On the one hand, they need to represent their members, those who pay to be in their organization and who may abandon the lobbyist if the latter is not seen as a faithful agent. On the other hand, they cannot easily advocate for the needs of these members if they do not have the support of lawmakers. Their capacity to mobilize bias on behalf of their members depends on their ability to persuade legislators to back their position on an issue, which in turn is contingent on whether their competitor does the same and supports a position closer to one ideally preferred ex ante by many lawmakers. The lobbyist must walk a tightrope in order to find the position that best balances these conflicting pressures. If group members are sufficiently flexible, or enough lawmakers prefer positions between the competing groups, or the advocacy resources held by the competitor lobbyist are great enough, a lobbyist has an incentive to support a position closer to the competitor. Essentially they minimize their differences on issues, perhaps erasing them entirely if the incentives to find common ground are strong enough.

I end with a few qualifiers. As happens when any human behavior is stripped down to a model, many other contextual factors and idiosyncrasies are lost. Sometimes too much is lost, which may explain why Gray and Lowery (2004) argue against using rational choice models to study neopluralist interest group politics. I see three shortcomings worth noting. The first is relationship context. An important line of research by Laumann and Knoke (1987), Heinz et al. (1993), and more recently Heaney (2004) emphasizes that the choices of lobbyists are shaped as much as anything by whom they know because they are deeply embedded in social and professional networks. Certainly this finding is true. One of the first things young Capitol Hill interns learn (after the importance of free buffets at interest group receptions) is that whom you know is as crucial to success as what you know. This basic truth is not incompatible with my model. Indeed, I assume interactive relationships between and among lobbyists and legislators as well as ideological proximity, both of which are fundamental to network analysis.

The other qualifier is that everything I have described is merely the second stage of lobbying campaigns. Tremendous advocacy has presumably been used already just to get issues onto the government's decision agenda. Indeed, a crucial element of competitive lobbying first highlighted by Schattschneider (1960) is that merely mobilizing competition, a form of conflict expansion, and getting policy alternatives heard is half the battle (Baumgartner et al. 2009). Although some may see it as too great a stretch, a quiet subgovernment dominated by ideologically homogenous elites is simply a degenerate form of my model. As Lacireno-Paquet and Holyoke (2006) describe in terms of education policy, an issue dominated by a subgovernment can still be conceived of as a continuum, but only one small portion that represents incremental change is active or recognized as a legitimate range of choices by participants. A group at odds with prevailing ideology can be identified off to the side, but given the distribution of legislator preferences over the status quo, it would either require truly vast resources to disrupt the subgovernment. Otherwise that outside group's lobbyist can take a position at the group member mean and be ignored by lawmakers and other interests enfranchised in the subgovernment.

Finally, my model appears to provide no option for "not lobbying" by forcing lobbyists to choose positions. I have two comments on this lack of option. First, it is true that I do not model that choice, though that would not be hard to do as too much member punishment, too little legislator support, or too much competition might lower a lobbyist's payoff curve vertically in figure 2.5 below some lobby/not lobby threshold. The model would then reduce to the noncompetitive version introduced earlier in this chapter. My second comment is more conceptual. What is to be gained by not lobbying beyond a near term saving of resources? Not much that I can see. Failure to be active on an issue important to members damages the lobbyist's reputation not only with members, who see their advocate asleep at the wheel, but with lawmakers who likely would no longer see the lobbyist as a player and part of their "enterprise." I doubt most lobbyists could sustain such reputation damage and still have healthy careers in Washington, DC.

Notes

1. Lobbyists themselves may often have a hand in shaping member preferences by controlling the information they receive regarding issues and possible outcomes. Many groups, however, use committee systems for determining official positions on issues or at least guiding principals their lobbyist is to use in staking out positions. These positions are developed as planks and submitted to the membership for approval, usually at annual conferences, and serve lobbyists as guides.

2. This form of constraint on the lobbyist is similar to Arnold's (1990) model of constituent constraint on members of Congress. On issues about which constituents feel strongly, legislators know they are being watched and are more likely to follow constituent preferences.

3. Lobbyists do build relationships with executive branch officials, but because most formal theories of advocacy focus on legislatures, it makes the model's presentation easier if I focus solely on legislatures as well.

4. All of the calculations behind the identification of legislators in CFA's access set, as well as all subsequent calculations for the various curves used later in this chapter and chapter 5, are available from the author on request.

5. If the equation yields a negative number, I record 0 for the relationship's value. In this case all four relationships resulted in 0. The values of these legislators to CFA are $l_7 = 13.5$, $l_9 = 12.5$, $l_{10} = 14$, and $l_{16} = 35$, so $239 - 13.5 - 12.5 - 14 - 35 = 164$.

CHAPTER 3

■

Studying Contentious Policies

PEOPLE in Washington, DC, love to count. House and Senate whips count votes to ensure that their party has enough to move legislation, block it with a filibuster, overturn presidential vetoes, or show party unity behind controversial policies. Pollsters count public opinion survey responses of the electorate to see how the latest political winds are blowing across the nation. Self-described good-government interest groups count the number of dollars the presumably less-good special interests contribute to legislators and presidents and draw conclusions as to whose votes are purchased. Scholars and pundits count presidential power by how many bills on executive agendas are passed within the first hundred days, and sessions of Congress are called "do-nothings" when fewer bills are passed than in other congresses. For a profession so often described as an art, there are many people in the nation's capital who appear to be trying to take all of the uncertainty they can out of politics through quantification. Then they use these quantities to determine power and status. Even the influence of foreign diplomats is measured by the number of cars and SUVs in their formal entourages that tie up traffic in the capital city.

Lobbying, however, is notoriously difficult to quantify. Lobbyists do not like to have their fascinating stories of struggles reduced to cold data points on a researcher's laptop where they will be lumped in with hundreds or, if the researcher is lucky, thousands of other data points. They would rather be the counters (counting votes in Congress or how many co-signers there are on a bill) than the counted. Interest group scholars for their part often have little choice but to slog their way through one interview after another because their subjects are less prone to public scrutiny and their actions are often missing from public records. We do not have access to very many large, truly comprehensive data sets capturing most of the really interesting decisions of lobbyists as do scholars who study voting behavior in the electorate and in Congress (Smith 1995). To pursue their work, interest group researchers often find they must make trade-offs between project tractability and their desire to explore the contextual richness of interest group politics. Thus projects tend to be "broad and thin" or "narrow and thick." The more researchers desire to probe the complexity of social interactions among lobbyists, group members, and lawmakers, and the political system surrounding them, the smaller the scale of their research designs (e.g., Smith 1984; Browne 1988; Rothenberg 1992; McFarland 1993).

The result, as Baumgartner and Leech (1998) point out, is that much of our literature has been built on case studies of single groups and issues. The few population-scale studies of national interest groups that do exist (e.g., Walker 1983; Schlozman and Tierney 1986; Baumgartner and Leech 2001) are thin in that they largely describe what the group community looks like but offer little data regarding what they and their lobbyist do to attract members or advance policy alternatives. The empirical studies that have made the most significant impacts in advancing theory strike a middle ground between these two extremes by utilizing comparative research designs. They study groups and lobbyists working on a limited number of carefully chosen issues or policy domains (e.g., Laumann and Knoke 1987; Heinz et al. 1993; Hojnacki and Kimball 1998). This approach makes it feasible to gather data on the choices of lobbyists and the attributes of interest groups from relatively well-defined subpopulations, and makes it possible to compare behavior from one policy domain to another. Although the results cannot be truly generalized to the population of interest groups lobbying in Washington, they capture the scientific aspirations of social research in a way that most one-issue case studies cannot.

I adopt this approach, with all of its limitations, to test the competitive model. The data I use to test aspects of the model and its implications is drawn from six issues, and the interest groups lobbying those issues, selected according to the criteria laid out below. I then tackle the most significant measurement issues raised in chapter 2, such as ideological measurement on a unidimensional policy space, and propose a solution.

Levels of Analysis in the Research Design

The predictions I lay out at the end of chapter 2 regard the responses of interest group lobbyists to pressures from their members, legislator allies, and, indirectly, other lobbyists, so I need to collect data on the choices of individual lobbyists. Specifically, I need data regarding their position-taking choices on specific issues and the attributes of their interest groups and the people in those groups. Although a comparison could be made of issues within just one area of policymaking (or "domains" such as agriculture, education, or transportation), a better test would be to compare several issues within one policy domain to several issues in another because this approach offers more opportunity to control for many issue and domain-level factors that have been highlighted in the lobbying and public policy literatures but which are not part of the competitive model.

Selecting Public Policy Domains

Public policies, Clausen (1973, 21) argues, tend to clump together by similar characteristics, usually by the issue problems they are intended to solve. The idea that networks of political organizations, lobbyists, and lawmakers concerned with the issues in these "policy domains" develop their own fairly unique systems of issue definitions and behavioral norms has its roots in both the public policy and lobbying literatures, almost to the point where it is taken as an article of faith that elite behavior varies from one policy domain to another (Browne 1988, 246; Victor 2007).

If all policy domains developed similar norms, then domain characteristics would not be an issue in my research design. Yet in his 1973 book, Richard Fenno argued that most policy domains, built around individual congressional committees as a result of the decentralization of Congress in the late 1940s (still considered true today, see May, Sapotichne, and Workman 2006), differ significantly by accepted norms of behavior. While some domains are characterized by norms of quiet, conflict-free distributive policymaking where players are expected to get along and work out deals when they disagree, others have long traditions of animosity and conflict (Ripley and Franklin 1980). Since this domain-to-domain variation in behavioral norms may exert a significant influence, I must control for them through a careful selection of policy domains if I am to isolate the influence of the variables crucial for testing the competitive model.

Theodore Lowi (1964, 1972) was the first to actually try to predict how lobbyists and lawmakers behave based on a general typology of policy domains and how the issues in them are perceived to impact society. As long as policies distributing public money to narrow sets of constituent interests are justified by definitions, arguments, and symbols that reinforce the importance of supporting these interests, he argued, then the result will be less public resistance to the status quo and less internal competition between stakeholders. Public quiescence is maintained through the broad (and therefore invisible) distribution of the costs that support these interests, usually through taxation. Successful justification of such policy prevents other social interests from realizing that they are harmed by it, thus creating a quiet and peaceful policymaking environment where elites are supportive of everyone's share of the policy benefits. This system of mutually beneficial, and therefore peaceful, relationships, of course, refers to the very subgovernments described in chapter 1.

Although the arrival of new groups with more ideological policy goals has broken up some of these benefit-distributing domains (Gais, Peterson, and Walker 1984), they are hardly extinct. Agriculture, William Browne (2001) argues, remains a bastion of public subsidization of crop producers under the guises of economic competitiveness and protection of the nearly extinct family farmer (but see Hurwitz, Moiles, and Rohde 2001). Lobbyists here rarely compete with each other. For these reasons I select agriculture as one of the policy domains I will study.

Redistributive policy often emerges and ultimately redefines a distributive domain when the norms of cooperation and symbols perpetuating a benign policy image break down and competition between interests erupts, forcing lawmakers to choose winners and losers. When the perceptions and justifications of a policy become contested rather than taken as gospel, and especially when one or more social interests perceive the subsidization of other interests to be at their expense, a domain becomes redistributive and competitive. As discussed in chapter 1, much of the mobilization of new, competing interests made many distributive policy domains redistributive. Environmental policy is often so characterized, especially by organizations forced to provide financial support for projects desired by others. For instance, under pressure from environmentalists, Congress requires producers to pay into Superfund to clean up brownfields polluted by industrial waste, even when the waste is produced by other companies (Church and Nakamura 1993). To control for domain-level norms different from those of distributive domains, I will also study environmental policy.

Lowi's third type, regulatory policy, lies outside of this subsidy framework. Instead, regulatory policy involves legal obligations placed on organizations, including for-profit corporations, to compel them to take actions they would not take otherwise. This compulsion normally makes these areas of policymaking quite contentious, especially when other interests are advocating for this regulation. For example, policy that requires banks to make home mortgage loans and other investments in low-income communities is a competitive regulatory policy (Holyoke 2004; but see Santiago, Holyoke, and Levi 1998). Not that all regulatory policymaking is unwanted by the recipients. A branch of economic theory argues that business interests sometimes solicit regulation to raise barriers to market entry by competitors and set price floors to guarantee certain levels of profits (Stigler 1971; Peltzman 1976). The setting of transportation rates on railroads by the now defunct Interstate Commerce Commission was regarded by Milton Friedman as just such a scheme (Friedman and Friedman 1979). This type of policymaking is very different from the other two types, legislators and lobbyists working on them may be constrained by norms and expectations quite different from those of distributive and redistributive domains.

For my third and final domain I choose the regulatory policy domain of banking and finance, but it is worth emphasizing that I am not starting my research this way just to ensure that competition and conflict between organized interests will occur in one but not another. That would introduce serious biases into my research design because I would be deliberately selecting areas of policymaking that enhance or suppress lobbyist conflict. I actually expect that competition and conflict can be better explained by group members and legislator motivations than domain-wide behavioral expectations. Yet it will be interesting to see to what extent, if any, group and lobbyist competition really does vary from domain to domain.

Issue Selection and the Salience Problem

Now I select six issues, two from each policy domain, but this selection brings up another question: Just what constitutes an issue? Is it a single, very precise question about what public policy ought to be, or might it involve a multitude of such questions? Is an issue a bill in Congress that takes up a number of different items deemed to be in need of legislative action, or is it perhaps no more than a single line in a bill creating a single new statute? This question is not trivial. Two interest groups lobbying a large omnibus bill that contains many unrelated proposals may be fighting against each other in the sense that one wants the omnibill to pass and the other does not, even though the policy one desires is unconnected to the policy feared by the other. By the definition of "competition" that I laid out in chapter 1, these groups are not competing against each other because policy benefiting one is not harming the other. The advocacy decisions of one impact the other only by chance, but their interests do not conflict. I need a definition of issue that captures circumstances where a specific policy aiding one interest can be perceived as harming another.

In his highly regarded book on public policymaking, John Kingdon offers the foundation of a working definition. In defining agendas, he writes: "The agenda . . . is the list of subjects or problems to which governmental officials, and people outside of government closely associated with those officials, are paying some serious attention to at any given time" (1984, 3). The key word is "problem," meaning a concern government lawmakers have decided they need to deal with, a question they must answer. Therefore, I define an issue as a specific question that Congress is being asked to answer, such as the following: "Should banks be allowed to sell insurance?" "Should Congress allow drilling for oil in Alaska?" "Should the federal budget be balanced by tapping social security funds?" Not only does a specific question scale the concept of an issue down to manageable size, it also fits well with my definition of competition and the competitive model because it is on a single, specific issue question where one group's members can stake out a position potentially threatening those of another.

Now I can identify discrete issues in the three policy domains, which I do with two guiding criteria. First, I want to include complete congressional cycles. Whether lobbyists view each other as potential enemies or allies, or whether they need to be concerned with each other at all, may vary from committee stages to floor stages of the lawmaking process (see chapter 6), so I want to capture the development of issues not only over one two-year cycle but over two so that the effect of "resetting" (all bills starting over) can also be observed. Therefore, I focus on issues addressed in the entire 106th Congress (1999–2000) and 107th Congress (2001–2).

To identify issues I collected articles published in the *CQ Weekly* (*CQW*), perhaps the most comprehensive coverage of the doings of Congress, over the course of the four years. I read and recorded every article published in *CQW* on every issue from each of the three chosen policy domains, which provided me with three lists of active issues. Yet while interest groups intensely lobby to get issues on to the decision agenda (which Baumgartner et al. 2009 carefully study), competition is most clearly seen, and thus most easily studied, when issues are being actively addressed with legislation or regulation. I therefore added three qualifiers for identifying issues. First, each issue must have manifested as legislation, which means more nebulous problems that might have only been subjects of hearings were not counted.[1] Second, each must have been actively worked on in Congress during the four years, although they did not have to be started or finished. Third, each must also have been the subject of a congressional hearing or have been marked up in committee or on the floor of either the House or Senate.[2] Environmental conservation produced the most issues at thirteen, agriculture the least at six, and banking in the middle with seven.

The second guiding criterion is issue salience. Apart from effects on competition stemming from policy domain type, lobbyist behavior may also be influenced by factors pertinent to individual issues as well, such as how aware the public is of the issue. As Kollman (1998) demonstrates, the degree of public attention focused on an issue can enhance incentives or impose constraints on the choices of lobbyists, changing their behavior from what it might be in the absence of such public scrutiny (also see Bacheller 1977). For instance, he found that groups on more or less the same side of an issue as a significant portion of the public are more likely to use grassroots lobbying tactics to pressure lawmakers. Lobbyists lacking such public support tend to keep lower profiles; they use more behind-the-scenes, face-to-face direct lobbying (Victor 2007). Of course, if the public is not focused on an issue, then a low level of salience may cause this difference in tactics to vanish.

Although the direct effect of salience on lobbyist competition has not been studied, the degree of public salience of an issue has been found to correlate with the level of legislative conflict over it (Price 1978). Only a small number of issues each year, of course, ever achieve anything approaching high public salience, and even fewer are actively tracked by even a portion of the public, yet the effect on how salience shapes policy debates can be substantial (Page and Shapiro 1983). Lobbyists on the wrong side of public opinion (if there is any) might negotiate when they might otherwise have fought, and vice versa. The effect can be so powerful that many lobbyists spend considerable resources in an attempt to raise public awareness of an issue, although the effects tend to be uncertain and they might unwittingly stir up a hornet's nest. In any case, the effect of an issue's public salience is important to a study of competition and conflict and should be part of issue selection.

To control for an issue's public salience and still respect the division between distributive and regulatory/redistributive policy, I drew two issues from the issue lists for each policy domain that differed from each other only in the degree of press coverage each received. Specifically, to measure the level of salience of an issue, I created an index score for each of the twenty-six issues selected based on the number of times an article was written about the issue in the *New York Times* (*NYT*) from 1999 to 2002.[3] Some may quibble with my choice of news outlet, but no publication better serves as a bellwether of issues before the public. Because only the most highly salient issues are likely to attract levels of public scrutiny intense enough to influence lawmakers and lobbyists, I chose to divide all of the issues in each domain into two pools. One contains articles with index scores more than one standard deviation over that domain's average; the other comprises the remainder of articles, that is, the low-salience pool. In all cases only one issue fell into the high-salience pool and was therefore automatically chosen for my study. From those in the low-salience pools, one was randomly selected out of each for a total of six issues.

The Issues Selected

I mention the issues selected here only briefly because they are described in detail in the case studies used throughout the rest of the book. For banking, the high-salience issue selected was reform of the nation's individual and corporate bankruptcy laws. The low-salience issue was money laundering. Both were ongoing issues through the entire 1990s, money laundering being endlessly recast in different types of debates ranging from the war on drugs and terrorism to relief for banks from "unnecessary" regulation. In the area of environmental conservation, the high-salience issue was the lightning rod centerpiece of the Bush administration's energy policy, namely, opening up the Arctic National Wildlife Refuge (ANWR) for oil exploration. The low-salience issue was an effort to increase the amount of royalties oil companies pay for offshore drilling transferred to the Land and Wildlife Conservation Fund, providing more money for states to use in managing wildlife preserves. Finally, the high-salience issue for agriculture, which had the highest score on the salience index overall, was the potential regulation of bioengineered food crops.[4] The low-salience issue, on the other hand, comes with a long distributive history—federal dairy price subsidies. For all of the history of accommodation in agriculture policy, this issue has become divisive as northeastern dairy farmers fight midwestern dairy farmers over what the federally subsidized price for milk ought to be and which region will be advantaged by it.

It is worth pointing out that not all of the issues selected clearly fall into one of Lowi's policy domain types. Specifically, whether an issue and the policy proposed to address it was regulatory, distributive, or redistributive depended on each interest group's point of view. Money laundering, bioengineered food, and drilling for oil in the Arctic National Wildlife Refuge were most clearly seen as regulatory by the lobbyists I interviewed. Banks by and large resisted any additional reporting requirements as simply more red tape and paperwork, whereas consumer and law enforcement groups saw greater disclosure as favorable to the public interest because it would help track funding for drug cartels and terrorist organizations. Similarly, the primary concerns in the debate over using technology to genetically enhance food products, particularly grains and beef, were not so much over whether it should be done but the level of safety testing to be required by the US Department of Agriculture and whether such foods should be labeled for the benefit of consumers. Finally, the ANWR issue was seen by all sides as a matter of how much, if any, of the refuge would be opened for oil exploration.

The use of oil royalties for conservation was considered by some as redistributive. Oil companies would be required to pay more in royalties to state conservation funds, but at the same time these companies anticipated greater revenue from expanded oil drilling in the Gulf of Mexico, making higher payments to the states palatable. Yet from the point of view of some of the more ideologically hard-core environmental groups, the issue was regulatory, that is, whether the US government should even allow expanded drilling. Bankruptcy reform was similarly mixed. The banking industry cast it as a regulatory matter, changing the threshold under which credit card holders would be required to pay back banks under Chapter 13 requirements rather than erase their debts under Chapter 7. It is not surprising that consumer groups advocating on the issue saw it as redistributive, banks making larger profits off consumers by forcing them, often low-income and minorities, to pay money they could not afford to lose or simply did not have. The revision of the nation's laws that set the wholesale price of fresh milk was the most clearly redistributive issue; it could be boiled down to whether a change would provide greater price supports and therefore higher profits for dairy farmers in New England at the expense of producers in the Midwest near the heart of the dairy world at Eau Claire, Wisconsin, or whether the status quo should prevail.

Selecting Interest Groups and Interviewing Lobbyists

With the issues selected, the next task was to identify the interest groups lobbying them. I adopted a strategy similar to the one used to identify issues, using the articles from *CQW* and the *NYT*. But not all groups are equally good at finding their way into press accounts of policy debates. Indeed, Danielian and Page (1994) found that coverage tends to be biased toward wealthier business and industry groups, although Berry (1999) actually found that media-savvy citizen's groups tend to be more adept at getting their names into the printed press. My concern, however, is to make sure that I am casting as wide a net as possible, which I do in a couple of different ways. First, I moved the beginning of the study time period from 1999 back to 1990 to recognize the possibility that an involved interest group, for whatever reason, did not end up mentioned in press accounts during just those four years. Second, I also used hearing witness lists and published reports on hearings by congressional committees during the same expanded time period to supplement my list of groups.[5] Every interest group identified in this material as actively lobbying the issue at some point was placed on issue-specific lists, six lists in all. I ended up with 103 interest groups.

To collect the quantitative and qualitative data necessary for testing the competitive model, I contacted each group for an interview regarding their advocacy on the relevant issue. In each case I attempted to speak to the most senior lobbyist specializing in that issue, although in many cases they were the organization's only lobbyist. The interviews covered a wide range of discussion topics, but I came to each with a survey of specific questions to ask, many of which required closed-end answers. (For a list of all the groups participating in my study, see appendix 1.) It is surprising that most everyone I interviewed was willing to comply with the answer format.[6] (For a copy of the interview survey, see appendix 1.) I tried to conduct as many interviews as possible in person, but many ended up being done by telephone.[7] In the end, 83 out of 102 attempted interviews were completed for a response rate of 81 percent. For all issues, a significant number of interviews were completed. Table 3.1 displays these groups using a reduced version of Schlozman and Tierney's (1986) typology.[8] Each cell in the table lists the total number of groups identified on the issue and the number who agreed to be interviewed.

Are the data at all biased because the number of responses from one type of group may outnumber those of another type of group? For the most part, the distribution of the groups in my sample is roughly similar to that of Baumgartner and Leech (2001). Of the groups in my sample, 34 percent were professional / trade associations compared to 39 percent they found in the population of all Washington interest groups lobbying Congress; labors unions at 5 to 3 percent; and intergovernmental

Table 3.1 Interest Group Types by Issue

Group Type	Arctic Oil Drilling	Bankruptcy Reform	Bioengineered Foods	Oil Royalties for Conservation	Dairy Pricing	Money Laundering	Total Group Type
Professional and Trade Associations	7 (5)	13 (11)	11 (7)	2 (1)	9 (7)	7 (5)	49 (36)
Citizen's and Public Interest Groups	11 (8)	5 (5)	9 (8)	12 (12)	5 (4)	1 (1)	43 (38)
Labor Unions	2 (2)	2 (2)	0	0	1 (0)	0	5 (4)
Intergovernmental Groups	0	3 (2)	0	3 (3)	0	0	6 (5)
Issue Total	20 (15)	23 (20)	20 (15)	17 (16)	15 (11)	8 (6)	103 (83)

Upper-cell value shows number of groups identified; lower-cell value (parentheses) shows the number of groups actually identified.

groups at 6 to 3 percent. The proportion of public interest/citizen's groups, however, was 45 percent rather than their 30 percent. The imbalance, however, was only in environmental policy, 62 percent of all groups in that domain. As the proportions were roughly correct for the other two, rather than not use this data I will use a citizen's group dummy variable in the relevant statistical analyses to control for any significant distortions from an overabundance of this type.

One other apparent omission might raise eyebrows: the lack of corporations or anything else interest group scholars tend to refer to as "institutions." In 1984 Robert Salisbury published another often-cited article that noted that the majority of the entities lobbying in Washington, DC, are not interest groups at all but corporations or entities such as hospitals and universities lacking memberships. Yet Salisbury also suggests why it is not surprising that none appears in my data set and why it should not be a great concern, although this part of his article is often overlooked. It is not surprising because corporations do not seek the limelight of the media and often avoid it. Calls by journalists to corporate lobbyists are often referred to their representative industry association, so my method of group selection is not likely to pick them up. Furthermore, as Salisbury points out, corporations and other institutions tend to lobby very intermittently. They often leave the job and cost of advocacy to their associations unless their interests conflict with those of similar institutions within the same association, so that association leaders cannot provide representation without running the danger of angering powerful members.

Regarding the issues included in my study, corporations, including large banks in the case of bankruptcy reform, did not have major conflicting interests and generally left advocacy to their associations. The American Bankers Association and Credit Union National Association represented financial institutions big and small on changing bankruptcy laws because they all had a common interest in forcing consumers to repay more of their debts. Similarly, the oil industry was united in their desire to open the Arctic National Wildlife Refuge and to expand drilling in the Gulf of Mexico (though these were not priority issues to many companies) so the American Petroleum Institute did most of the lobbying. Even dairy pricing, which sets regional dairy producers against each other and creates conflict within the American Farm Bureau Federation and National Milk Producers Federation, was nonetheless spearheaded on both sides by regional associations such as Western Dairy Farmers and Associated Milk Producers. On none of the issues did I hear of any corporation actively lobbying with the exception of the Monsanto Corporation advocating in favor of genetically engineered food. Monsanto, unfortunately, would not be interviewed.

Competitive Choices and Ideological Measurement

I develop and use a large number of variables in the chapters to come, but a few crucial measures that figure prominently throughout the book are highlighted in this section. For the sake of clarity, I discuss how these measures were constructed and save the others for their respective chapters.

Choosing Positions

In the competitive model conflict and cooperation between lobbyists manifest as the result of decisions to support or oppose policy proposals addressing issues over which their groups are competing. Therefore, my main dependent variable is whether the lobbyists in my sample supported or opposed a series of bills and the positions on the policy outcome space they represent on my six issues. To build this measure, I identify discrete pieces of legislation or executive agency regulation that every lobbyist had to confront from 1999 to 2002 and decide whether to support or oppose. I picked the proposals from the *CQW* articles used to identify issues; the only criteria were that they either had to be (1) bills that had been reported from a congressional committee, or rules proposed by an agency, or (2) proposals to change policy that were specifically mentioned in the *CQW* and *NYT* articles as being supported or opposed by an interest group. In a few cases an amendment to a bill qualified as a proposal, but on no issue did I identify more than four items that met these criteria during the four years. The complete list is in appendix 1.

In the interviews I asked each interest group lobbyist identified as advocating for a particular issue to indicate whether they supported or opposed each bill, amendment, or rule tied to that issue (see appendix 1) and whether this opposition or support was "strong" or "reluctant." "Strong" was explained to mean that the lobbyist found the proposal strongly objectionable or desirable and was more than willing to lobby against or for it. "Reluctant" meant the lobbyist still had reservations about the proposal but agreed to support or oppose it. Answers to these questions form a simple, ordinal indicator of opposition or support.

The differentiation between intense and reluctant lobbying, whether in support of or in opposition to a bill or regulation, produces some interesting results. In figure 3.1 I graph averages of the responses (ignore the distinction in gray for a moment), which revealed two findings. First, no clear indication exists that any more lobbying occurs in opposition to the various proposals than in support of them. On the majority of issues proponents and opponents were more or less balanced, though it is worth remembering that the results in figure 3.1 are averages and which group lobbied on which side may have changed from one bill (an issue iteration) to another. But on two issues no semblance of balance occurred. On dairy pricing, most lobbyists opposed all attempts made to strike a balance between regional dairy interests, whether on questions of new price weights or interstate price compacts. On the flip side, the vast majority of groups that lobbied for the transfer of offshore oil royalties to conservation programs supported this proposal in its many forms. On the latter issue, the fact that a large and enduring coalition of oil interests, sportsmen's groups, and moderate environmental groups supported legislation that ultimately failed to pass reflects the classic political maxim that it is easier to defend a status quo than move new policy.

The second finding is seen in the difference between strong and reluctant lobbying, reluctance distinguished in figure 3.1 by the darker colored portions of the bars that show the proportion of advocacy in support or opposition conducted reluc-

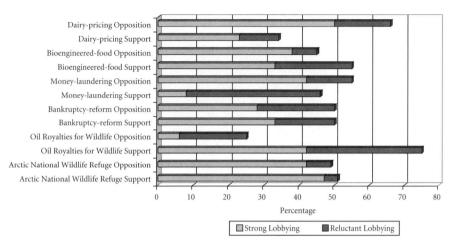

Figure 3.1. Percentage of lobbyists reporting strong and reluctant lobbying by issue

tantly. In all cases, except lobbying in support of money-laundering legislation and in opposition to state wildlife funding, the majority of advocacy was fairly strong. Granted, the lobbyists interviewed may have been inclined to overstate the intensity of their efforts, reluctant to admit any pro forma effort intended to give the illusion of effort (Holyoke 2003). Nonetheless, it appears that most of the lobbying on these six issues was meant to make a difference.

Measuring Ideological Space

Testing the competitive model means creating a policy outcome space allowing me to distinguish between the potential policy positions on a unidimensional scale. As far back as Hotelling (1929) in economics and Clausen (1973) in political science, scholars have been trying to construct dimensions on which actor preferences and choices can be identified as liberal and conservative. Most of this spatial model research relies on interval-level data to mark positions on a continuum whose magnitudes are known, the best known being Poole and Rosenthal's (1997) DW-Nominate scores for Congress. Although interest group politics also tends to be conceptualized in terms of a left–right, unidimensional continuum (e.g., Kollman 1998; Bowler and Hanneman 2006; Baumgartner et al. 2009), we simply do not have such finely tuned measures (but see McKay 2008 for a good effort). Yet to test my hypotheses, potential policy solutions addressing my six issues must be mapped onto a unidimensional continuum ranging from liberal to conservative solutions in a manner analogous to the competitive model in chapter 2. With my data the best I can do is to create a simple ordinal scale that ranks the different iterations of policy proposals from liberal to conservative without measuring how much more liberal (or conservative) one proposal is from another.

I create the scale by taking all of the bills or regulations I asked lobbyists about in the interviews and compare them to each other in terms of the direction they would change current policy. One proposal is ranked as more "liberal" than another if it changes the status quo by providing an increase in public funding, providing more government support to a public welfare program, or imposing more regulation on business. The status quo, or the current position on each issue in 1999, can also be ranked in comparison to the bills and regulations vying to replace it.

An example of this procedure is in bankruptcy reform where four different iterations of the issue, a status quo and three alternative proposals, are identified. The status quo gives consumers a fair amount of flexibility in deciding whether to restructure and repay their debts under Chapter 13 of the US Bankruptcy Code or have most of their debts erased under Chapter 7. Business, especially large retail stores such as Sears and mid-to-large banks, claimed in the 1990s that they were losing millions because the majority of debtors chose Chapter 7. In response, banks and retailers supported legislation in Congress to require all consumers, except under the most severe circumstances, to only file under Chapter 13, which in the 106th Congress was bill H.R. 833. The Senate, however, crafted its own proposal, S. 625, which allowed much greater flexibility for consumers to still opt for Chapter 7; thus it falls between the House bill and the status quo in terms of how conservative a solution it is vis-à-vis the status quo. In the 107th Congress, under pressure from banking interests and House and Senate leaders, senators introduced a new bill, S. 420, which removed some of the exceptions to the Chapter 13 repayment requirements but still left more filing flexibility than the original House bill, making S. 420 more conservative than S. 625, but more liberal than H.R. 833.

As is perhaps clearer now, the status quo and these three bills, all iterations of the issue of bankruptcy reform, can be ranked by how tough they are in terms of repaying consumer debt, arguably a form of economic conservatism. The status quo is the most consumer friendly and therefore is on the most liberal side of the policy outcome space, coded 1. The original Senate bill is more consumer friendly than H.R. 833 or S. 420 but not as much so as the status quo, so it is coded 2. The new 2001 bill, S. 420, is still more pro-consumer than the House bill but not as much as the first Senate bill or the status quo, so it is coded 3; thus the House bill is at the most conservative position, so it is coded 4. Figure 3.2 illustrates what this scale looks like, listing each proposal along with the status quo and its code. I have no illusions about the scale's shortcomings. Reducing a theoretically infinite continuum of possible policy outcomes in this way greatly reduces its utility. The scale is merely an ordinal measure, so I cannot make any claim as to how much more liberal or conservative one bill is than another, merely that it is more or less so. Yet it does allow me to make the distinctions between positions on a continuum in terms of liberalism and conservatism analogous to the policy outcome space in the competitive model.[9]

Ideal Interest Group Positions

I can also use this four-point ordinal scale to roughly locate the ideal positions of the members of the groups lobbying the issue, defined in chapter 2 as the mean of the distribution of member preferences. The first question in the general section of

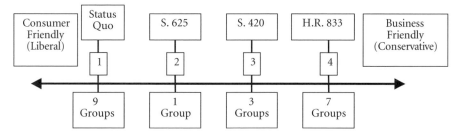

Figure 3.2. Distribution of proposal iterations for bankruptcy reform

questions in the interviews (the first question after the set of questions asking about specific policy proposals, for specific issues see appendix 1) asks what the ideal policy outcome for their members would be on the issue at hand. Their response is easily linked to current policy or one of the alternatives already asked in the first section of the survey. It is a rough measure, but the responses allow me to place every group (but not their lobbyist) on the relevant issue outcome space so that I can get a sense of distance between what each group's members ideally prefer and the positions of bills and rules actually being considered, bills and rules each lobbyist must decide whether or not to support if they are at positions other than their members' ideal position.[10] In the lower part of figure 3.2 I list the number of interest groups working on bankruptcy and show where on the four-point scale I place their ideal member positions.

Some Initial Results

I repeated this coding process for every interest group on every issue, and thus the codes and graphs provided in appendix 1 are similar to figure 3.2. But in figure 3.3 I show the overall distribution of all groups in the study irrespective of issues. A majority appears on the ends of the continuum, but a significant number also occupy the inner positions. Interestingly, it is the two environmental issues that appear to be the most and least polarizing. Drilling for oil in the Arctic National Wildlife Refuge is the most polarized; groups occupy only the extreme positions. But on the state wildlife funding issue the environmental community was fractured; the more liberal groups, such as Defenders of Wildlife and the Wilderness Society, opposed most legislation because they favored more qualifiers on how the money was to be used and fewer incentives for new drilling. Other groups, including the National Audubon Society and the National Wildlife Federation, were willing to use oil-leasing revenue to fund state wildlife preserves.

In chapter 1 I argued that it may be a mistake to assume that all citizen's and public interest groups fall on the liberal side of the ideological continuum in opposition to more conservative business and trade groups. Now it is possible to see whether this is true on my six issues. Figure 3.4 breaks out the groups in my sample by organizational type in two different ways. The first, figure 3.4A, shows the percentage

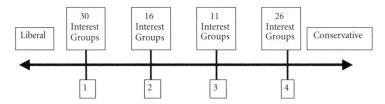

Figure 3.3. Distribution of all interest groups

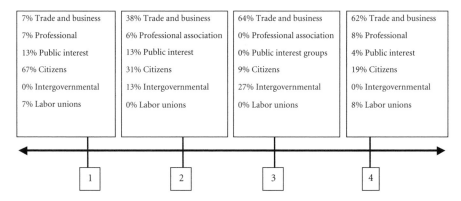

Figure 3.4A. Distribution of all interest groups across all issues by type

of each type of group supporting that position. For example, of all the interest groups ideally preferring position 1 (the most liberal position), 67 percent were citizen's groups but only 7 percent were business and trade associations, while only 19 percent of all of the groups supporting the highly conservative position 4 were citizen's groups but 62 percent were business and trade associations. In figure 3.4B I present the distribution of each group type across all four positions. Of all trade and business associations, only 7 percent supported the most liberal position whereas

Group Type (no. of groups)	Position 1	Position 2	Position 3	Position 4
Trade or Business Association (31)	7	19	23	52
Professional Association (5)	40	20	0	40
Public Interest Group (7)	57	29	0	14
Citizen's Group (31)	65	16	3	16
Intergovernmental Group (5)	0	40	60	0
Labor Unions (4)	50	0	0	50

Figure 3.4B. Distribution of group type by position (%)

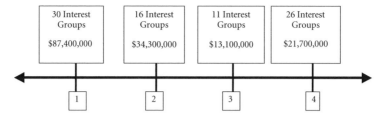

Figure 3.5. Distribution of all groups across all issues by average annual budget

52 percent supported the most conservative. In contrast, 65 percent of citizen's groups support the most liberal position and only 16 percent the most conservative.

The number of labor unions and intragovernmental groups in the sample is too small to draw any conclusions, but there does appear to be some evidence of a liberal–conservative split between trade and business associations on the conservative side and citizen's and public interest groups on the liberal side. Nevertheless, groups of both types do appear at every position. Business-oriented groups are not uniformly conservative, and plenty of citizen's groups have mobilized in support of conservative interests. Public interest and citizen's groups such as Arctic Power, Americans for Tax Relief, the National Taxpayers Union, and Citizens Against Government Waste advocated for very conservative positions on the Arctic National Wildlife Refuge and bankruptcy reform issues. The American Farm Bureau Federation and the National Milk Producers Federation also took the most liberal position on the milk-pricing issue.

This spatial measure also makes it possible to see whether traditional indicators of interest group power, annual budgets, and political action committee contributions are evenly distributed or, as McFarland (1984) and Berry (1999) argue, tend to favor more conservative interest groups.

In figure 3.5 I present the average of the annual budgets of all groups at each position, budget data coming from the 2002 edition of the publication *Washington Representatives.* Similar figures for average budgets by issues are in appendix 1. At least in terms of ideological position, more money is actually associated with the liberal left position on the outcome space than with the other three positions combined. Much of this, however, comes from the support of wealthy groups such as the American Bar Association, the AFL-CIO, and the United Auto Workers (UAW), all of whom opposed bankruptcy reform. Although none of the citizen's groups lobbying this issue, such as the Consumer Federation of America, Common Cause, and the National Women's Law Center, were especially poor, they still could not draw on this same level of internal financial support. Their median annual budget was $4,500,000 whereas the median budget for all trade and business associations was $7,500,000, the average being $37,900,000. Although a clear financial inequality exists between business-oriented groups and consumer and environmental interests, the financial resources measure of power is much more balanced ideologically.

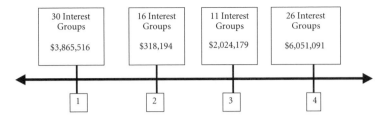

Figure 3.6. Distribution of all groups across all issues by PAC contributions

Of course, annual budgets are a fairly poor measure of group power because only a portion, perhaps a very small portion, of those resources is used for advocacy. A better measure may be PAC contributions, though real power for many groups, such as AARP, comes from the grassroots advocacy they can unleash. For this I collected data on all contributions made by the PACs for these interest groups, at least the thirty-three who had them, to congressional candidates from the Federal Election Commission. The distribution of contributions by issue position is portrayed in figure 3.6 (with the issue specific distributions in appendix 1). The data reveal that the advantage here is clearly on the conservative side of the collective issue dimensions, with groups at position 4 contributing a total of $6,051,091 in the 2000 congressional elections, though only $2,706,445, or 45 percent, was to majority party Republicans in the House and Senate. The remainder was given to minority party Democrats, largely by the United Auto Workers and AFL-CIO, who took the most conservative position on the Arctic oil-drilling issue, that is, they were in favor of opening the refuge to drilling. By contrast, groups lobbying for the most liberal position made contributions of only $3,865,516, and only 5 percent of that sum went to Republicans.

Overall, trade and business associations, along with professional associations, gave $5,950,440, or 65 percent, to Republicans, whereas labor unions gave $5,799,573 (remember that only the AFL-CIO, the International Brotherhood of Teamsters, and the UAW are in my data set), 95 percent of which went to Democrats. Citizen's groups contributed a rather paltry $508,967, and 92 percent went to Democrats. It is surprising that well-known liberal groups such as Friends of the Earth and the League of Conservation Voters gave $651 and $25,503, respectively, to Republicans. This fact may not be as important as the relative imbalance ideologically in contributions, but it is still interesting to see the vast contributing disparities between arguably pro-business interests and those traditionally opposing them.

Concluding Remarks

Without a doubt, these measures are very rough, and great care must be taken in their use, and even more in the interpretation of results based on analyses using them. Nonetheless, the social sciences and science in general have a long history of using rough proxies when ideal measures are not available. In this chapter I am attempting to devise measures that will allow me to test new hypotheses throughout the rest of this book that have not been previously explored in interest group research. It is hoped that better measures will be available in the future, but in the meantime I have tried to use the best methods available to build acceptable measures. If I have failed, then the entire enterprise fails because the analysis chapters that follow are dependent on these measures. I will interpret my statistical results as carefully as I can, but as always, it is for the informed reader to judge whether I have made my measures rigorous enough and whether my findings should be permitted to stand.

Notes

1. No issue was cut from the list for lack of legislation. All issues discussed in *CQW* were introduced as specific bills.

2. As *CQW* frequently provides bill numbers for issues that have taken the form of legislation, it is easy to use the Library of Congress's THOMAS database to ascertain whether or not an issue has been acted on.

3. The LexisNexis database of news articles was employed using key search terms to turn up a fairly complete list of stories on each issue. News summaries were not counted.

4. For comparison, bioengineered food was the subject of fifty-six *New York Times* articles from 1999 to 2002, whereas ANWR was written about in only fifty-one.

5. It is unfortunate that the congressional sources do not go back as far as the other databases do. I was only able to find hearing witness lists for committees back to 1996.

6. No lobbyist refused to answer the closed-end questions, though many embellished their answers.

7. A few times I was not initially referred to the correct lobbyist, but in every case I ended up completing an interview with an individual knowledgeable regarding advocacy on the issue. I learned as much as I could about each issue before interviewing lobbyists, which helped me get to the right person and made the interviews much more productive.

8. Schlozman and Tierney (1986) develop a detailed typology of organizations. Many of their distinctions are fairly cosmetic, so I collapse several categories together to create six types: corporations and institutions, trade and professional associations, labor unions, public interest groups, citizen's groups, and intergovernmental groups. The main difference between public interest and citizen's groups is that the latter have members and the former do not, but I combine the two types throughout most of this book.

9. My assistant recoded these bills, regulations, and status quos, and we compared the results; they agree 92 percent of the time. Thus I have confidence in the measure's reliability.

10. In nearly all cases lobbyists had no problem lining up the ideal positions of their members with one of the proposals we were discussing or the status quo. Perhaps the lobbyist exaggerated somewhat, wanting to claim that members ideally preferred the position he or she had chosen, but in many cases lobbyists acknowledged that what they chose and what members wanted were not the same. Some compromise was made because "that was how politics in Congress worked." Based on the research I did on each group and issue before the interviews, I do not believe that I was lied to at any time. Nonetheless, the measure is still very rough.

CHAPTER 4

An Empirical Analysis of Group Competition

Tʜᴇ introduction of the Conservation and Reinvestment Act (CARA) in 1999 to fully fund state and federal wildlife protection programs cracked Washington's environmental community. At first glance CARA seemed like an environmentalist's dream; it promised a wealth of funding for a new Land and Wildlife Conservation Fund and for state wildlife programs. The dark side of this otherwise wonderful proposal, the League of Conservation Voters (LCV) lobbyist told me, was the source of all of this new money, what it might mean for the future, and its potential to lure her into compromising principles deeply held by the people she represented. That funding for CARA would come from the royalties oil companies paid for the right to drill on public lands was not the problem; oil companies ought to compensate the public for drilling, she believed. No, the problem was that she feared enactment of this legislation would create an irresistible incentive to expand oil drilling, especially in the Gulf of Mexico, to generate even more conservation funding. Nothing in the minds of LCV's members could ever justify such a giveaway to "big oil," but for lobbyists and legislators it would be awfully tempting.

Unfortunately, from a more personal standpoint, to oppose the bill would risk her career as a professional lobbyist. The proposal was the pet project of several important legislators, most notably Rep. Don Young (R-AK), the powerful chair of the House Appropriations Committee. Lobbyists crossed Young at their peril, and to lose the access she now enjoyed to such a senior member of Congress would undermine her ability to play an influential role in this and future environmental policy debates. She was also under pressure from other interest group lobbyists to support CARA. Some of the more left-leaning environmental groups such as Defenders of Wildlife and the Wilderness Society had chosen to oppose it, but many in the environmental lobby, including the National Wildlife Federation and the Izaak Walton League of America, were supporting it. They, in fact, were backed by an astonishingly large coalition of well over one hundred interest groups. The National Governors Association, the US Conference of Mayors, and the International Association of Fish and Wildlife Agencies had brought state and county officials into the game, and of course, the oil lobby through the American Petroleum Institute was backing CARA. In the face of such unified support for the measure, combined with pressure from CARA's 315 congressional cosponsors, LCV's lobbyist found she did not dare fight Young's proposal and lent her organization's support.

This story is not too different from that of the insurance agent lobbyist at the opening of this book; both stories reflect the theoretical arguments made in chapter 2. Members of an interest group may want their lobbyist to remain ideologically pure and wage a fierce battle, even an ultimately doomed one, rather than support a policy proposal significantly different from their ideal. Other organized interests may pressure the lobbyist to join them in support of the alternative, implicitly or explicitly threatening a costly lobbying campaign if they do not. Coupled with the fear of angering powerful lawmakers, this latter pressure overcame the LCV lobbyist's fear of losing members or his or her job. The story lends anecdotal evidence in support of my theoretical arguments regarding the pressures on lobbyists specified in the competitive model. Now it remains to be seen if supportive empirical evidence can also be found by examining the choices made by all of the lobbyists described in chapter 3.

This chapter is really the culmination of the first half of the book. Here I provide a basic test of my hypotheses regarding the incentives and constraints lobbyists are under from group members, their allies in Congress, and the interest group community as they decide which positions on issues to support. For this purpose, I divide the chapter into three sections. First, I describe several additional measures essential for exploring the behavior of individual lobbyists. Second, I explore these measures to gain some empirical insight into the world of competitive lobbying. Third, I use these measures to test hypotheses in a multivariate model of position taking in a competitive environment.

A Quick Look at Competition and Conflict

Any empirical measure of a concept as abstract as "competition" that is based on proxies such as group type (e.g., citizen's groups versus business associations) is not likely to be valid because it assumes that all groups of one type are united in their opposition to groups of the other type and that groups of the same type do not compete with each other. Neither of these assumptions is true. I need an empirical definition that is clearly grounded in the theoretical definition presented in chapter 2, one that emphasizes spatial distances between the positions ideally preferred by members of two or more groups on an issue's outcome space.

In chapter 3 I explained how these positions were coded, and now I use them to build a simple measure of competition. I create a data set by pairing every lobbyist interviewed once with every other lobbyist working on the same issue. The result is a matrix of dyads, or pairs of lobbyists.[1] I then subtract the ideal member position of one lobbyist's group in the dyad from the ideal position of the other and take the absolute value. The result is the degree of (though not the intensity of) competition between those two groups. I then average the position differences between every pair of

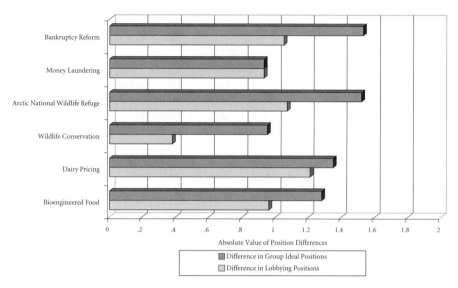

Figure 4.1. Interest group competition and conflict between lobbyists

groups connected to the same issue. The resulting average, graphed as dark bars in figure 4.1, is the total group competition on each issue.

It is not surprising that drilling for oil in the Arctic and bankruptcy reform were the most competitive issues during these four years; on these issues more interest groups had ideal positions further from each other than they did on money-laundering reform and wildlife conservation. These were also the high-salience issues for their respective domains, suggesting a connection between public awareness of issues and the level of group opposition to the positions favored by members of other groups. Of course, it is not clear whether the greater differences between positions were caused by, or were the causes of, the issue's high salience. Lobbyists who seek to raise their group's profile to appeal to potential members might convince existing members to support more ideologically extreme positions. Alternatively, more intense media scrutiny may put leaders in positions where they feel they have to take more extreme positions to keep their credibility. Perhaps more surprising is that the two issues from the distributive policy domain of agriculture, dairy pricing and the regulation of bioengineered food, are not the least competitive as the policy literature predicts. Granted, these issues have more of a regulatory (bioengineered food) or redistributive (dairy pricing) flavor to them, whereas generating more revenue for wildlife conservation is arguably more distributive and, consequently, less competitive. Yet no evidence supports the existence of domain-wide norms of cooperation or conflict.

This measure only reveals the degree of competition on each issue, that is, the differences between the collective interests of group members. It says nothing about how much conflict exists between their lobbyists. To get this information, I find whether both lobbyists in a pair chose to support the proposals they were asked about in the interviews, the same proposals used to build each issue's outcome space in the previous chapter. If one lobbyist in a pair supported a proposal and the second did not, I took the absolute value of the difference between the position of the proposal and the second lobbyist's member-ideal position; I assume the second lobbyist supported the member-ideal position if he or she did not support the proposal, or vice versa if the second supported the bill but the first did not. The difference is 0 if both supported the same proposal; if neither supported it, I took the difference between both of their groups' ideal positions. These positions are those that they chose to fight for, the positions they are trying to convince legislators to support instead of their competitor's chosen position. I did this for every lobbyist pair and repeated it for every proposal associated with the issue, and then did the same for the other five issues. The averaged spatial difference of all the lobbyist pairs for each issue is my measure of total issue conflict, which I graph as light gray bars in figure 4.1.

The results are striking when compared to the dark bars. The differences in positions supported by lobbyists on bankruptcy reform and ANWR are smaller by nearly a third, and nearly no conflict exists at all on wildlife conservation because most lobbyists chose to support the same bills (and therefore the same positions). On bankruptcy reform 33 percent of lobbyists supported proposals at positions on the policy outcome space other than what their members ideally preferred; 36 percent on ANWR and 54 percent on wildlife conservation also did so. Only the money-laundering issue exhibited no change from competition to conflict, but then there was not much competition on this issue to begin with (most of the financial industry was united). Again, the distributive domain issues showed less change from competition to actual conflict. Only 20 percent of lobbyists working on milk pricing supported positions other than their groups' ideal, although 32 percent did on bioengineered food. It is dairy pricing, not the Arctic National Wildlife Refuge, that turns out to be the most intractable issue of my six, whereas the environmental issue of wildlife conservation appears to be the one exhibiting the most compromise.

Looking more closely at this data, simple though it is, reveals something arguably more interesting. In figure 4.2 I graph the percentage of times that at least one lobbyist in a pair chose to support a bill at a position other than the one ideally preferred by his or her members. Lobbyists, it would seem, are frequently supporting positions quite different from those that their members desire, essentially compromising their members' interests. State wildlife funding still exhibits the most position compromise, and dairy pricing the least; however, bioengineered food regulation, the other distributive policy, exhibits the second-highest level of compromise.

The competitive model predicts that when lobbyists choose positions other than those ideally preferred by their members, they should be toward the center of the policy outcome space, not the extremes. Even with the outcome spaces reduced to only four positions, it is possible to see whether this prediction is true. Lobbyists for groups at positions 1 and 4, of course, can only move inward, but those at 2 could support a bill at 1 rather than at 3 or 4, just as lobbyists whose members prefer

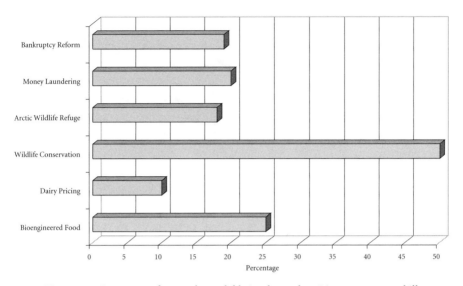

Figure 4.2. Percentage of cases where a lobbyist changed positions to support a bill

position 3 could support bills at 4 rather than 1 or 2. But they rarely do. Looking at groups preferring position 3, I find that their lobbyists only support position 4 in 1 percent of cases and lobbyists for groups desiring position 2 supported position 1 in only 3.5 percent of cases (all on the Arctic Wildlife issue).

The last question now is whether advocates for groups whose members prefer more extreme positions, 1 and 4, are more or less likely to compromise their members' interests by supporting proposals at alternative positions than are lobbyists for groups that prefer the moderate "interior" positions. The statistics presented in table 4.1 are the average spatial differences between the ideal member positions listed in each column heading and the positions actually supported by their lobbyists but only of those groups' lobbyists supported positions other than their members' ideal. The results vary from issue to issue, but the average position change by lobbyists whose members prefer positions 2 and 3 is not significantly greater than it is for lobbyists representing more ideologically extreme members. In other words, no clear evidence exists to support the conclusion that lobbyists for groups at one position are more likely to make compromises by supporting alternatives further from what their members ideally prefer than any other.

Taking a Closer Look at Group Competition in Environmental Policy

Oil-drilling revenue for wildlife conservation through the Conservation and Reinvestment Act (CARA) and drilling in the Arctic (ANWR) are the two issues that, respectively, exhibited the least and second greatest level of lobbyist conflict in figure 4.1 (light gray bars); CARA also shows the most flexibility in the positions taken

Table 4.1 Difference between Group-Ideal Positions and Proposals Supported by Lobbyists

Issue	Ideal Position 1	Ideal Position 2	Ideal Position 3	Ideal Position 4
Bankruptcy Reform	0	0	1	1.5
Money Laundering	—	1	.75	1
Arctic National Wildlife Refuge	0	—	—	1.5
Wildlife Conservation	1.76	1	1.5	0
Dairy Pricing	1	1.24	1	0
Bioengineered Foods	1	1	1	1.5

Cell values are the average differences in positions for lobbyists who chose a position other than their group's ideal position.

by lobbyists, so comparing these issues is a good first step in exploring competitive pressures on lobbyists. Keep in mind that the purpose here is to explore why the level of lobbyist conflict shown in figure 4.1 is often less than the level of competition between their respective interest groups (the dark gray bars) and to consider whether the explanations suggested by the competitive model, that legislative allies and competing groups with greater resources often pressure lobbyists into compromising member interests, might be true.

Funding State Wildlife Conservation

I start by exploring legislator pressure for CARA. In the early 1990s lobbyists from several of the more moderate interest groups (position 2 on the outcome space), notably the National Wildlife Federation (NWF) and the International Association of Fish and Wildlife Agencies (IAFWA), conceived the idea of replenishing state wildlife conservation funds with royalties the oil industry pays for leasing drilling sites on the continental shelf. But great care would be needed to move environmental legislation through a Republican Congress. Their first step was to make the bill highly distributive by crafting authorization language favoring Alaska, western states, and states around the Gulf of Mexico, including Senate Majority Leader Trent Lott's home state of Mississippi (Cushman 1994). Money for state conservation agencies, as opposed to federal agencies, proved palatable enough to attract Alaskans Rep. Don Young (R) and Sen. Frank Murkowski (R), who were perhaps happy to find an environmental bill they could support for natural resource and wildlife-rich Alaska without any new restrictions on resource extraction from the Tongass National Forest or the Arctic National Wildlife Refuge. Their support was a great coup for conservation lobbyists because they chaired the House and

Senate Natural Resource committees where the legislation had to begin. When she gained Young's support, the IAFWA lobbyist told me, she realized her idea might actually have a chance of becoming law.

The next hurdle was how to raise revenue. Originally, NWF and IAFWA proposed an excise tax on sporting goods; their rationale was that those who used nature recreationally, such as hunters and anglers, ought to pay for it when they purchased equipment and licenses. Pragmatic minority party Republicans such as senators Robert Dole (R-KS) and Malcolm Wallop (R-WY) had been willing to consider such targeted taxes for conservation in the 1980s (Healey 1993), but majority Republicans in the 1990s felt less inclined to raise taxes of any kind, especially for anything environmental. By changing the funding source to oil-leasing royalties, reframing their issue as one of "conservation" rather than "environmentalism," and referring to themselves as "conservation groups," the lobbyists were able to draw Republicans (and Democrats) in droves. By 1999 conservation lobbyists and Chairman Young proudly touted bill H.R. 701 in the 106th Congress, with 315 cosponsors ranging from George Miller (D-CA) to W. J. "Billy" Tauzin (R-LA). Only a few dyed-in-the-wool anti–public lands legislators such as senators Conrad Burns (R-MT) and Larry Craig (R-ID) and Rep. Helen Chenoweth (R-ID) were left to oppose CARA (Pope 1999).

The 5,000 or so interest groups listed as publicly supporting CARA not only included like-minded conservation groups such as the Nature Conservancy, Americans for Our Heritage, the Izaak Walton League, and the US Conference of Mayors, but also many nonconservation groups such as the Sporting Goods Manufacturers Association (at least after the excise tax on sporting equipment was dropped) and the National Governors Association along with the Western and Southern Governors associations and even the Camp Fire Girls (Monoson 2000). In an interview, the Sporting Goods lobbyists admitted that many of his members were dubious about supporting conservation legislation, even with its proposed benefits for outdoor sports. But impressed with the groundwork laid by conservation lobbyists, the resources these lobbyists had invested, and the stunning coalition of legislators they had assembled, the Sporting Goods group feared being left out of what they thought was a sure-to-pass bill.

The more unabashedly environmental lobbyists interviewed, such as those with Defenders of Wildlife and the Sierra Club, were also impressed, and even a little intimidated, by the size of these legislator and lobbyist coalitions. They supported CARA, however reluctantly, because this broad ideological support made it likely to pass and they wanted a seat at the implementation table after it did. Selling the issue to their more ideologically committed members, however, was difficult as long as the bill contained the offshore oil-drilling provision, but fortunately (for the lobbyists) their members varied significantly in their feelings about the issue. This variance can be seen in my interview data. For interest groups at position 1 on this issue, the average of responses to closed-end question 2-2 on the relative importance of the issue was 2.33, meaning that CARA was only fairly important to the members of these groups. The lobbyist for the League of Conservation Voters (ideally supporting position 1) even told me that, after having been personally convinced to support

H.R. 701, she found it possible to persuade members because they were fairly "scattered" on the issue and generally ill informed.

For conservation groups with ideal scores at position 2, the average issue-importance score was 3. This issue was their most important one, and the original CARA was the member-collective ideal of NWF, IAFWA, and other conservation groups. When the Clinton administration began pushing for its scaled-back version of CARA in 2000 (often referred to as "CARA-Lite" by the lobbyists I interviewed), the issue in the version that ultimately became law was how much flexibility members allowed their lobbyists. Clinton wanted less revenue redistribution overall, and some of what would be available he wanted put through federal agencies rather than the states. Question 2-5 in the interview protocol measures the flexibility lobbyists believe they have from members to support alternative positions. The average flexibility score for conservation lobbyists was 2.14, indicating some flexibility; so they were able to get away with supporting CARA-Lite at position 3, albeit with a stinging sense of disappointment. More surprising is that the six more liberal environmental groups, with a low member flexibility score of 1.5, also supported CARA-Lite. In an interview the US Public Interest Research Group (USPIRG) lobbyist admitted that intense pressure from the White House was the reason they supported the bill.

The only group in my survey to consistently oppose CARA in any version was the highly conservative American Land Rights Association (ALRA). Its group-member issue-importance score was 3 (high importance) and its flexibility score was 1 (members not tolerating any alternatives). "Don Young really seems to have gone off the rails [with CARA]," a lobbyist for a like-minded interest group I did not interview, the Competitive Enterprise Institute, told the CQW (Pope 1999). Even the scaled-down CARA-Lite legislation was too much for them to swallow, and the ALRA lobbyist told me he would throw everything he had into fighting the "government land grabbing" CARA in all of its forms. In regard to the Republicans supporting the bill, the lobbyist stated, "We're going to be in [supporters'] faces, every week, every day if necessary, for the next two years," he told the CQW (Adams 2001).

Arctic National Wildlife Refuge

As odd as it may seem to anyone tuning into the media coverage of the ANWR debate in the late 1990s, this issue was not really all that important to the oil-extraction and oil-refining industries. Although most environmental groups lobbying the issue drew a clear line in the arctic tundra, it was Alaskan lawmakers who were the most fervent proponents of opening the refuge, especially Republican Ted Stevens, chair of the Senate Appropriations Committee. It also fit with the broader energy policy being pushed by congressional Republicans and was an opportunity to score points against the Clinton administration (Plungis 2000). Thus the majority of Republican lawmakers were at position 4, along with local, state, and even Native American tribal leaders in Alaska, who were all represented by the single-issue group Arctic Power (Pope 2000b; Hebert 2002).

In contrast, lobbyists for the Independent Petroleum Association of America, the Alaska Oil and Gas Association, and even the American Petroleum Institute reported in interviews that the issue was not overly important to their members, though all preferred position 4 (completely opening the refuge). These groups were interested in opening up plenty of other areas in Alaska and the Rocky Mountains for oil and natural gas exploration (Hebert 2002). The average member issue-importance score for the eight groups at position 4 is only 1.88 (lower intensity) and the member flexibility score is 2.25 (higher flexibility), whereas for the environmental groups clustered at position 1, the average importance score is 2.86 and flexibility only 1.14.

Thus group members exercised real constraint over their lobbyists on the political left; they kept them from considering any compromises, including at least whether to explore the refuge to see how much oil was actually there. The Sierra Club compared drilling there to tapping Yellowstone Park's Old Faithful or damming the Grand Canyon (Pope 2000b), and a lobbyist for another environmental group said in his interview that he only wanted "bad things to happen to oil companies." Yet some environmental groups hinted that they took firm stands against any compromise reluctantly. The Audubon Society's lobbyist told me that many of her members were not overly concerned with protecting the refuge, but they took the hard line anyway to please their allies in Congress and to sustain relationships with other environmental groups. "Everybody else was doing it," I was told, "so we did it too." Certainly many Democratic members of Congress were taking the uncompromising approach and pressuring their interest group allies to do so as well, incorporating this high-profile, value-laden issue into their general oppose-the-majority party strategy.

In sum, the rigid position on the left was set by legislators and interest groups whose members were unified in their desire to stamp out any talk of compromise; they pressured other, less ideologically intense environmental groups, whose members did not see ANWR as a life-or-death issue, into also supporting this unyielding position. On the other side, any compromise suggested by oil industry groups, themselves only reluctant combatants, such as supporting exploration-only language in the 2001 Interior Appropriations bill, was only permitted when Republican leaders saw it as a way to embarrass Democrats. More than the other five issues, ANWR was high politics driven more by the legislators than by most of the involved interest groups. Even Arctic Power's lobbyist told me that they just "follow the lead of their congressional delegation; they call the shots, and Arctic Power provides the grassroots support."

Pressure from group members, legislators, and even indirectly from competing groups all conspired to shape the choices of the lobbyists advocating on these two issues. Broad support from legislators of both parties for CARA helped pry many lobbyists away from what their members ideally preferred to support these alternatives, as did the choices of so many competitor groups to form a broad alliance backing those bills. Only property rights groups had members so angry that their lobbyists dared not support any proposals. Some of these same pressures also manifested on ANWR but with different results. In this case the intensity of pressure from environmental group members and their congressional allies kept their lobbyists fiercely opposed to any drilling, and even more intense legislator pressure on the other side kept the oil industry from dropping out of the fight. "It got too political for us," one industry lobbyist told me, "but we had to keep [House Majority Leader Tom] DeLay happy and he wouldn't let us quit." The indirect competitive effect laid out in chapter 2 actually did not occur on ANWR. Rather than move towards each other to make compromises and conserve resources, which is what the indirect competitive effect predicts, lobbyists backed into ideological corners and refused to budge. Of course, the indirect effect assumes that most legislators prefer less extreme positions than interest group members, thus pulling lobbyists towards the middle of the outcome space, but in this case the opposite was true and it was lawmakers who kept lobbyists apart.

A Statistical Look at Interest Group Competition

If a lobbyist's freedom to balance competitive pressures in the policy positions they choose is shaped by members, legislators, and competing groups, then I should be able to find systematic evidence of these incentives and constraints at work in a statistical analysis. The first step is to create an indicator of whether each lobbyist actually chose to support a position reflecting their members' interests or, if both are not at the same position, an alternative proposal. I create a binary variable for every proposal in the survey I used for each lobbyist interviewed and code it 1 if he or she supported the proposal and the proposal was not at his or her group members' ideal position. For example, a lobbyist on the money laundering issue is coded 1 if he or she supported the Federal Reserve's Know-Your-Customer Rule because it is not what his or her members ideally wanted. If he or she supported reform bill S. 1663, the next proposal listed in the survey protocol for that issue, I coded the dummy variable 0 because it is at the same position as his or her members' ideal. I repeated this process for every lobbyist on this issue, and then for every lobbyist on every other issue to create a data matrix of 281 observations. In 35 percent of cases lobbyists supported proposals that were not their members' ideal position, though only on the wildlife conservation issue did lobbyists support alternative positions more frequently than those preferred by their members.

Measuring Legislator Pressure

Pressure from legislators should pull lobbyists toward proposals at alternative positions if the former also support those alternatives. To make this hypothesis operational, I need a measure of pressure that will exhibit a positive effect on a lobbyist's likelihood of supporting a proposal at a position other than what his or her members ideally prefer on the outcome space if a preponderance of legislators also supports it. I cannot use Poole and Rosenthal's (1997) ideology scores to plot interest groups' ideal positions, but I can use them to begin creating a measure of legislator pressure. Common Space scores are comparable from House to Senate (Poole 1998), and from the 106th Congress to the 107th Congress, so I use them rather than DW-NOMINATE scores. For each congress I divide the scores of all House members into quartiles, calculate the percentage of all representatives in each quartile, and assume that those in each quartile support the corresponding position of the four positions marked on each policy outcome space in chapter 3 (see figure 3.3). For example, the 106th Congress had 127 House members, or 29 percent, with ideology scores in the liberal-most quartile, so I assume that 29 percent of House members were generally disposed to support position 1 on all six issues. I repeat this quartile calculation for House members in the 107th and for senators in both congresses.

But 29 percent is not my measure of pressure to support a proposal at position 1. In chapter 2 I assumed that legislators redistribute themselves on specific issues according to their preferences for that issue (the difference between figure 2.2 A and B), perhaps because of pressures from constituents, institutional norms, or party leaders. Common Space data do not capture issue-specific preferences, so I use sponsorship and cosponsorship of the same bills lobbyists were asked about in the interviews as indicators of legislators' "revealed" policy preferences. In a few cases roll-call votes were actually cast by House members or senators on these bills providing data on the issue preferences of all legislators, so in those cases I use roll calls rather than sponsorships to identify supporters of that bill and its position on the outcome space.

All legislators in a quartile who are supporting a proposal corresponding to a different quartile are subtracted from the total number of legislators in their initial quartile and added to the number in the quartile containing the observed proposal. On bioengineered food, H.R. 3377 would impose labeling and testing on all genetically modified foods sold in stores. The bill is at position 1, the most liberal, but 7 of the 87 House members with Common Space scores placing them in the second (liberal-to-moderate) quartile cosponsored the bill. I subtract these seven from the number of legislators in the second quartile, 87 minus 7, and add them to the 127 in the quartile corresponding to position 1, thus increasing the number of supporters to 134. The same is done for the third and fourth quartiles, adding cosponsoring (or "aye"-voting) legislators from those quartiles to the total in quartile 1. The quartile containing the bill does not lose any legislators, at least for this bill. The percentage of legislator supporters in that quartile is recalculated and becomes my measure of legislator pressure on lobbyists to support that bill at that position. The more legislators in the quartile, the more likely it is that lobbyists for groups whose members prefer different positions will support the proposal anyway. Details on this measure's construction are in appendix 2.

Interest Group Member Constraint

The competitive model also predicts that lobbyists are more likely to be constrained to support group-ideal positions when their members feel strongly about the issue and individual member preferences for policy outcomes are similar (preferences are clumped rather than dispersed over the outcome space). It was not possible to gather data on the preferences of all interest group members, so I asked a battery of questions in the interviews regarding lobbyists' perceptions of member preferences. This approach may be best anyway because it captures what lobbyists believe about the intensity and unity of member preferences. Referring to the interview questions asked of all lobbyists (appendix 1, page 155), I build the scale out of answers to questions 2, 3a, 4, 5, and 6. I reverse the answer coding of the last three so that on all questions higher values mean greater constraint on the lobbyist. I employ a confirmatory factor analysis (see table A2.13 in appendix 2 for more details) of the five variables and find that they all load on one, and only one, dimension, which I use as my index of group member pressure.[2] Bankruptcy reform yields the highest member-constraint score and reform of milk pricing regulations the least. The highly polarizing ANWR issue is only the third most constraining issue. Less surprising is that interest groups classified as citizen's groups have an average member-constraint score nearly one standard deviation greater than the average for all other group types.

The Indirect Competitive Interest Group Effect

This variable is the heart of my research, and like the legislator-pressure variable, it has to be designed to pull the observed lobbyist toward a bill at a position other than what his or her members prefer. Chapter 2 characterizes competition between a pair of interest groups on an issue as a combination of the spatial distance between their member-ideal issue positions and the advocacy resources each can draw on to influence the legislators who ultimately decide whether to pass or reject a proposal at one of these positions. Now, however, I have more than two groups striving to influence legislators, so the indirect competition variable must be an aggregation of the spatial distance between one observed group and all of the others in the direction of the proposal multiplied by those groups' financial resources. It is possible that groups that prefer positions on the other side of the observed group might also exert some countervailing pressure, but for the purpose of designing this variable, I am concerned only with pressure pulling a lobbyist in the direction of the observed proposal.

For example, on oil revenues for wildlife conservation, seven groups are at position 2, but the CARA-Lite proposal is at 3 where there are only two groups (and one more at 4). The need to counter the advocacy of competing groups at position 3 should pull a lobbyist whose members supported the original CARA (position 2) toward CARA-Lite. So, for an observed group at 2, I take the absolute value of the difference between its position and the first group at 3, and then the other group at 3 and then the group at 4, and multiply each of these three differences by each competing group's annual budget. This weights the distance between them by the resources competitors could potentially bring to the advocacy conflict to sway legislators if the lobbyist chose to support his or her member-ideal position (position 2) instead of CARA-Lite at position 3. Groups further away, or with larger budgets, have greater influence.[3] Then I average the products of distance and budget for all of these competing groups to produce the indirect competition score for all lobbyists whose members prefer position 2 on the wildlife conservation issue when CARA-Lite was being considered. Aggregate group-competition scores for all positions on all issues are in appendix 2, but the highest score appears on ANWR and the least on the wildlife conservation issue.

Multivariate Analysis

Several control variables were created for the multivariate analysis. The competitive model shows how the indirect competitive effect can be mitigated by the observed lobbyist's resources, at least those he or she will commit to counterpressuring legislators. Interview question 2-8 asked lobbyists to rank their commitment of resources to the issue relative to other issues they might be working on, to create an ordinal indicator of "less than," "about the same as," or "more than" other issues. Coding "less than" as 3, "same" as 2, and "more than" as 1, I divided the group's annual budget by this variable so that the organization's financial resources are weighted by the level actually committed to this advocacy campaign.[4] Another resource variable I use is the number of lobbyists actually employed by the interest group, which comes from *Washington Representatives.*

Binary variables are coded 1, indicating whether the issue is highly salient, whether it is from the distributive policy domain of agriculture, and whether the lobbyist's organization is classified as a citizen's group. Although not the focus of my work, contributions to majority party Republicans should at least be controlled for, so each group's 2000 cycle campaign contributions discussed in the last chapter are averaged into a single variable. Older interest groups with more well-established reputations and experienced lobbyists may also act somewhat differently from younger groups, so the year each organization was founded was acquired from *Washington Representatives* and subtracted from the year of the observed proposal. Finally, the passage of time across these four years might also matter, so I use an ordinal variable to simply mark the order in which each of the proposals used in this book appeared in time so that the first is coded 1 and the last is either 3 or 4.

The dependent variable, whether a lobbyist supported a proposal, is binary, so I use the probit method to estimate the statistical model and present the maximum likelihood estimates for each explanatory variable in table 4.2. The key variables appear to perform as predicted by the competitive model. The more important the issue is to group members and the more unified they are in their preferences for policy outcomes, the less likely their lobbyist is to support legislation at a different position. Nor is he or she likely to deviate from member wishes when they commit more resources to the effort, which reflects their greater capacity to persuade legislative allies to support the member-ideal position. Perhaps it also shows a greater need on the lobbyist's part not to be seen making compromises when members may be asked to replenish organizational coffers. Alternatively, more congressional allies who support a proposal at a position on the outcome space other than the one group members desired does make it more likely that lobbyists will compromise their members' interests to support the interests of these legislators.

Most important, interest group competition also exhibits the predicted effect. More aggregate competition from groups supporting positions at or near the proposal in question makes it more likely that any single lobbyist will do the same. In figure 4.3 I break out the first-difference influence of this variable by issue (all other variables held at mean and modal values). It is important to understand that the effect seen

Table 4.2 Likelihood That a Lobbyist Will Support Positions Other Than Member Ideal

Explanatory Variable	Maximum Likelihood Estimate (Standard Error)
Group Member Constraint Index	$-.45^b$
	(.14)
Pressure from Members of Congress	$.02^a$
	(.01)
Aggregate Competition from Other Interest Groups	$.04^b$
	(.01)
Resources Interest Groups Commit to This Issue	$-.01^a$
	(.00)
Highly Salient Issue	-1.04^b
	(.21)
Distributive Policy Domain Issue	$-.32$
	(.22)
Number of Lobbyists Employed by the Interest Group	$-.04^a$
	(.02)
Citizen's Group Interest	$-.77^b$
	(.22)
Interest Group Age	.01
	(.01)
Amount of Contributions to Republicans in Congress	$.01^a$
	(.01)
Issue Iteration	.11
	(.08)
Constant	$-.80^a$
	(0.35)
Wald χ^2	82.59^b
Pseudo R^2	.26
N	281

$^a p < .05;\ ^b p < .005.$

here is not the amount of interest group competition; it is the effect competition has on the lobbyists working each issue. Something interesting is revealed here when the curves here are compared to the dark gray bars in figure 4.1. Here we see that lobbyists who advocate on money laundering and wildlife conservation are more likely to support positions other than their group member ideals because of competition than are advocates on the other issues. Yet figure 4.1 shows that these were the two issues exhibiting the least interest-group competition as measured by differences in ideal positions. The reverse is true for ANWR, milk pricing, and bankruptcy reform, the issues with the greatest competition in figure 4.1 but exhibiting the smallest indirect competitive effect in figure 4.3 (although an effect ranging from .02 to .40 is still substantial).

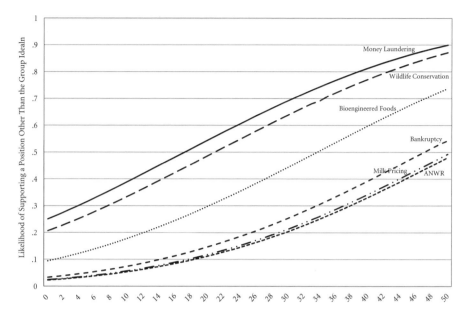

Figure 4.3. The competitive effect by issue

This variation in the indirect competitive effect is the result of variation in the other constraints on the lobbyists from issue to issue. Variables operationalizing other constraints are held constant within the context of each issue as the marginal effect of interest group competition is calculated, but are held constant at different values from one issue to the next. Group members felt more intensely about ANWR, bankruptcy reform, and milk pricing than they did about wildlife conservation and money laundering, so this constraint on lobbyists was weaker and allowed for competing groups to have a greater influence on lobbyists. In other words, what figure 4.3 shows is not only the relative influence of interest group competition, but how this effect is sometimes diluted by other pressures, such as the need to keep group members happy.

The indirect effect is still just that, competing groups indirectly affect a lobbyist's choice of positions because they can force him or her to spend more resources on counter advocacy. So lobbyists for wealthier groups should be in better positions to resist this competitive pressure because they can draw on more resources to persuade legislators to reconsider their support for alternative policy outcomes. The statistical model is not capable of capturing all of these intricacies, but I can explore the interplay of group resources, legislator pressure, and competition. In figure 4.4 I plot the marginal effect of group competition on a lobbyist's decision to support an alternative proposal when he or she is committing only a low level of resources (one standard deviation below the mean) under more intense legislator pressure, and then again when he or she has abundant resources and faces little legislator pressure. When there are no group competitors trying to influence many of the same

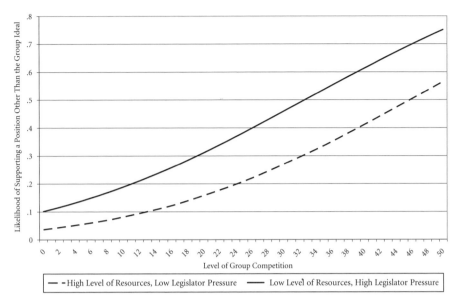

Figure 4.4. Effect of group competition by resources and legislator pressure

legislators (on the left end of the horizontal axis), the difference in the effect of resources and legislator pressure (difference between the two curves on the vertical axis) is small. When competitive pressure rises, the gap expands from about 5 percent to about 19 percent. Low resources mean the lobbyist has less ability to resist competitor advocacy, which in turn increases legislator pressure. The increase in the gap to 14 percent may also reflect greater pressure from legislators because they themselves are being pressured by competing lobbyists to support alternative positions, pressures they pass on to the observed lobbyist.

In addition to interest group competition and legislator pressure, the competitive model in chapter 2 holds that the other main pressure on lobbyists is the intensity and unity of their members' preferences. All things being equal (meaning all other independent variables set at mean or modal values), in the statistical model an increase of one standard deviation in group member pressure decreases the likelihood that lobbyists will support an alternative position by 11 percent, whereas an increase of one standard deviation in legislator pressure increases this likelihood by 7 percent. Yet all of these pressures are frequently changing, so the best approach to understanding their influences and to complete my basic test of the competitive model is to study their interplay as well.

In figure 4.5 I explore the influence of group competition within the context of legislator and group member pressures, calculating the likelihood a lobbyist will support an alternative proposal for every value of the competition variable when member constraint is one standard deviation lower than average and legislator pressure one deviation higher, and then vice versa. The dashed curve shows that when a

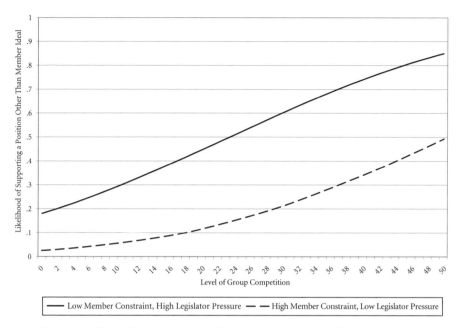

Figure 4.5. Effect of group competition by member constraint and legislator pressure

lobbyist's group members feel strongly about the issue and are relatively united in their collective positions and the countervailing pressure from legislators is low, then interest group competition appears not to matter much at all. If the .5 mark in figure 4.5 is the cut-point between not supporting and supporting an alternative proposal, then when member pressure is low but legislators support the alternative, adding in competition from other interest groups rapidly changes the lobbyist's calculations, increasing the likelihood of support from 18 percent at the lowest level of competition to 86 percent at the highest. This result is hardly surprising as the competitive model predicted that the influence of group competition was tied to the preferences of legislators.

Every combination cannot be explored here. Instead I merely point out a few other interesting results in table 4.2. Perhaps most important is the influence of issue salience. Because of the negative effect member pressure has on lobbyists' willingness to support alternatives, it is not surprising that when issues are highly visible to both group members and the public (some of whom are potential members), lobbyists are significantly less inclined to support any positions other than the one their members prefer. The very promotion of some issues by the media or perhaps by concerned lawmakers through the media might contribute to this ideological purity on the lobbyist's part. Of course this issue salience also serves to make compromise among competing lobbyists nearly impossible, a theme I take up in the next chapter. Whether or not the issue is in a distributive domain is not significant, but this finding is unsurprising given the lack of evidence for such an effect seen earlier in this chapter. Also unsurprising is the citizen's group dummy. Lobbyists for these ideological groups, whose members are attracted by purposive incentives, appear decidedly less willing to compromise member interests, perhaps because more of them pay close attention to politics, are aware of what their lobbyist is doing, and are less tolerant of anything smacking of compromise.

Conclusion

For all of the time spent on developing measures and graphs, this chapter had only one real purpose, to see if empirical support existed for the main mechanisms of the competitive model as laid out in chapter 2. And support was found. Keep in mind that in a subgovernment it would probably not have been necessary to choose between policy proposals and member interests or to balance conflicting pressures. Group member desires and legislator goals would be largely aligned and competing groups would not have existed (or been considered legitimate). The null hypothesis that the key variables measuring competitive group politics pressures are not significant could not have been rejected. The lobbyist would quietly be helping lawmakers serve member interests, what Milbrath saw happening in the late 1950s and 1960s.

Instead legislators who were normally disposed to serve a group's members are finding that they must now support bills at other positions and serve other interests and want their lobbyist ally to do so as well, even when it comes at the expense of the lobbyist's members. This pressure is only exacerbated when lobbyists for competing groups take the field and use their resources to persuade legislators, often the very legislators the first lobbyist has built exchange relationships with, to support positions detrimental to his or her members' interests. Now the lobbyist is hard-pressed to wisely use resources to find a position that keeps at least some members moderately happy but from which he or she can still retain influence in Congress. Wealthier groups have an edge and thus need make fewer compromises, though lobbyists for more extreme groups are in less tractable positions. Only when members really care about an issue and are united in their preferences are lobbyists likely to feel the need to faithfully represent the desires of their real employers.

These results are modest. The theoretical model in chapter 2 was fairly abstract, and just because empirical evidence now supports it does not make it fully capable of explaining all advocacy behavior. It has yet to shed new light on current questions in the literature. What can it actually contribute to interest group scholarship? What, really, are the consequences of competitive lobbying for interest group politics? I spend the remainder of the book trying to find out as I use the model to extend other research agendas.

Notes

1. For example, on ANWR I start with the first group in my list, the AFL-CIO, and create the first observation in the data matrix by pairing it with the second group, Alaska Oil and Gas Association. Then I pair AFL-CIO with the third group, the American Association of Petroleum Geologists, and continue until I have paired this umbrella labor organization with every other group lobbying the issue.

Then I start again with the second group, Alaska Oil and Gas, and pair it with every group except AFL-CIO because I have already paired these two. This process is reiterated until every group lobbying the issue has been paired only once with every other group. Then I repeat this process for the remaining five issues to create the data matrix.

2. In cases where the same group was interviewed on multiple issues, separate interviews were conducted with separate lobbyists so that the answers of groups, such as American Bankers Association or Natural Resources Defense Council, and their member-constraint scores vary from one issue to another. In cases where a group lobbied on two of my issues, I conducted separate interviews with separate lobbyists to preclude the possibility of one interview influencing another and thus to preserve the integrity of the different groups' member-constraint scores. As a result, these scores from the American Bankers Association and the Natural Resources Defense Council vary from one issue to another.

3. Annual budgets come from *Washington Representatives* (2000 edition), although in a few cases the data was not available so I requested it from the lobbyist who was interviewed. The budget data was also widely distributed, running from small budgets of a couple hundred thousand dollars up to many millions, such a wide variation that I "smoothed" the difference by taking the natural logarithm to convert the data that I use throughout the book. This helps reduce the influence of some very substantial outliers in the data on the statistical estimates.

4. I did not use it to reduce the resources the competitor lobbyists can bring to bear in the indirect competitive effect measure because the first lobbyist only anticipates the resources his or her competitors can draw upon, not what they will actually commit.

PART II

Consequences of Interest Group Competition

CHAPTER 5

■

Competition in Coalition Politics

AGRIBUSINESS lobbyists knew 2001 was going to be a year of trouble. An issue they had kept off the congressional agenda for years was erupting, and this time they would be hard-pressed to defend the status quo. Ever since a 1992 decision by the US Food and Drug Administration (FDA) not to label genetically modified (GM) grains, and meat from cattle fed on those grains, consumer protection lobbyists had been assembling a coalition strong enough to convince Congress to mandate exactly that. Already facing growing resistance in European markets, Monsanto, Cargill, and Con-Agra did not need a new anti-GM foods campaign to shake consumer confidence at home. Unfortunately (for them), the Genetically Engineered Food Alert coalition, comprising lobbyists from Consumer Federation of America, Consumers Union, USPIRG, and a dozen similar groups, were gaining traction with their Frankenfoods campaign, which equated artificially enhanced food with Mary Shelley's famous artificial monster. Pooling their talents for made-for-media grassroots activism, these groups were spreading a message of doubt, even fear, among consumers. Agribusiness lobbyists only needed to look across the Atlantic to see how quickly such campaigns could poison markets for GM foods.

Appreciating the truth of "united we stand, divided we fall," agribusiness lobbyists decided they also needed a united front, not only among GM-food manufacturers but distributors and producers as well. Distributors, including the Grocery Manufacturers of America and the National Food Processors Association, proved easy to bring on board, but producers vacillated. Many corn, wheat, and soy farmers had no particular objections to planting GM grains, but they feared embracing the agribusiness position lest consumer advocates gain the upper hand and terrify shoppers and wholesalers into rejecting their products. Many, including the American Corn Growers Association and American Soybean Association, felt the better strategy might be to make common cause with the other side; by embracing tests and labels they might gain consumer confidence and thus better resist efforts at a ban.

Biotech lobbyists knew they were unlikely to win without swing-group producer support. The social and political values symbolized by the American farmer were too potent a weapon to let fall into the Alert's hands. Ultimately their ideological compatibility and greater resources persuaded producers to back away from the rival coalition; however, the delay allowed consumer interests to make headway on Capitol Hill, and the issue became the subject of hearings and legislation. The pro-GM side finally "got its act together," as one producer lobbyist told me in an interview; but to persuade lawmakers and win, they had to compromise their own interests by accepting producers' demand that they all support FDA's new rule creating a modest GM food approval process and a labeling system that producers could opt out of.

Coalitions are a way of life today in Washington, DC. Whether in Congress, the Supreme Court, or interest group lobbying, policy change is rarely achieved without the support of other, often many other, players. The literature on lobbying coalitions is now relatively well developed; it reveals how resources, both financial and informational, act as attractors, and at first glance it may not appear to fit easily into an analytical framework that emphasizes competition. For lobbyists who represent cohesive memberships supportive of the same policy outcomes, such as consumer groups or agribusiness groups on GM food regulation, coalitions are a "no-brainer." But what of producer lobbyists? More sympathetic to the position of biotech companies in their desire for less regulation, why would they be willing to consider partnering with consumer interests by supporting policies that might leave some of their members scratching their heads in bewilderment? And why would technology firm lobbyists form a coalition supporting a new regulatory scheme just to keep producer groups out of the consumer interests' camp? Coalitions often turn out to be ideologically stranger the closer one looks them, but with the core elements of the competitive model now in place and somewhat verified empirically, I can start using it to explore and perhaps untangle interest group coalition politics a little more.

Coalitions in Interest Group Politics

Interest group coalitions are hardly a new phenomenon, and scholars have not failed to recognize it. Key (1942, chapter 2), Truman (1951, 362–68), Milbrath (1963, 206–7), Bauer, de Sola Pool, and Dexter (1963, 325–28), and Greenwald (1977, 75–76) all take a little time to mention occasions on which groups formed alliances to push forward or push back against new policy. Yet none really explores the strange logic behind coalitions, perhaps because in the subgovernment age of less ambiguous (if not actually clear) lines of demarcation between policy jurisdictions, as well as between groups' member and issue niches, coalitions were less necessary, emerged less frequently, and were thus less interesting to study. But as more groups representing new and more varied interests appeared and as subgovernment boundaries blurred into cross-jurisdictional issue networks, Schlozman and Tierney (1986, 48, 278, 306) and Salisbury (1990) argue that lobbying coalitions are rapidly becoming a normal way of life and studying them is essential if scholars hope to understand modern interest group politics.

The literature on coalition formation is arguably small in comparison to the importance of the topic. It addresses two questions: (1) why coalitions form and (2) how they function once they do. Kevin Hula (1999) tackles the first with an eye toward the second. Lobbyists find coalitions attractive, he argues, because they provide a low-cost way to advocate on more issues and policy domains than they can otherwise afford. Thus, joining a coalition can enhance their organization's reputation with group members, potential members, and show lawmakers that they are key players in policy debates—even though their real level of activity and influence is less than meets the eye. Participation in coalitions, he argues as he moves toward the second question, or line of research, also helps lobbyists keep abreast of the activities of their colleagues and other players in exchange for whatever tactical information they can provide. More about how lobbyists participate has been explored through network analysis by Carpenter, Esterling, and Lazer (2004) and Heaney (2004, 2006), who find that more "central" players wield more influence. Although competitive pressures almost certainly shape these communication structures, I restrict myself to exploring the foundational question of why they join in the first place.

Hula (1999, 38) was certainly aware that it is sometimes advantageous for lobbyists to not join coalitions, but it was Marie Hojnacki (1997) who really framed joining as a calculated decision with potential costs. Within that frame she stresses that what lobbyists risk in coalition formation is their organization's "autonomy"; that is, it is easier to impress current and potential members when they show that they do not need to lean on others to successfully promote member interests. She portrays resources as compensation for the risk to their group's autonomy that lobbyists take by joining a coalition, which in turn depends on how likely potential coalition partners are to actually provide resources.

To study coalition formation in a competitive framework, I begin with this notion of compensation. If differences in member interests exist between groups, then greater the distance on the outcome space separating them, the more autonomy their lobbyists sacrifice by working together and the more compensation is required to make alliances worthwhile. After all, joining a coalition is essentially a declaration as to who a lobbyist's "friends" and "enemies" are on an issue, and some group members might be surprised to learn just who some of their lobbyist's friends are. Of course, the less members care about the issue, the freer their lobbyist is to have increasingly strange bedfellows. Thus a competitive framework should not only shed new light on strategic coalition-joining decisions, it should also help explain the size and ideological breadth of coalitions.

A Look at Competitive Coalition Formation and Stability

First consider the following two questions: Are lobbyists crossing policy space to form coalitions, or are coalitions simply composed of lobbyists for groups with the same ideal positions on issues? A reexamination of coalition politics in a competitive context is not needed unless a coalition has strange bedfellows to explain. To find out I counted the number of times that the lobbyists in my data set chose to support each policy proposal listed in appendix 1. I then average these percentages for a measure

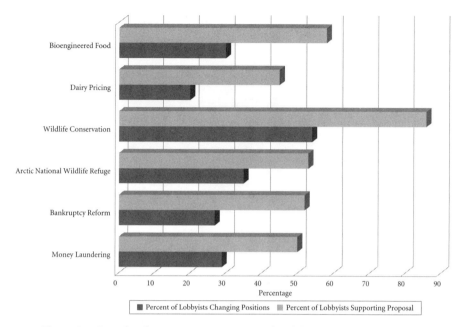

Figure 5.1. Size of coalitions supporting a proposal and the spatial distance crossed

of cooperation on each issue and graph the results as light gray bars in figure 5.1. The figure, for instance, shows that 58 percent of the lobbyists working on the bioengineered food issue chose to support one or more proposals rather than their member-ideal position (unless the proposal was at their member-ideal position).

I assume, of course, that everyone supporting the same proposal actually worked together for it in a coalition, even though some coalitions existed only a short time. Some coalitions were actually very formal, with their own letterhead and website, such as the Genetically Engineered Food Alert. Others were informal but endured over time from proposal to proposal, such as the one backing the Conservation and Reinvestment Act discussed in chapter 4. Still others were entirely ad hoc, lobbyists (respondents told me) quickly trading information and developing tactics as they passed each other in the Capitol building. I also do not assume that all opponents of a proposal coordinated their efforts in a coalition. Supporters all backed the same position (a coalition can only support one position), but opponents supported a variety of alternative positions.

The average sizes of these coalitions are fairly large, especially on wildlife conservation, where the majority of lobbyists supported H.R. 701 (the original CARA). More interesting, however, are the dark bars in figure 5.1. They capture the percentage of lobbyists who supported proposals at positions not ideally preferred by their members, who crossed policy outcome space to form coalitions with their competitors to back a proposal. Again, the data is too rough to know just how strange these bedfellows really were, but coalitions based on compromises among competitors occurred to some extent on all six issues. Asking why competitors would cross policy outcome space and join others to back a proposal links the coalition literature to the competitive model.

Another point to consider is coalition stability. Figure 5.1 tells us nothing about whether lobbyists working together on one proposal continued to work together on the next. To see whether they did, I use the same issue-specific lobbyist pairs I created for chapter 4. I calculate the percentage of lobbyist pairs where both did not support the same position on one proposal but did so on the one next in time (pairs coming together) and where at least one chose not to support a later proposal after both supported an earlier one (pairs coming apart). On ANWR and bankruptcy reform, partnerships were completely stable; that is, pairs of lobbyists either chose to work together on all proposals, or never did on any. On money laundering, 47 percent of all partnerships came later in time, but once they formed they held (no pair came apart). Coalitions were less enduring on GM food; 50 percent of lobbyists came together at some point in time during the four years, whereas 23 percent of them parted ways later. Wildlife conservation was similar; 34 percent partnered after the first proposal, but 34 percent parted later. On dairy pricing, 11 percent came together, but then 24 percent came apart; thus fewer lobbyists were actually working together at the end of the four-year period than at the start.

The question then arises: Is there a timing element to coalition formation, one that perhaps favors a point later in time to ease the passage of legislation? On state wildlife conservation, 79 percent of all cooperating pairs occurred on the middle proposal, which was in mid-2000 and helped the Clinton administration enact CARA-Lite as part of its environmental legacy. On bioengineered food, 44 percent came together on the final proposal to support the FDA's compromise rule on labeling. On milk pricing, 60 percent occurred on the final proposal, which was a compromise that compensated some dairy farmers but eliminated an old, region-based pricing system. It was all but one group (ACLU) on the final money-laundering proposal, though in this case the September 11 attacks convinced groups such as America's Community Bankers and Financial Services Roundtable to put aside their differences and support legislation to fight the laundering of terrorist money. In other words, on three of these four issues large coalitions formed later in time and appeared crucial for enacting new laws resolving these issue questions (I explore this further in chapter 6). On ANWR, coalitions never expanded, but no new policy ever passed. On bankruptcy, coalitions were also small but stable, and it would be four more years before new legislation was enacted.

The Direct Competitive Effect

Explaining why lobbyists would put aside differences in member interests to form coalitions requires returning to chapter 2. Although it was possible in my milk-pricing scenario for the CFA and NTU lobbyists to advocate together for the same position, no reason was given why they would (beyond coincidence). More development of the model is needed. Recall from figure 2.3B that a lobbyist's "alternate set" consists of positions on the policy space he or she values more than the one ideally preferred by a majority of group members. Moreover, the set's range changes as support and pressure from group members and legislators grows or diminishes, the latter changing partially in response to advocacy by other lobbyists (the indirect competitive effect). Yet these pressures are often insufficient to get competitors to support the same position. A new incentive is necessary to increase the height of both lobbyists' payoff curves so that the range of positions they are willing to support as alternatives to their group member ideal positions in figure 2.3B will extend further toward the outcome space's center. Perhaps they will intersect and reveal a set of positions both prefer to member ideals *cfa* and *ntu* and yield payoffs greater than for their competitive optimal positions identified in figure 2.5.

Hula (1999, 26–27, 34) identifies just such an incentive. He argues that perhaps the most important incentive for lobbyists to form coalitions is the sharing of advocacy resources, both tangible financial resources and the nontangible exchange of political intelligence and access. This makes sense when considering Salisbury's (1990) argument that an increase in the number of interest groups that lobby Capitol Hill reduces the influence of every individual lobbyist and the resources he or she wields. If the CFA lobbyist combined resources *r* with NTU, which would happen only if both chose to support the same position, then both now possess more resources for persuading legislators. In fact, by lobbying for the same position, the cost of persuasion and the relationship damage endured should they fail might be even less for CFA than it was before NTU decided to lobby (remember that supporting different positions means they expend even more resources in conflict with each other, but the indirect competitive effect disappears when they support the same position).

Assume for a moment that both the CFA and NTU lobbyists are willing to share their resources at every position on the milk-pricing continuum. The greater advocacy costs both incur for lobbying against each other, the indirect competitive effect, now vanishes. Furthermore, with resources now combined, they find that they can obtain the support of more legislators, perhaps all of them, so that significantly less payoff loss occurs for breaking legislator–lobbyist relationships at any position. I show the result of this in figure 5.2, which is based on figure 2.5. Here I take CFA's competitive joint curve from figure 2.5 (the lower dashed curve where *ntu* = 20) and smooth it and alter it so that it peaks (balances pressures) over position 7 rather than 15 (it is now the solid curve for CFA in figure 5.2). I then add a similar competitive joint curve for NTU with that lobbyist's optimal position at 15. The dashed curves lying over these competitive curves represent the hypothetical payoffs each would receive if they agreed to share their resources in a coalition at every possible dairy-pricing position. Shared resources mean both lobbyists can persuade more legislators to support them rather than fewer at all positions and no indirect competitive effect, so these new coalition curves are higher than the competitive curves. The CFA lobbyist, benefiting from NTU's resources (and vice versa), now finds that positions 2 through 13 all yield greater payoffs than his or her competitive optimal position of 7.[1] Except that the CFA lobbyist does not actually have the option of

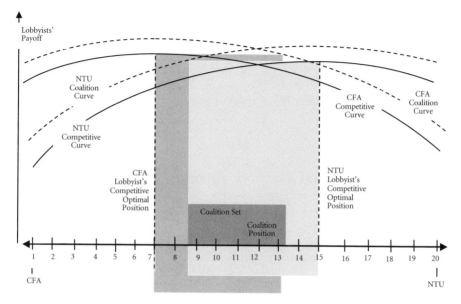

Figure 5.2. Change in payoffs and optimal positions for cooperating in a coalition

working with NTU at positions 2 through 8 because the latter has no incentive to support any position leftward of 9.

In figure 5.2 the dark gray box marks those positions that the CFA lobbyist would be willing to support rightward of 7 if resources were shared, and the light gray box marks the alternatives leftward that the NTU lobbyist could support. The area where they overlap (darkest gray box) is the coalition set; both lobbyists find positions 9 through 13 more rewarding to support than their respective competitive optimal positions of 7 and 15, but only if both agree to share resources in a coalition. This pull toward the coalition set is the direct competitive effect because the incentive to overcome spatial differences in interests and cooperation comes straight from competitors holding out the hope of sharing resources rather than anticipating a long and costly battle. CFA's new coalition payoff curve does not just return the lobbyist to precompetitive levels (the solid noncompetitive joint curve in figure 2.5), it exceeds it for most positions on the outcome space because the resources he or she can now employ to persuade legislators are even greater than when CFA's lobbyist did not have a competitor (who is now a coalition partner). Of course, the direct competitive effect decreases group members' ability to constrain their lobbyists, and the incentive for lobbyists to deviate from what members prefer increases (the alternate set has expanded). But a coalition can only support one position. Which position in the milk-pricing coalition set will these two lobbyists actually choose to support?

The Coalition Position

So far, I have not made any assumptions about whether competing lobbyists communicate and negotiate with each other as they select positions. Noncooperative game theory, in which the competitive model is cast, assumes that one actor makes decisions based on what they observe others doing, what they are likely to do within certain probabilities, or what they have done in the past. This approach has often been favored by scholars because it more readily lends itself to modeling strategy (Rubinstein 1982). Now, however, I utilize the cooperative approach by assuming that lobbyists coordinate their strategies through communication for three reasons. First, noncooperative models assume that participants do not speak meaningfully to each other, and this assumption is at odds with Hula's description of coalition building (1999, 7, 31). He describes coalition formation as the result of extensive negotiations, everyone trying to find common ground and still bring home something for their members even if they cannot get everything their members want. Second, the cooperative bargaining solution developed by Nash (1953) was proven to produce a result equivalent to those of noncooperative bargaining models, even without incorporating the sticky issue of side payments (Binmore, Rubinstein, and Wolinsky 1986). Finally, it produces an intuitive result.

Applying Nash's bargaining solution, Robert Axelrod (1967, 1970) found that negotiators will only agree to a compromise if it simultaneously gives both of them the greatest realizable payoff. It may not be the one each desires most, but it will be greater than any payoff either could hope to receive by choosing to support competing positions. In figure 5.2 the greatest payoff for the CFA lobbyist for cooperating still appears to be at 7, the peak of his or her coalition curve, just as it is for his or her competitive curve. Unfortunately (for CFA's lobbyist), this payoff is impossible to attain because it assumes that NTU will also support position 7, but it is not to that lobbyist's advantage to do so because for him or her that position yields less than what he or she could gain by cooperating at other positions (follow the arc of NTU's coalition curve) or by choosing to fight at position 15. If the CFA lobbyist chose 7, the payoff could only be as great as that marked for his or her competitive curve (the same, of course, is true for the NTU lobbyist at 15). The only position where both coalition curves are simultaneously highest and therefore produce the mutually best outcome is where they intersect over position 12. It is the only outcome both lobbyists would support together in a dairy-pricing coalition.

I have discussed elsewhere how this works in scenarios with more than two lobbyists (Holyoke 2009). The main point here is that because coalition formation is now portrayed as an outcome of the competitive model, whether a lobbyist chooses to join one is a function of the same variables empirically explored in chapter 4. The direct competitive effect predicts that the more resources a lobbyist wields, the more likely that a competitor will want to join him or her in a coalition rather than fight. Also, assuming the coalition position is not at a lobbyist's member-ideal position, greater unity and intensity of member preferences will make it harder for that lobbyist to join one. However, the more resources one lobbyist holds over the competitor, the closer the coalition position will be to the former's group-ideal position. Finally, if prior to lobbying lawmakers collectively prefer a position, they will be able to pressure competing lobbyists to support that position in a coalition. Legislator–lobbyist pressure in combination with the direct competitive effect forcing a compromise is what happened to the insurance agent lobbyist in the introduction.

Ideological Purity or Just Getting Something Done

Can this abstract depiction help explain actual coalition formation? Some supportive statistical evidence is provided later, but it is also useful to explore the model's predictions through the case studies. An ideologically broad coalition was already described as forming in support of wildlife conservation funding under pressure from influential lobbyists and powerful lawmakers. A more interesting case of coalition politics, however, is the biotechnology issue discussed at this chapter's opening because while alliances formed, they changed over the life of the issue.

Coalitions as Sides

The FDA's 1992 rule that required little more than consultation with companies regarding the safety of their GM products and essentially assumed that all products are safe until proven otherwise was enthusiastically embraced by biotechnology giants such as Monsanto and DuPont. Large grain processors Cargill and Archer Daniels Midland, along with their trade associations National Food Processors Association and Grocery Manufacturers of America (GMA), I was told, also hailed the rules as a fair approach laying the groundwork for a revolution in how America produced food. Genetic modification of fruits and grains, they argued, was little different than and therefore just as safe as the ancient technique of selective plant breeding. It would result in food that was tastier, healthier, safer, and a potential solution to world hunger, and they were pleased that FDA recognized such potential.[2]

Consumer protection and environmental public interest groups, however, were less enamored with the FDA's approach, or the similar approach taken by the Environmental Protection Agency.[3] Not only were GM foods potentially dangerous because the science was so new, I was told in interviews, but by starting with the assumption that they were really no more or less safe than "normal" foods, the government was putting the American consumer and environment at considerable risk. Splicing foreign genetic material into a plant's genome was "random" in that scientists did not know where in its DNA the new genes would end up. Consequently, neither they nor the government really knew whether this new process might contaminate soil, how it might enhance insect resistance, or whether GM foods could really be harmlessly consumed.

The Center for Food Safety, Friends of the Earth, Organic Consumers Association, USPIRG, and others formed the Genetically Engineered Food Alert coalition in the late 1990s to "raise public awareness" regarding the dangers of GM foods and push for a public boycott. They even attempted to persuade the chief executive officers (CEOs) of PepsiCo and Kellogg to boycott all products containing *Bacillus thuringiensis* (Bt), a bacterium that produces a toxin found to be a natural insecticide.[4] Both they and the biotechnology industry thus began this study's first year, 1999, supporting positions desired by their members both for and against FDA's status quo. Other consumer groups, such as the Center for Science in the Public Interest (CSPI) and Union of Concerned Scientists (UCS), were not as interested in turning the public against GM technology, but fear of a dangerously easy regulatory scheme pushed them to overcome minor competitive difference and be the Alert's allies.

For the most part, farmers and grocers had few philosophical concerns with bioengineered food and preferred a loose regulatory structure. Yet they had learned to be wary. The National Institutes of Health and the American Medical Association insisted that milk produced by cows given Monsanto's bovine hormone to increase production was indistinguishable from ordinary milk, but midwestern dairy farmers and grocers across the nation were still afraid. They knew from bitter experience that public interest groups had the resources and experience to turn the public against GM foods, just like they had in Europe (Gaskell et al. 1999; Botelho and Kurtz 2008). In 1994 several large grocery and convenience store chains, including Southland Corporation which owned 7-Eleven, even announced that they would no longer sell milk from cows injected with the hormone (Schneider 1994).

Strategies and Arguments

The fight was over the level of government regulation, whether from the FDA, the EPA, or a broad new framework imposed by Congress, and it is the key to understanding interest group competition on this issue. A lobbyist for the technology industry's advocacy group, Biotechnology Industry Organization (BIO), explained its position as "we only want the FDA to focus on content, not the process; to approach these foods just as they do any other foods." For BIO and food producer and processor groups, FDA's guidelines, the status quo since 1992, were "reasonable," "streamlined," full of "common sense," and essential for promoting business profits and job creation. It was their ideal policy outcome, even more so than no regulation at all since public acceptance, and thus higher profits, would likely be greater with the government's imprimatur of safety. Consumer group's claims they wrote off as "unscientific," "Luddite," and even "hysterical" (Barboza 1999b). Trying to keep any safety debate out of the public eye, they relied heavily on their connections to members of Congress, especially delegations from California and midwestern agriculture states, to hold off any efforts to create any new regulatory scheme threatening the status quo.

Consumer groups in the Alert portrayed GM products as "untested," "unnatural," "likely dangerous," and, of course, "Frankensteinian." Their arguments gained traction with lawmakers and the public in 1999 and 2000 when researchers at Cornell University found that Monarch butterfly caterpillars were dying after eating Bt corn, and that some Bt corn not approved for public consumption was finding its way into food products (Bettelheim 2000). Although the more science-oriented consumer groups UCS and CSPI were willing to support biotechnology under a tough regulatory scheme than were members of the Alert (who wanted an outright ban on GM foods), they initially supported the coalition with its resources and connections as the best chance to overthrow the status quo. As these congressional connections were minority Democrats, they and their legislative allies did what Berry (1999) says public interest groups do well; they launched a media campaign to pressure majority Republicans by souring the public on GM foods.

Farmers and grocers vacillated between these two sides for years, but during the fight over the bovine milk hormone when biotech companies were still politically disorganized, they found it practical to side with the stronger consumer groups, forming an alliance of convenience with them in the early 1990s called the Pure Food Campaign. And they were successful, at least on the issue of GM-enhanced milk production. In 1990 the Wisconsin and Minnesota state legislatures and in 1993 Congress through the efforts of Sen. Russell Feingold (D-WI) imposed temporary moratoriums on the use of hormones (Schneider 1993). Much of this alliance of strange bedfellows survived into the time period of my study. Again, farmer motivations were different from consumer and environmental groups, but they feared that consumer resistance might create a backlash that hurt all crop producers—their worst possible outcome. This fear was put on display when the large food distributor Archer Daniels Midland told its suppliers in 1998 to sort GM products from non-GM products for sale in European markets. The high-profile protests in Seattle against the World Trade Organization in late 1999, said a National Corn Growers Association lobbyist, also went a long way toward pushing grocers and farmers to support more stringent regulation and labeling (Kirchhoff 1999).

Congressional Pressure and Response

After the negative reaction by members of Congress and state legislators to the bovine hormone, ag-friendly lawmakers and technology groups began trying to organize and change the way biotechnology was viewed. Rep. Nick Smith (R-MI) pushed for more federal research and development support to demonstrate how safe GM foods were. Rep. John Tierney (D-MA) requested the US Department of Agriculture (USDA) and the National Academy of Sciences to report to Congress on whether more data on GM foods was really needed (Bettelheim 2000). Given that the academy and USDA had already declared GM foods safe and were unlikely to change their conclusions now, the effort was more of a move to strip consumer groups of their most potent weapon, public doubt, and gain the political support of farmers and grocers.

Little evidence exists that this scientific reassurance strategy worked. A survey in December 2000 found that two-thirds of the public did not approve of the idea of GM foods (Brody 2000), numbers that remained largely unchanged in 2006 (Weiss 2006). Reacting to negative public opinion and the persuasive power of farmer and consumer groups, members of Congress of many ideological stripes became increasingly critical of FDA and EPA. At the urging of these groups, forty-seven House members, including Republicans Christopher Shays (R-CT) and Jack Metcalf (R-WA), wrote to the FDA commissioner to express their frustration with the original regulatory scheme and demanded something more stringent. More pointed letters expressing concern over the FDA's lack of transparency and use of sound science came from the chair and ranking member of the House and Senate Agriculture committees (Pope 2000b) and even soon-to-be Senate Majority Leader Bill Frist (R-TN).[5]

An especially good example of the pressure on farmers to ally with consumer groups against the status quo was their support of H.R. 3883 by Rep. Dennis Kucinich (D-OH) in 2000. His Genetically Engineered Food Safety Act would mandate an extensive regulatory scheme to thoroughly test all genetically modified foods before permitting them to be sold at market. Farmers, their lobbyists told me, did not especially like Kucinich's proposed regulatory hoops, and they even found some language regarding liability to be frightening. But FDA approval based on testing would, they hoped, be better than the status quo for it might make their products acceptable to US and European consumers. Even Sen. Barbara Boxer's (D-CA) mandatory labeling bill, the American Corn Growers Association's lobbyist explained to me, would be acceptable over FDA's current policy. FDA tested and labeled so many other things, he said, that his members did not see why there would be a problem with one more test and one more label. The more anti-GM consumer groups in the Alert were also reluctant supporters of the Kucinich bill, said the USPIRG lobbyist (who helped the congressman's staff write it). They preferred a ban, but that would cost them the support of farm groups and their resources. Kucinich's bill was a compromise both could live with and was preferred to the status quo.

Final Coalitions

However, Kucinich's proposal was not the policy finally put in place. Finding their position eroding because consumer groups had "crossed the line" with their "misinformation campaign," biotech lobbyists tried counterattacking with their own public relations campaign (Bettelheim 2000). Grocery Manufacturers of America (GMA) and BIO formed the Alliance for Better Foods to publicly promote the safety and benefits of GM foods without any new regulation. It proved too little, too late. After being bombarded by letters from Congress and over 50 consumer, environmental, and farm groups, in the last days of the Clinton administration FDA proposed a new regulatory framework that required companies to give 120-day notification before selling any GM products, as well as making public all scientific documentation regarding the technology used.

Most of the lobbyists I interviewed were less than thrilled with FDA's new proposal, being more stringent than the 1992 rules though not as tough as Kucinich's proposal. BIO's lobbyist told me these regulations would slow down the technology's development by years and cost the industry millions in unrealized profits. The GMA lobbyist told me it was a "job killer" for small technology companies and large-scale farmers. But members of Congress in large numbers approved and the incoming Bush administration showed no interest in withdrawing it (Hosansky 2001), so the industry lobbyists largely gave up and threw their resources behind the farmer and more science-oriented consumer groups, their strange bedfellows, in their effort to make it the final rule.

FDA's proposal split the consumer group coalition. Although UCS, CSPI, and Consumers Union and farmer interest groups supported it along with the biotechnology companies, most lobbyists in the Alert campaigned against it. But with Congress satisfied and the preponderance of other groups that were mending competitive differences to back it, the policy window of opportunity (as Kingdon [1984] might have put it) closed. The new, ideologically broad coalition of interest groups remained more or less intact over the years that followed, and no significant change in policy or position occurred. Indeed, FDA's policy remains the same at the time of this writing.

Reflecting

Out of the fifteen groups that lobbied on the GM-foods issue that I interviewed, seven switched coalitions during the four-year period. Five of them did so twice. Moreover, of all cases where a lobbyist told me he or she supported a regulation or bill in the interview protocol for this issue, 25 percent did so by participation in a coalition where the proposal, the focus of the coalition's advocacy, deviated from their members' collective ideal position. The largest coalition, the final one backing the new FDA rule, required nearly every lobbyist involved to compromise their members' interests; only members of the farm lobby were more or less happy with the new status quo. The GMA lobbyist told me that he supported it largely because it was a better alternative than the Kucinich bill, downplaying the new rule as "just formalizing what the process has been."

Many of the anti–GM foods consumer lobbyists, including everyone in the Alert, believed his words to be true and branded FDA's proposal as "new window dressing" (as one of their lobbyists called it in an interview). Although the outside advocacy tactics they had successfully used early on had done much to change GM-food regulations, their members, I was told in numerous interviews, would never forgive them for supporting any compromise, even one that was better than the old status quo. For these lobbyists, member anger made any compromise worse than the status quo. Consumers Union, Center for Science in the Public Interest, and Union of Concerned Scientists, however, did find it to their advantage to support the new rules. "It was a very modest improvement, though a step in the right direction," said the UCS's lobbyist. She also added that a significant portion of their membership was not overly concerned with this issue, which made it easier for them to support the new rules, especially because so many members of Congress and farmer and technology interest groups were willing to throw their resources into supporting it.

The broad, successful coalition of consumer, farmer, and most reluctantly, biotech groups appears to have had three crucial characteristics, all consistent with the extension of the competitive model laid out previously. First, the coalition possessed crucial resources each group could take advantage of, scientific knowledge (from UCS and CSPI as well as BIO), money (largely from some of the farmer groups and the industry), and the support of one of the most sacred icons in politics, the American farmer (or at least their interest groups). Second, many of these groups did not have members who cared strongly about the issue. The UCS's lobbyist told me that this issue was simply not as crucial to his members as, say, global warming. All of the farm organization lobbyists except the National Cotton Council told me that less than half of their members used GM seed and were reluctant to do so (most of the Cotton Council's members did use GM seed and had found it to be quite lucrative). They simply did not want the issue to taint consumer perceptions of their non-GM crops. Lobbyists for GMA, BIO, and the National Food Processors Association did have members who felt strongly, but they were also pragmatic in the end and most endorsed their lobbyists' strategic choice to accept a compromise that many other lobbyists favored. In their view, the alternative was likely to be the worse Kucinich bill (or possibly something even more reprehensible). Finally, the coalition supported the position favored by a majority of the concerned members of Congress.

Multivariate Analysis

Pressure from group members to remain ideologically "pure," pressure from legislators to make compromises in support of positions they desire, the draw of competing group resources, and the distance on each policy space between the collective interests of different group memberships are all variables in the competitive model that are also factors in coalition formation (or lack thereof). Each of these played a role in the biotechnology issue, but empirical measures that capture them should also exhibit significant effects in a statistical analysis of coalition formation. Only the appeal of sharing resources among competitors, the direct competitive effect, is a new explanatory variable, although I will need a new dependent variable.

Lobbyists who support members' ideal positions that are all at the same position almost certainly work together and share resources (though Hojnacki 1998 notes some may free ride), but they do not overcome competitive differences to do so, so this partnership is theoretically uninteresting. Coalition formation where some or all participants make compromises through support of a collective position that is not what their members want is where the variables from the competitive model should exert significant influence. To study this type of coalition formation, I continue using the data matrix from the first part of this chapter, pairing every lobbyist with every other working on the same issue with one observation of a pair for each proposal ($N = 1{,}945$). My dependent variable is a binary indicator coded 1 if both lobbyists in a pair supported a bill at a position that was not ideally preferred by the first lobbyist's members, which was true in 20 percent of cases. Thus, in each observation I am observing the first lobbyist's reaction to the other. Given that a competitive difference exists between the positions both of their members ideally prefer, the question arises: Did the first choose to support the same position as the second (who may or may not be supporting his or her members' ideal) because of the resources the second offers or because of pressure from legislators?[6]

The variable that captures the direct competitive effect is the level of advocacy resources the second lobbyist in the dyad, the competitor, has and is presumably willing to share if both support a proposal at the same position. This effect is measured by dividing the annual budget of the competing lobbyist's group by the ordinal indicator from the interviews of the level of resources committed. Thus a high level, coded 1, does not reduce the budget amount. Medium is coded 2 and minimal is coded 3, both of which reduce the resource enticement respectively. My hypothesis is that the greater the resources committed by the competitor, the more likely it is that the first lobbyist will compromise member preferences by choosing to work with that competitor. The other variables should exhibit the same effect as in the previous chapter.[7]

The results of a probit estimate of the likelihood of the first lobbyist crossing ideological space to work in a coalition with a competitor are displayed in table 5.1 and

Table 5.1 Estimates of One Lobbyist Cooperating with a Competitor

Explanatory Variable	Maximum Likelihood Estimate (Robust Standard Error)
Level of Competing Lobbyist's Committed Advocacy Resources	.03[b]
	(.01)
Constraint on the Lobbyist from Interest Group Members	−.18[b]
	(.05)
Pressure on the Lobbyist from Allied Legislators	.83[b]
	(.14)
Distance between the Lobbyist and the Competitor on the Issue Continuum	−.63[b]
	(.04)
Highly Salient Issue	−.56[b]
	(.08)
Observed Bill Occurs Later in Time	.15[b]
	(.04)
Size of the Interest Group's Advocacy Staff	−.01[a]
	(.01)
Amount of PAC Contributions to Republican Legislators	.01[b]
	(.01)
Interest Group Age	.01
	(.01)
Citizen's Interest Group	−.62[b]
	(.01)
Constant	−.63[b]
	(.01)
Wald χ^2	380.11[b]
Pseudo R^2	.25
N	1,945

[a] $p < .05$; [b] $p < .005$.

conform to expectations. All things being equal, the more resources the competitor has to potentially share, the more likely the first lobbyist is to partner with him or her instead of faithfully advocate the position preferred by most group members. Lobbyists are also more likely to work together in support of a bill favored by legislators, which reflects Ainsworth's (1997) argument that lawmakers often pressure their lobbyist allies to back the compromises they desire. This legislator–lobbyist pressure may even be evidence for Herrnson's (2009) argument that many interest groups are being integrated into the party organizations seeking to control Congress; that is, they are often pressured into helping to promote the agendas and therefore to share the fates of their patron parties. The constraints on coalition formation, of course, are the unity and intensity of group members for their ideal positions and thus the spatial distance, or degree of competition, one or both lobbyists must overcome.

The interaction of competitive differences (spatial distance between group ideal positions) and the enticement of a competitor's resources deserves a closer look. In figure 5.3 the solid black curve is the likelihood the first lobbyist will ally with the second given increasing levels of resources offered by the second (the horizontal axis) when no competitive difference exists between the two, given that all other variables remain constant at their mean or modal values. The influence of competitor resources in this baseline curve ranges from 26 percent likelihood of joining a coalition to 46 percent, but when a competitive difference of one position on the

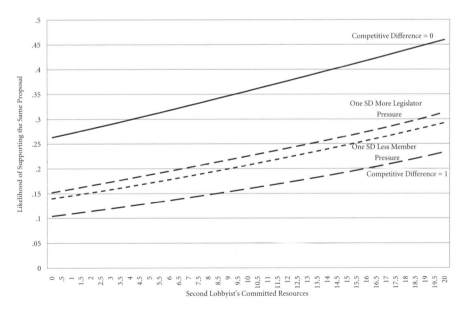

SD = standard deviation.

Figure 5.3. Effect of competitor's resources and other variables on cooperation

policy outcomes space is introduced, shown as the curve with the longest dashes (the lowest curve in figure 5.3), the range falls to 10 percent from 23 percent. A two-position difference (not shown here) drops the range even further to 3 percent to 10 percent, and a three-position difference reduces it essentially to 0 percent for all values of the resources variable. The enticement of sharing a competitor's resources is powerful, but competitive differences are still hard for lobbyists to overcome. It is simply harder to form ideologically broad coalitions, but not impossible as evidenced on CARA (chapter 4) and FDA's final GM-foods rule; it just takes more combined group resources and legislator pressure.

Changing the other two main variables, group member and legislator pressure, also alters this range as predicted by the competitive model. The curve with the shortest dashes in figure 5.3 holds group competition at a one position difference, but the level of member pressure on the lobbyist is reduced by one standard deviation. The result is that the likelihood range for all values of competitor resources, as compared to the heavy, dashed curve, increases across the board by 5 to 6 percentage points. Similarly, greater pressure from Congress on the first lobbyist to support a proposal increases the height of the second highest curve over the largest dash curve by 5 to 8 percent. Lowering member pressure and increasing legislator pressure at the same time (not shown) increases the likelihood-of-partnering range from 20 percent to 38 percent. This range is still not as high as when no competition exists between the pair but it is clearly a shift from fear of member retribution to prioritizing the need to please legislators and benefit from pooling resources with potential allies; thus it is more likely that negotiation and coalition formation take place.

Conclusion

Coalitions are prominent in interest group politics, but only in the last fifteen years have scholars considered coalition formation an important advocacy tactic worth rigorous empirical scrutiny. Evidence presented in this chapter that cooperation can occur among lobbyists for competing interests and that competing interest groups make compromises to do so, it may be argued, makes studying coalitions an even more important topic in the interest group literature.

The question of whether any of the lobbyists who worked on the biotechnology issue (or on any other of my six issues) and chose to support the same position as a competitor ever truly sat down and negotiated these compromises remains unanswered. The data does not allow me to state definitively that the give-and-take of bargaining between interests actually took place or that the positions they collectively supported yielded the greatest payoff to all coalition members (as per figure 5.2). I can only infer it based on the theoretical model's logic as supported by results in the data analysis and by evidence gleaned from case studies such as the battle over GM foods.

Many of the lobbyists I interviewed mentioned negotiating compromises, but they also shied away from talking too much about them. It may not have been something they were eager for outsiders to hear about, just as they were most likely reluctant to tell their members too much about it. Farm lobbyists reported talks with the biotechnology industry several times during the debate, including over whether to support the new FDA rules. The more science-oriented consumer groups told me that even in 2003, two years after FDA's final rule, they continued talking with farmer and industry lobbyists about modifications. They even tried to get the more anti-GM consumer groups to support them as well but had little success. Monsanto even made an interesting, if futile, effort to negotiate with Greenpeace in 1999, to convince the environmental group that GM foods had great potential (Barboza 1999a). This effort may have been a naïve gesture on Monsanto's part, but it does show how difficult it is to build alliances when it requires bridging large competitive divides.

A good example of negotiation between competitors to build a coalition and move policy took place on bankruptcy legislation, though again the differences between the interest groups were not large and took place under intense pressure from members of Congress. They also occurred at later stages of the legislative process, which suggests a timing factor in the decision to overcome competitive differences and form coalitions. Perhaps group competitive differences are more likely to be set aside by lobbyists later in time. I turn to this question in chapter 6.

Notes

1. This graph is based on the assumption that pressure on CFA from group members is $M = 5$.

2. See www.gmabrands.com/news/docs/WhitePaper.cfm?DocID=425.

3. The EPA regulates all pesticides, so GM modifications designed to create pest resistance in crops are subject to its authority.

4. According to Friends of the Earth, only Utz Quality Foods responded to this letter-writing campaign; Utz explained that it was safe to use GM foods because it was not considered by FDA as different from other foods. See www.foe.org/safefood/nfpapr.html.

5. I have copies of these letters and will share them upon request.

6. Although the second lobbyist is theoretically making the same choice, all of the group-level independent variables capture characteristics of the first lobbyist's group with the exception of the incentive of the second lobbyist's resources. Although this reduces coalition formation to an aggregation of decisions by one lobbyist to work with another and then another, I argue that this is not an unrealistic way to think about coalition formation.

7. I eliminate the dummy that indicates whether the issue is distributive because the case studies strongly suggest that issues do not break down by Lowi's typology.

CHAPTER 6

Institutional Constraints
on Lobbyist Conflict

Up to this point I have described legislator pressure in the competitive model as simply a distribution of individual preferences for positions. Some legislators may feel more strongly about their positions than others and thus be more costly to persuade, but no one member of Congress is assumed to have more influence over the positions lobbyists strategically choose than any other. But even a casual political observer knows that this description vastly oversimplifies the way Congress works. Legislative institutions invest disproportionately greater power in committee and party leaders, powers they can use to pressure rank-and-file legislators into supporting committee and party issue positions. Because the competitive model assumes that legislators and lobbyists are connected to each other through mutually supportive relationships, it is possible, even likely, that pressure on legislators from the leadership to toe the party line will translate into pressure on lobbyists as well. Lobbyists may find themselves indirectly pressured by congressional leaders to put aside competitive differences and cooperate when they might prefer to fight, or vice versa.

But legislative leaders must use their powers carefully, for it is also well known that institutions such as Congress operate under intricate sets of rules and norms protecting rank-and-file legislators from being abused by committee and party leaders. So not only may lobbyists be subject to the same pressures from congressional leaders as their legislator allies, they might enjoy some of their institutional protections as well. And when lobbyists decide to resist pressure from their congressional allies to support compromises because they fear a revolt by group members, they are defying the House or Senate leadership as well, which may end up putting their legislator allies in awkward positions. By carefully studying lobbying at the committee and floor stages of the lawmaking process in this chapter, I explore the extent and limits of the institutional power of legislative leaders on lobbying in the context of the competitive model.

For example, consider the following case in California. In a state known for polarized politics, no issue is fought over more fiercely than the control of water. A largely arid state, California's enormous agricultural regions in the Central and Imperial

Valleys and megalopolises such as Los Angeles would have dried up long ago without enormous federal and state investments in systems that capture and move Sierra Nevada mountain snowmelt hundreds of miles away through a maze of canals (Hundley 2001). But by 2009, both physically and legally, this distribution system was on the verge of collapse. Expanding populations, greater agriculture demand, eroding levees in the Sacramento–San Joaquin River Delta (which collects much of the mountain runoff), coupled with new legal requirements to divert water for environmental and species preservation and several years of drought, had created one of the greatest economic, environmental, and political crises in the state's history.

Interest group competition was fierce because the stakes were enormous. Agriculture interests lobbied Sacramento for more water for farming and greater ease in circumventing environmental restrictions. Environmental organizations wanted to prevent the building of large, new dams and canals, instead pushing to divert even more water to protect dwindling fish and bird species. Southern cities and water districts wanted guaranteed supplies, while northern California cities, farmers, and water districts feared that all of these demands could only be met by taking more of the water originating in their regions, their water.

Into this political quagmire stepped Republican actor-turned-governor Arnold Schwarzenegger and Democratic state senate leader Darrell Steinberg, both of whom had staked their reputations on passing new water legislation. Both had struggled to broker compromises between these competing interests in 2007 and 2008, only to see their efforts fall to pieces amid bitter accusations and even more bitter recriminations. But they had new advantages in 2009: A three-year-old drought had coupled with new diversions of agriculture water to save several fish species in the delta ordered by a federal judge under the Endangered Species Act. Doing nothing suddenly looked far worse for most interests than making compromises with reviled competitors.

As Steve Wiegand (2009) of the *Sacramento Bee* chronicled it, in 2008 Gov. Schwarzenegger and Sen. Dianne Feinstein (D-CA) had pushed agriculture, urban, and environmental lobbyists to all sit down and hammer out a compromise. Lobbyists balked at the proposals that were made. Environmentalists and some cities wanted the state to take a stronger role in regulating groundwater, but agriculture interests argued that this proposal would intrude on private property rights. Central Valley farmers, southern cities, and even some environmentalists wanted to build a new tunnel under the delta to move more clean water south, but this proposal was anathema to northern Californians and other environmentalists. The effort at compromise failed because the mutual distrust of group members simply could not be overcome, but the pressure to negotiate laid the foundation for even more intense talks the following year.

The governor applied even more pressure in 2009 by announcing that he would start vetoing the more than 700 bills dearly desired by interest groups on his desk if no comprehensive water legislation was produced. This made legislative leaders like Steinberg furious, but the governor had done it before so his threat was credible.

The leaders pushed their allied interests even harder to compromise, and several bills were written that gave something to each of the many interests in the debate. However, the bills were all "linked" so that if one failed, they all failed. Lobbyists who were successful in getting their priorities embedded in one bill now had a powerful incentive to support the entire package, even if other bills contained changes harmful to their members.

By November 2, 2009, enough ducks were in rows to put all of the bills up for votes. Compromises continued to be made, so much so that by midnight one lobbyist, according to Wiegand, did not even know whether or not he was supporting the package at that moment because he had lost track of what was actually in it. Early in the morning of November 3, Sen. Steinberg forced environmentalists to support lighter penalties for illegal water diversions to appease agriculture interests, the last road block to overcome. A few refused, but most unhappily agreed; they were still getting the greater water regulation they desired. As the sun rose a few hours later, the package passed. Noses were held, but the disaster of doing nothing was avoided.

Competitive Lobbying in an Institutional Context

Political leaders in the Golden State may have their own strong personalities, but they are also powerful because political institutions give them great power. They can sometimes use this power to pressure lobbyists into supporting unpopular compromises, not because they have forged close relationships with them all (through which pressure is directly exerted in the competitive model) but because they can control agendas and discipline errant party members. And they often need to. Bill-passing majorities must be assembled if laws are to be made, which is hard to do when fierce interest group lobbying pulls rank-and-file legislators away from the positions leaders prefer. Legislators must be pushed into pressuring their lobbyist allies to set aside competitive differences and form ideologically broad, bill-supporting coalitions, which is what happened on the water bills. Institutional rules and courtesies, however, also require leaders to carefully choose when to use such coercive powers.

I have so far neglected to include any asymmetry in legislator power or institutional constraints on that power in the competitive model, but this omission ignores a large body of literature showing how such structures shape and constrain human behavior. Rules and norms exist because they help "boundedly rational" actors manage complex environments by limiting some choices (like conflict) while making others (like compromise) more likely (Kollman, Miller, and Page 2000; Jones 2001; Page 2008). Shepsle and Weingast's 1994 *Legislative Studies Quarterly* article chronicles the development of this research in regard to how Congress's rules shape choices and policy outcomes. Other research explores how procedural rules shape the way bureaucrats respond to congressional oversight (Epstein and O'Halloran 1996) or require Supreme Court justices to bargain over the precedents set in their opinions (Maltzman, Spriggs, and Wahlbeck 1999). Very little work, however, explores how institutional structures shape lobbying behavior.

Perhaps this influence has been neglected because lobbyists are not members of any institution and so are not directly bound by their rules and norms of procedure, leadership, and courtesy. Yet the competitive model provides a framework for understanding how lobbyists can still be subject to institutional pressures and constraints as a result of their need to find positions that can be supported by their legislative allies, whose aid lobbyists require in order to influence the lawmaking process. If congressional leaders need bills to pass (or not to pass if they are minority party leaders trying to embarrass the majority), then they may pressure junior legislators to back party positions. Defiance by legislators means risking their own bills, committee assignments, party electoral support, or funding requests for district projects. And when these junior legislators bow to pressure from the leadership, they may in turn expect their lobbyist allies to do the same and will cut off their access if the lobbyists refuse to fall into line.

Recall from chapter 2 that the more intensely legislators prefer their ex ante positions, the more costly it is for lobbyists to convince them to support any other. So if a legislator's prelobbying position is determined by committee and party leadership pressure, lobbyists will have to commit even more advocacy resources to convince that legislator to support the interest group. They risk severe punishment if they fail to be persuasive because they will have tried to convince their allies to take dangerous risks by defying the leadership. Instead, lobbyists are more likely to choose positions closer to those of the legislators and thus to the leadership, even if it is further from what their group members prefer. Thus, lobbyists are indirectly pressured by institutional leaders. Yet these same leaders may sometimes feel that it is not prudent to pressure the rank-and-file and their lobbyist allies if it means violating norms that protect the rights of individual legislators and help the institution function smoothly. As House Speaker Joseph Cannon (R-IL) discovered in 1910 when the rank-and-file stripped him of his authority, abuse of power has its consequences.

Competitive Lobbying of Committees

This chapter focuses on the influence of institutional structure on competitive lobbying, so it makes sense to explore it at the two institutional levels of congressional policymaking: the committee stage and the floor stage. Committee lobbying has been the subject of considerable research for the simple reason that it is where agendas are formed and bills developed. Lobbyists themselves make it a high priority to build relationships with legislators on committees with jurisdiction over issues important to their members (Hall and Wayman 1990; Hojnacki and Kimball 1998). Given this crucial plenary function, it would be surprising not to observe every lobbyist with a stake in an issue striving as hard as they can to ensure that their members' interests are embedded in a bill before it leaves committee (it is much harder to add or strip provisions out later). In other words, given the stakes, we ought to see more conflict than cooperation between competing interest groups at the committee stage. Or should we?

A couple of institution-based reasons exist for why we might not see more conflict at the committee stage. One reason comes from the way legislators are assigned to committees. Kollman (1997) explains that legislators are "high demanders" in that they seek assignments giving them opportunities to shape policies important to mobilized constituencies in their districts (Jewell and Chi-Hung 1974; Benson 1981). Congressional rules allow members to have the assignments they want, provided slots for their party are available and they are senior to other claimants. If most of the constituencies benefiting from committee largess have similar preferences, then the preference range of committee members serving them should be similarly narrow. Lobbyists representing these same electorally important constituencies can easily, or "cheaply," build relationships with committee legislators because the latter's preferences will be similar to those of the group members. Consequently, groups closely connected to the committee will have few competitive differences with each other. Lobbyists for interests not so privileged will find it prohibitively difficult to overcome this preference gap and will either not lobby or will target other venues (Holyoke 2003). Thus, we should see little conflict among groups lobbying any particular committee.

As seen in chapter 1, however, this description of committee lobbying really applies to the subgovernment era when there were fewer constituencies mobilized to lobby and thus fewer conflicts of interests. Subgovernments broke up partially because more groups representing more diverse interests mobilized as they found young, sympathetic legislators willing to champion their interests in order to create electoral foundations for their own careers (Costain 1981; Meyer 2004). After the Legislative Reorganization Act of 1946 reduced and then largely froze the number of congressional committees (Davidson 1990), junior legislators looking to serve new constituencies found they had to do so on existing committees, which resulted in a broadening of both committee jurisdictions and the collective policy preferences of committee members. Many committees became quite ideologically diverse, Krehbiel (1990) finds, so we actually should observe more lobbyists for competing groups expressing their members' demands as they fight to shape policy at this plenary stage, not less.[1]

The other reason why we might see less conflict between competing groups at the committee stage is more compelling and has to do with the asymmetry in power that gives committee leaders disproportionate influence over their committee members and agendas. The revolt against Speaker Cannon led to a decentralization of power-giving chairs such as Wilbur Mills (D-MS), Wayne Aspinall (D-CO), and John Stennis (D-MI) near dictatorial control over both committee agendas and members (Davidson 1981). The partial recentralization of power under the Republicans in 1995 may have reduced it somewhat (Deering and Smith 1997, chapter 2), but chairs still retain considerable influence over which issues are taken up and which bills are moved forward and can marginalize committee members who refuse to support them (Fenno 1973).

Chairs who are in need of bill-passing committee majorities and who desire to impress other House and Senate members with a show of stakeholder unity may use their influence to compel rank-and-file members and, through them, their lobbyist allies, to form coalitions backing chair-determined positions whether they want to or not. Yet Heitshusen (2000) finds evidence of lobbyists who engage in wide-ranging conflict before one committee even as they all appear to fall in line behind the chair of another committee, which suggests that chairs are sometimes unwilling or unable to compel competing lobbyists to cooperate.

Conflict and Cooperation at Committee Hearings

Simply looking at who contacts whom, a frequently used research strategy, cannot tell us whether or not lobbyists are changing their positions to cooperate in coalitions under pressure from committee leaders. For this we need to look at advocacy content, to learn what positions lobbyists actually say they are supporting. One rarely exploited opportunity to study content is committee hearing testimony. Committee hearings themselves have long been regarded simply as opportunities for chairs to showcase carefully screened lobbyists to bolster predetermined agendas and convince floor leaders of a bill's merits with a show of stakeholder unity (Huitt 1954; Milbrath 1960). This view presumes, of course, that hearings only feature lobbyists whose members' ideal positions already reflect the chair's position. Ross (1970), however, found instances of lobbyists testifying against committee bills in the 1960s, and Tichenor and Harris (2002) found lobbyists testifying in opposition to each other many times in the twentieth century, which would not be possible if they were all supporting the committee. So, when unity exists among testifying lobbyists, does it reflect a true lack of competition or a suppression of real differences by the committee chair?

To make this determination easier, consider four possible scenarios of outcomes and explanations. In scenario 1, few differences exist between the member-derived positions of the testifying groups (little competition) or between these groups and the committee to begin with. When these lobbyists all testify in support of the committee, they are sincerely expressing their members' preferences and nobody is exerting any pressure. The other scenarios occur when competitive differences exist between the interests of the groups lobbying the committee. In scenario 2, the chair and majority party staff (who usually create hearing invitation lists) screen groups to make sure that they only invite lobbyists whose members already support the chair's position. Lack of expressed conflict now only reflects a lack of competition between invited groups, not between all groups lobbying the committee. The chair's control of hearing invitations is used to give the appearance of stakeholder unity, though he or she may be ignoring courtesies of allowing other minority and even majority party members to invite their favored interest groups.

In scenario 3, the chair invites competing groups but pressures their lobbyists into supporting his or her issue position. Perhaps the issue is highly visible and the minority party sees it as an opportunity to embarrass the majority, so the chair tries to defang the opposition by compelling support from competing groups, some of whom might actually prefer minority party positions. Now the unity observed in testimony is the result of lobbyists who strategically choose to change their positions and cooperate. Finally, scenario 4 is simple. Chairs of committees with diverse preferences are not pressuring invited lobbyists to compromise. Perhaps the committee has a tradition of extending invitation courtesies to the minority, and the chair is accommodating the ranking member, or perhaps the chair just wants a frank airing of differences between constituencies affected by legislation he or she is developing (or preventing). Yet only in this pressure-free scenario would we expect to see conflict expressed at hearings by competing interest groups.

During my four-year study period there were twenty-seven hearings held by eight committees on the six issues. Not all are usable, however, because I need committees to take clear positions on the issues against which I can compare the positions lobbyists take in their testimony as well as their members' ideal positions. I could not identify any committee position in five hearings, in which chairs claimed in opening statements that the hearings were merely "fact finding." Two more had to be dropped because only one lobbyist testified and, of course, it takes at least two to compete. In the end I had twenty usable hearings by eight committees: thirteen in the House, six in the Senate, and one joint hearing (details are in Holyoke 2008).

Finding each committee's position is essential, and it must be on the same scale as the interest group ideal positions developed in chapter 3. To do this I used the chair's opening statement at each hearing as an indicator, based on the assumption that it more or less reflected the preferences of at least the chair. Because the group-ideal-position scale is built from observations that are specific bills, it was relatively easy to attach the chair's statement to one of them; usually a chair promoted a specific bill, thus establishing the committee's position at that hearing. For example, at a hearing on wildlife conservation by the House Natural Resources Committee, Chair Don Young (R-AK) started off by announcing his support for H.R. 701 (his bill), which also happened to be in my survey. It has a position code of 2, so the committee's position at this hearing was also coded 2, though committee positions at other hearings on the same issue were at other positions.

Whether each invited lobbyist (or some important group member giving testimony written by the lobbyist) supported the committee was found by coding his or her testimony.[2] All testimony, including chair statements, was obtained either from committees' websites or the LexisNexis database. If they did support the committee they were assigned the same position code as the committee, otherwise they were assigned their group's ideal member position code so that a sense of distance between the committee's position and the one collectively preferred by his or her members can be identified.[3]

Scenario 1 of no competitive difference between the testifying groups can be immediately dismissed because we have known since chapter 3 that there is competition between interest groups on all six issues. Differences between the ideal positions of a lobbyist's members and the chair are also not impediments to receiving invitations. Only 29 percent of all groups with ideal positions identical to the committee's were invited to testify. Of those who were invited but whose members opposed the

Table 6.1 Lobbyists Supporting or Opposing the Committee in Testimony

Issue	Lobbyists Opposing the Committee	Lobbyists Supporting the Committee and Members	Lobbyists Supporting the Committee by Opposing Members
Arctic National Wildlife Refuge	1	10	0
Oil Royalties for Wildlife Conservation	7	11	10
Bankruptcy Reform	6	10	5
Money Laundering	3	1	1
Dairy Pricing	17	8	5
Bioengineered Food	1	9	5
Total	35	49	26

committee, 42 percent supported a position one position away from the committee on the outcome space, 46 percent were two spaces away, and 12 percent had a three-space difference. And many lobbyists expressed differences with the chair and, by extension, each other in testimony. Only 68 percent of those with a one-position difference from the committee testified in support, and only 38 percent of those with a two-position difference. No group with a three-position difference offered support, all of which suggests support for scenario 4 of freely expressed conflict.

I take a closer look by breaking out this data by issue in table 6.1. On four issues more lobbyists testified in support of the committee's position than against and, in many cases, supported the committee at the expense of their members' interests by changing their group's official position. But I also find that on four issues significant numbers of lobbyists still testified in opposition, which supports scenarios 3 and 4 and a conclusion that very limited pressure came from chairs. On ANWR, however, nearly every lobbyist supported the committee, but only because committees almost exclusively invited groups already supporting greater oil drilling, per scenario 2. But this issue was also of tremendous importance to the majority party and was opposed by the minority; it may be argued that pressure came more from party leaders than from committee chairs. Only on bioengineered foods did half of all lobbyists change their positions to support the committee. I cannot say exactly why position change occurred at the hearings on these issues, but it is hard to imagine an explanation other than pressure from the chair. Other lobbyists refused to publicly compromise members' interests, and consistent with the competitive model, I find an overall negative correlation ($r=-.25$) between position change in committee testimony and greater group member pressure as measured by the variable I developed in chapter 4.

Another way to study these scenarios is to determine whether competitive differences between group positions expressed at hearings is less than the total level of competition between all of the interest groups lobbying that issue regardless of

Table 6.2 Actual and Expressed Interest Group Competition

Issue (scenario supported)	Average Difference between Positions of Members of All Groups Lobbying the Issue	Average Difference between Positions of Members of Groups Invited to Testify	Average Difference Expressed between Testifying Lobbyists
Money Laundering (2)	.93	.56	.50
Oil Royalties for Wildlife Conservation (4)	.95	1.11	1.53
Bioengineered Food (4)	1.28	1.21	1.27
Dairy Pricing (4)	1.35	1.40	1.33
Bankruptcy Reform (4)	1.53	1.50	1.86
Arctic National Wildlife Refuge (2)	1.60	.55	.36
All Issues	1.27	1.06	1.14

whether they were invited to testify. For this purpose, I calculate three sets of statistics. The first is the average absolute value of group position differences on each issue. The second is the position differences of all groups invited to testify. The third is a measure of the difference between positions expressed in testimony. To create this last measure I pair all of the lobbyists who testified and assigned to both in every pair the committee's position code if he or she testified in support of the committee. If only one in the pair supported the committee and the other did not, then the first was assigned the committee code and the other his or her group member ideal position code. If neither supported the committee, then both were simply assigned their group member ideal position codes. I then take the absolute value of the difference and calculate the average for all testimony on each issue. The results for all three measures are in table 6.2.

Now we see that the ANWR issue fits scenario 2, in which committee staff members invite groups that already support the majority Republican position of expanded oil drilling so that the level of competition between them is much less than it is between all groups. In this scenario, the chair's power of invitation control (rather than his or her ability to pressure other committee members and their lobbyist allies) is likely being used to give the appearance of broad public support. Republicans were trying to build momentum to overcome resistance from environmentalists, few of whom were invited to testify. Money laundering looks similar, closer to scenario 2 than in table 6.1 (where it resembled scenario 4), but the small number of groups on this issue makes the result unreliable.

The other issues largely conform to scenario 4 where, contrary to the traditional view of hearings, chairs appear to be exerting little, if any, pressure on lobbyists to support committee positions. Some lobbyists supported the committees at the expense of their members' interests, but others were comfortable voicing their objections. In other words, like table 6.1, table 6.2 shows that on all but the most partisan and highly visible issue of all, ANWR, competition between lobbyists is still frequently expressed rather than suppressed in committee hearings. Perhaps chairs could not force every lobbyist to toe the line. Or perhaps chairs chose not to apply pressure out of respect for norms of courtesy, such as when House Judiciary Committee chair John Conyers (D-MI) reluctantly allowed Zoe Lofgren (D-CA) to invite comedian Stephen Colbert to testify on farm workers' rights.[4] Or perhaps indirect pressure from chairs was simply not enough to outweigh the pressure lobbyists were under from their own members when the issue at hand was important and their members united.

Beyond Committees

So far, the investigation in this chapter has produced little evidence of institutional constraint on competitive lobbying, at least at the committee stage. In the issue case studies, some evidence exists of significant cooperation among lobbyists at both the committee and floor stages on the wildlife funding issue, but this cooperation was the result of extensive negotiations between lobbyists and legislators before the first committee was even lobbied. Bankruptcy reform may be a more instructive case. On this issue, legislators fought at the committee stage but put their conflict aside at the floor stage under pressure from their leaders. Lobbyists did not.

Conflict over Bankruptcy Reform

Since the early 1990s the Holy Grail for the banking and credit industries was to make it harder for businesses and individuals to erase debts under Chapters 11 and 13 of the bankruptcy code. Consumer debt and personal bankruptcies had been rising, and the industry wanted to ensure that more debtors would fully repay their obligations under Chapter 7, even if they had to sell property and assets to do so.[5] To advocate for these changes, credit card companies, large bank groups such as the American Bankers Association (ABA), small bank groups such as Independent Bankers Association, and even their long-time nemesis, Credit Union National Association, came together to form the National Consumer Bankruptcy Coalition (Seiberg 1997).[6] With personal bankruptcies on the rise and profits from other lines of business starting to decline, I was repeatedly told in interviews that for great banks and small, bankruptcy reform was their most important issue.

Bankruptcy reform had not been an overly partisan issue; many Democrats supported it along with most Republicans (Michaelis 1994), but little happened until banks were shaken in 1997 by the release of the Congress-created National Bankruptcy Review Commission's recommendations for reform, reform that the industry deemed too forgiving of consumer debt (Seiberg 1997).[7] After senators and representatives, and especially Republican and Democratic leaders, were bombarded with protests about the commission from bank CEOs, several bipartisan, industry-friendly bills were introduced (Hosansky 1997a). "Congress is already convinced we need a needs-based bankruptcy system," ABA lobbyist Philip Corwin was quoted as saying. "Now they're debating how that is going to be implemented" (Hosansky 1997b).

Evidence of bipartisanship, however, was nowhere to be found at the 1998 markup session by the House Judiciary Subcommittee on Commercial and Administrative Law. Subcommittee Democrats had close ties to consumer groups that, in an odd twist of fate, were fiercely defending the status quo. For the Consumer Federation of America, National Consumer Law Center, the National Women's Law Center, and United Auto Workers, bankruptcy reform was also their most important issue. It was "mean-spirited" legislation, they told me in interviews, and "cynical" because it was the banks who had created the consumer debt problem in the first place by marketing charge cards to people with poor credit and little experience in credit management. On party-line votes subcommittee chair George Gekas (R-PA) turned back twenty-one Democratic amendments that sought to attach more consumer protection provisions (Nitschke 1998). Yet consumer advocates saw Democrats flipflop when the bill came before the full House. Gekas and his cosponsor, Jim Moran (D-VA), made a few concessions to the minority, and the bill passed with sixty-six Democrats votes and little debate (Nitschke 1998).

The same thing happened in the Senate. Bill sponsor Charles Grassley (R-IA) fiercely debated Richard Durbin (D-IL) and other Judiciary Committee Democrats, but in floor debate these two senators made bargains leading to the withdrawal of nearly all forty-two consumer group-backed amendments, including several by Edward Kennedy (D-MA), who had been a critic of the bill but now let it pass without opposition. Under pressure from Majority Leader Trent Lott (R-MS), who needed a supermajority so senators could "really move on to other things," the Senate occasionally debated the bill for less than two weeks (short by Senate standards) and it passed 97 to 1 (Hosansky and Nitschke 1998). National Consumer Law Center lobbyist Gary Klein expressed dismay at such overwhelming bipartisan support in spite of intense consumer advocacy (Seelye 1998), but President Clinton's veto threat saved him, stalling the conference report until the bill died at year's end.

This pattern of intense committee debate between congressional supporters of bankers and consumer interests followed by easy passage on the floor of a bank-friendly bill repeated itself in the next two congresses. A joint hearing by House and Senate judiciary committees in 1999 saw Gekas and Democrats again snipe at each other with consumer groups denouncing the bill. "The reality is that more debtors use the bankruptcy system because more debtors are having serious financial problems," Klein testified, while banking lobbyists continued to emphasize the need to move a bill quickly (Seiberg 1999). A battle erupted in the House Judiciary Committee when Chair Henry Hyde (R-IL) tried to make the bill more consumer friendly only to see his efforts promptly undone by other Republicans in an unusual intraparty battle before passing it on a party-line vote (Parks and Kolb 1999). Then it again passed the House with little debate and a large, bipartisan margin of 313 to 108 after Gekas cut a deal to accept a few Democratic amendments (Nitschke 1999). During Senate floor debate, consumer lobbyists could only get three Democrats to appear with them at a rally as the bill passed 83 to 14 after Grassley and Durbin cut deals and withdrew nearly all consumer-backed amendments under pressure from Lott and Minority Leader Tom Daschle (D-SD) (Ota 2000a). Some Democrats, such as Rep. Patrick Kennedy (D-MA), even urged the president to sign the bill, though Clinton pocket vetoed it (Ota 2000b, 2000c).

And the cycle was repeated again in the 107th Congress where Republican and some Democrats hoped to move the bill quickly to a supportive President George Bush. The Senate Judiciary Committee fought off twenty-eight Democratic consumer protection amendments, but the only real conflict on the floor was over language placed in the bill by Sen. Charles Schumer (D-NY) regarding bankruptcy penalties for individuals convicted of violence at abortion clinics, a minor issue for most consumer groups (Blackwell and Heller 2001). Then it passed by now typical bipartisan majorities, 83 to 15 in the Senate and 306 to 108 in the House, which perhaps explains why America's Community Bankers issued exactly the same press release after floor votes in 1999, 2000, and 2001. A consumer group lobbyist summarized it for me differently, "Same [expletive], different year."

The only reason the bill did not make it to President Bush was a squabble over conference committee appointees when Democrats took control of the Senate after James Jeffords (I-VT) left the Republican Party. Then an abrupt shift of political attitudes toward support for consumers came after the September 11 attacks caused the economy to falter (Atlas 2001). Finally, in 2005, Bush signed an industry-supported bankruptcy bill.

Little compromise took place between the finance industry and consumer advocates on this issue; it was simply too crucial to the members of these groups to permit much give-and-take. The only ground given was by the banking industry, which reluctantly agreed to provisions making it easier for some consumers to continue to file under consumer-friendly Chapter 13 and to protect the equity in their homes if they did file Chapter 7. In sum, after fighting in committee, House and Senate members set aside their differences and made deals to get legislation passed at the floor stage, but lobbyists apparently felt no such compulsion.

Conflict and Cooperation at the Floor Stage

Was bankruptcy reform atypical, or were lobbyists generally free to continue fighting from committee stage to floor stage even in the face of institutional pressures to compromise? Using data from my issues, I can track cooperation and conflict by both lobbyists and legislators through both stages, although it requires some care. A bill reported by one committee may end up being re-referred to another or sent back to committee by the floor. Even more confusing is the end of the two-year Congress when all bills that fail to reach the president's desk (most of them) die. Bills must be reintroduced and the process starts all over again. To keep it simple I take each proposal discussed in my interviews (from which the ideological scale was built in chapter 3) and arrange them chronologically. Some were debated in committee, others were considered on House or Senate floor, though bioengineered food regu-

Table 6.3 Lobbyist and Legislator Conflict over Stages

Stage of Process	Average Intensity of Lobbyist Conflict	Legislator Ideology Standard Deviation
Dairy Pricing		
First Committee	1.85	.35
First Chamber	2.00	.35
Second Committee	1.53	.33
Second Chamber	1.85	.33
Bioengineered Food		
First Committee	1.90	.19
Second Committee	2.04	.26
Third Committee	2.02	0
Fourth Committee	1.68	.11
Money Laundering		
First Committee	1.60	.28
Second Committee	1.67	.50
First Chamber	1.60	.30
Second Chamber	1.53	.27
Bankruptcy Reform		
First Committee	2.08	.31
Second Committee	1.72	.33
First Chamber	1.94	.34
Wildlife Conservation		
First Chamber	1.57	.35
Second Chamber	.83	.34
First Committee	1.57	.32
Arctic National Wildlife Refuge		
First Committee	2.08	.25
Second Committee	2.13	.31
Third Committee	2.11	.31

lation and ANWR never made it to the floor stage. Each proposal's stage is listed in the left column of table 6.3.

The first data column in table 6.3 shows how intensely competing group lobbyists engaged in advocacy conflicts with each other from one stage to the next. Lobbyists were asked in the interviews how intensely they opposed or supported observed proposals; responses were coded 2 for strong support, 1 for moderate support, −1 for moderate opposition, and −2 for strong opposition. Once again I use the dyadic data set of lobbyist pairs for each proposal, but now I use this measure of conflict intensity between the two on that proposal. If one lobbyist in the pair strongly supported the observed bill with a code of 2, and the other moderately opposed it, −1, then that pair's conflict score is 3 but would be 4 if the second was strongly opposed. I then take the absolute value of each pair's difference, average the scores for all pairs on each proposal (each being at either the committee or floor stage) and present the results in the column. Larger scores indicate more conflict on that proposal at that stage.

Fowler (2006) argues that bill cosponsorship is perhaps the best way to measure the breadth of legislator support for bills and issues, so I identified every sponsor and cosponsor of my observed bills along with their Common Space scores. Then I calculated the standard deviation of all cosponsor scores for each bill and entered the result for that bill in column three, larger values indicating broader legislator support for the proposal at that stage.[8]

As it turns out, the mean level of lobbyist conflict at the committee stage is 1.87, but only 1.60 at the floor stage; not a large difference though a statistically significant one ($p < .10$) in a difference-of-means test. However, on just the low-salience issues, bioengineered food, money laundering, and wildlife funding, clearer evidence exists that conflict between competing lobbyists did decline over time. On wildlife funding conflict between lobbyists (though not legislators) fell as the issue shifted from the House floor to the Senate floor but rose again when it came back to the House Natural Resources Committee in 2000. Deals that had been cut among lobbyists regarding the amount of funding fell apart when the issue was reset to square one. Conflict at the floor stage on money laundering was also somewhat smaller than in committee. So some evidence exists that the committee stage of the lawmaking process matters; lobbyist conflict, at least on the low-salient issues, occurred more at the committee stage than at the floor stage as lobbyists staked-out and fought for positions.

As for the high-salience issues, no clear pattern emerges. Bankruptcy reform was highly salient but did not polarize members of Congress as much as ANWR. The Republican leadership wanted reform, and although Rep. Barney Frank (D-MA) and Sen. Charles Schumer (D-NY) opposed it, many Democrats were supportive of it. Perhaps it is not surprising, then, that conflict between legislators (if not lobbyists) decreased a little from committee stage to floor stage on this issue. ANWR, of course, was one of the most polarizing issues; it is unsurprising that lobbyist conflict remained unchanged, perhaps even increasing somewhat over time, although the issue never got beyond the committee stage. Dairy pricing was also highly salient and highly polarized, although by geographic region rather than by party, and shows no more decrease in lobbyist conflict over time than ANWR.

Overall, the stage-by-stage increase in legislator cooperation does not strongly correlate with a decrease in lobbyist conflict ($r = -.21$), but when looking at just the low-salience issues, I find a more significant negative correlation ($r = -.46$). At least on these issues, perhaps of less importance to the minority party, majority leaders had an easier time forging unity among legislators and lobbyists at the floor stage. Of course, while I have been attributing this unity to pressure from leaders, broad legislator support may also be the result of the institutional norm of logrolling that protects most bills from amendments contrary to the wishes of committee members. Other lawmakers may have qualms about a bill, but if they hold their noses and vote for it, they can expect the same courtesy when their committees' bills hit the floor.

As for lobbyists, if being granted access really commits them to supporting the enterprises of their patron legislators, then these same allies may pressure them also to respect the logrolling norm or bow to party leader pressure. Lobbyists might want to push their congressional allies to oppose or at least amend a bill coming out of another committee only to find themselves pushed to keep quiet. If lobbyists try to persuade their allies to go against the leadership or deeply ingrained norms, it may end up hurting their access. Thus, while conflict may be common before committees as lobbyists and legislators all position themselves, the time for fighting passes as bills move to the floor regardless of its consequences for member interests, at least on low-salient issues.

But the politics of highly-salient issues appears to be different. Considerable debate has taken place in the legislative literature regarding the real influence of parties (Krehbiel 1993; Binder, Lawrence, and Maltzman 1999), but Cox and McCubbins (1993) argue that legislation crucial to party fortunes may move leaders to run roughshod over institutional norms. On those issues most in the public eye, majority leaders may seek to pass bills quickly to bolster their electoral fortunes while the minority may try to stop them or at least make passage embarrassing and painful. Thus, where the majority prefers a show of interest group unity as a proxy for public unity, minority party leaders may desire conflict and will pressure their rank and file to, in turn, pressure their lobbyist allies to keep fighting, as happened on ANWR. And on bankruptcy reform, even while both Republican and Democratic leaders successfully pressured their colleagues to set aside conflict after bills came out of committee, most of the lobbyists continued to fight even though they risked alienating legislator allies. Consistent with the competitive model, it was simply lobbyists' needs to be seen as faithful advocates for member interests on especially crucial issues where members were united that trumped the need to please congressional allies and their leaders and respect institutional norms.

Legislative Timing of Lobbyist Conflict

The evidence in this chapter offers only tentative, conditional support for the influence of institutional rules and norms on lobbying but does suggest a timing element to competition and conflict. At least on my issues, the committee stage, the formative part of the lawmaking process, was clearly a time for expressing differences between competing groups. Given the control committee chairs and their staff have over lobbyist participation in hearings, a highly visible and very public form of committee advocacy, one might have expected lobbyists to be unanimously backing the chair's position, but that was not the case. Some lobbyists did appear willing to change their positions to support the committee; perhaps they hoped to be invited back because hearings are a low-cost but highly visible means of showing lawmakers and members that they are key players on an issue and have lots of access (Schlozman and Tierney 1986; Leyden 1995). But in many cases lobbyists who opposed the chair were also invited, perhaps because of institutional norms of courtesy to other majority and minority party committee members. Only on ANWR, an issue crucial to Republican leaders, did chairs appear to have forcefully pressured lobbyists or at least only invited lobbyists for groups supportive of opening the refuge.

Lobbyist conflict was a little less prevalent at the floor stage, though it hardly vanished, even on low-salience issues. The need to please congressional allies by giving their support to bills inconsistent with group member preferences to please leaders and support mutual "back-scratching" norms led to somewhat greater cooperation later in time. On highly visible issues like ANWR and bankruptcy reform, however, lobbyists were less inclined to give contentious bills a pass. Fighting between the parties may well have lead to greater conflict between lobbyists on ANWR. Institutional needs to pass bills with majorities, 60-plus in the Senate, gave minority leaders incentives to pressure their members and, indirectly, lobbyist allies to fight, even as the majority applied pressure on everyone to fall in line behind their position. On issues such as bankruptcy, however, while lawmakers of both parties were pressured to cooperate, lobbyists were not. The issue was just too important to too many members of too many interest groups for them to bend under congressional pressure.

All of these findings are consistent with the competitive model; the push and pull on lobbyists from group members and allied lawmakers is simply portrayed as being a little more complex by recognizing that allied legislators are themselves reacting to a variety of institutional pressures they can pass on to lobbyists. Yet readers may be bothered by my assumption here that the legislator–lobbyist relationship appears to assume that pressure largely flows only one way, from legislators, who hold the keys to institution access, to lobbyists, who need access to be influential. The popular view, of course, is the opposite, that it is the lobbyists who are pressuring legislators. Actually, in the competitive model I assume that it flows both ways, and in chapter 7 I explore the consequences for the lawmaking process when pressure flows in the other direction.

Notes

1. Election of more members of Congress who serve more constituencies should also lead to the enactment of more government programs, which, as Leech et al. (2005) find, leads to advocacy by more interest groups.

2. A total of 463 participants attended the hearings, only 54 percent of whom were lobbyists. Beyond that, 11 percent of those testifying were senators or House members, 12 percent were executive branch officials, 10 percent were state officials, and 11 percent were loosely classified as policy experts from think tanks in Washington, DC, or from universities around the nation.

3. A research assistant recoded all of the testimony, and we agreed 92 percent of the time.

4. See the *New York Times* blog at http://thecaucus.blogs.nytimes.com/2010/09/24/the-whole-truth iness-and-nothing-but/?scp=2&sq=colbert&st=cse. *Sesame Street* puppet Elmo also testified before Congress in April 2002, the only nonhuman to ever do so.

5. According to the Administrative Office of the US Courts, 473,000 individuals filed for personal bankruptcy in 1986–87, but 1.2 million by 1996–97. Much of it was attributable to credit card debt, but gambling was also a cause (Hosansky 1997a).

6. The coalition also included Mortgage Bankers Association, US League of Savings Institutions, American Bankers Association, Independent Bankers Association, America's Community Bankers,

American Financial Services Association, Consumer Bankers Association, Credit Union National Association, National Retail Federation, Visa USA, and MasterCard International (Seiberg 1997).

7. For instance, one of the Commission's 172 recommendations was to allow individuals to exempt up to $140,000 in personal property and home equity if they filed Chapter 7. Banking industry officials pointed to the 5–4 split on the Commission's vote as evidence that it was far from a unanimous support and therefore not a justification for adopting more pro-debtor reform legislation (Seiberg 1997).

8. This information came from the THOMAS system at the Library of Congress.

CHAPTER 7

■

Competition and Gridlock

COMPETING interest group lobbyists who chose conflict over compromise apparently helped bottle up legislation to open the Arctic National Wildlife Refuge to oil drilling and delayed bankruptcy reform, but their shift from conflict to cooperation may have led to the opposite result on the revamping of money-laundering laws. Scandals involving drug money and the illegal movement of currency by foreign governments such as Russia, Mexico, and Gabon through major American banks had convinced policymakers, and even many bankers, that new rules on tracking and enforcement were badly needed. Even before the September 11 terrorist attacks made tracking laundered money a matter of national security, lobbyists for the Financial Services Roundtable, American Bankers Association, other industry groups, and several consumer groups were negotiating compromise legislation; the tragic event simply hastened cooperation and put the bill on the fast track when it became apparent that the nation needed better ways to locate and confiscate terrorist money in the banking system. By late 2001 banking and consumer interests had helped Congress hammer out and pass a comprehensive new money-laundering law. Whereas group conflict on some issues leads to gridlock, on others compromise generates momentum.

In the last chapter I began exploring how and when legislators might pressure lobbyists into cooperating so that the wheels of the lawmaking process, already designed to move slowly, could at least turn a little. Yet the popular view of lobbyists is that it is they who decide whether to gum up the gears or grease the skids by pressuring legislators into conflict or compromise. The competitive model may provide a more nuanced understanding of lobbying and gridlock by engaging the theoretical literature on the topic and exploring how the need to please both group members and legislative allies pushes lobbyists into bill-stopping conflict with each other when lawmakers and concerned group memberships are themselves polarized.

Partisan and Preference Views of Gridlock

The causes and implications of legislative gridlock, Congress's apparent inability to produce meaningful new policy, became a major research agenda for political scientists in the 1990s. For decades scholars argued that unified control of government by a single political party was essential for enacting substantive policy agendas (Key 1942; Schattschneider 1942; Cutler 1988; Sundquist 1988).[1] Implicit in this argument was a normative belief that government ought to be unified so that parties wielding a mandate from the public could enact a comprehensive agenda that voters could evaluate at the next election.[2] The frequent inability of one party to exercise unified control reflected a fundamental weakness in the Madisonian system because the jockeying between parties for control brought the system to a standstill and made it impossible for the public to hold elected officials accountable. This consequence, in turn, was believed to exacerbate the alienation of the electorate (Burns 1963).

Given the strength of this belief in the value of unified government, it is not hard to understand the impact of David Mayhew's 1991 study of gridlock. Examining the fates of what he identified as landmark legislation, Mayhew drew the stunning conclusion that whether government was divided or united made no difference as to whether such legislation became law. His finding jump-started an intense research agenda on the causes and consequences of gridlock with scholars following one of two tracks. The first focuses on confirming or refuting Mayhew's conclusion with theoretical or methodological variations on his research design (Kelly 1993; Fiorina 1996; Howell et al. 2000); the other searches for alternative explanations for gridlock.

Research in the latter vein assumes that divided government explanations are unlikely to hold because of the relative weakness of the political parties. In parliamentary democracies where executive and legislative leadership are vested in the same individual and where the choices of rank-and-file members are tightly constrained by party leaders, the policy preferences of individual legislators on bills often take a backseat to party agendas. A bill is passed (or not) because it is in the interests of the majority party to do so, not because of individual legislators or other factors peculiar to the issue at hand. But in a system where parties cannot easily control individual members because power and electoral responsibility are highly dispersed, this party-based explanation is less likely to be true. Scholars looking beyond Mayhew thus turned to explanations rooted more in institutional structure and the distribution of individual legislator preferences.

Much of this work has its roots in Duncan Black's median voter theorem (1958), which holds that the policy preference of the legislator at the median of a distribution of lawmakers determines the outcome of a majority vote. Keith Krehbiel (1991) showed how differences between the preferences of the median legislator on a committee and the median of the parent chamber may prevent that committee from reporting legislation, a type of gridlock unconnected to party. Cox and McCubbins (1993, 2002) injected parties back into Krehbiel's purely preference-based model; they argue that when a bill is important to the electoral fate of the majority, the party leadership will use institutional rules to ensure that any policy enacted will reflect the preference of the majority party's median member rather than that of the floor or committee median. Wiseman and Wright (2008) go further; they argue that the closer the party and floor medians are, the less likely gridlock is to occur because the majority will be largely getting what it wants. Groseclose and McCarty (2001) and Beckmann and McGann (2008) argue that gridlock is more likely when preference differences exist between the majority party and the president. Brady and Volden (1998) and Krehbiel (1998) go further yet; they argue that particular features of legislative and executive institutions, such as the Senate filibuster and the presidential veto, permit the president or a minority of legislators with preferences significantly different from other lawmakers to thwart majority will and impose gridlock.

On the empirical side perhaps no work has been more influential than that of Sarah Binder (1999), who finds that preference differences within and between the House and Senate, unconstrained by party though perhaps shaped by institutional traditions of courtesy, may determine the fate of legislation. She also argues that lawmakers face external incentives, such as demand for legislation that addresses an issue highly salient to the public or constraints on what is feasible given budget availability. Although she finds that demand only exerts an influence on the likelihood of gridlock, I nonetheless take political context as my point of departure.

Interest group competition, I have been arguing, results when the members of one organization want to see an issue they care about resolved with policy in a manner different from, and perhaps harmful to, the way members of other groups want it resolved. This competition is part of an issue's context separate from legislator preferences because, while membership differences may be quite similar to, and may even indirectly cause, differences between legislators, I have assumed throughout this book that differences from one social interest to another are not influenced by the desires of their elected officials. Both influence the choices of lobbyists, and thus gridlock, because conflict results when members and legislators independently pressure lobbyists to fight.

Competitive Interest Groups and Gridlock

The idea that interest groups contribute to gridlock is hardly a new argument. Indeed, in the minds of many Americans it seems that interest groups are the real culprits behind Congress's apparent inability to act. Journalist accounts of policymaking tend to support this view. Birnbaum (1992), for example, blames interest group intransigence for the failure to enact transportation safety laws, and Drew (1999) lays blame for the death of campaign finance reform at the feet of self-interested lobbyists. Rauch (1995) and Moss (2008) make big-picture arguments that interest groups are defenders of the status quo, not forces for policy change. As long as legislation threatens their hard-won special benefits, they will vigorously lobby to bottle up such bills, and lawmakers will ultimately be unable to enact any policy threatening the status quo, even when there is a crisis. Not only do lobbyists create gridlock, Mancur Olson (1982) argues, they may ultimately force a revolution.[3] It is clear that these explanations are not grounded in any notion of interest group competition; they are actually reminiscent of the old subgovernment belief that lobbyists exert so much influence over the narrow policies that supply their members with benefits or protectionist regulation that government is no longer free to act.

In their attempt to empirically explore a possible link between interest groups and gridlock, Virginia Gray and David Lowery (1995) reject this theory of stasis resulting from the partitioning of policy domains by interest groups, arguing that there is simply too much diversity among groups for such an explanation to be true. Instead, they argue that the greater the diversity of interests, the more directions in which policy will be pulled and the harder it will be to build widespread support for new policy. Since legislators are unwilling to alienate any constituency or source of financial support, they end up taking no action at all. Evidence from their cross-sectional study of legislative productivity relative to public demand (as reflected in legislation introduced) in the states largely supports their argument that greater group diversity leads to more gridlock. Similar state-level work by Bowling and Ferguson (2001) reaches a similar conclusion.

Oddly, Jeff Berry's (2002) national-level study that examines the connection between organized interests and gridlock produces the opposite result. Like Gray and Lowery, he argues that because parties are weak, it makes sense to look to the community of groups lobbying each issue for an explanation for gridlock. Again, like Gray and Lowery, he argues that conflict between groups, when relatively balanced in terms of influence and resources, should bring a system already designed to move slowly to a complete halt. Although Berry argues that citizen's and public interest groups are those most likely to complete with business interests, his analysis of the relationship between the proportion of citizen's and public interest groups and legislative activity at three different time periods fails to uncover any significant correlation. Rates of bill passage, or even activity on bills such as committee hearings and markups, appear unrelated to the composition of the group community that lobbies the issue.

The explanation for these contradictory findings is unlikely to be just the result of significant differences between state and national interest group communities. For the most part, the contours of state interest group systems have become nearly as diverse as the national system (Thomas and Hrebenar 1992; Lowery and Gray 1994; but see Berkman 2001). One explanation is how dependent variables were measured. Berry looks at total bills passed, as well as selected activities on bills such as hearings, whereas Gray and Lowery's primary dependent variable is a ratio of introductions to enactments. Another is that simply pitting citizen's groups against professional and trade associations is too poor a proxy for competition and conflict. I have already shown how moderate environmental citizen's groups allied with the oil industry to provide more funding for wildlife conservation, bringing them into conflict with more ideologically extreme citizen's groups. On bioengineered food regulation, professional associations of crop growers initially allied with citizen's groups, but then jumped sides to ally with wholesaler and agribusiness groups.

Competition just does not always break along citizen's and professional group lines. It exists when groups desire different outcomes, and conflict exists when the lobbyists for these groups choose to fight for these outcomes rather than negotiate and cooperate.

Yet another explanation for these conflicting results is that these studies do not engage the rich theoretical and empirical work that has been done by scholars specializing in congressional and presidential politics, perhaps because it is difficult to link legislator preferences to those of interest groups and their lobbyists. Using the competitive model to explain gridlock, however, means that I must make this connection because the distribution of legislator preferences has already been shown to be an integral part of how lobbyists for competing groups decide whether to fight or cooperate. What I need to do is to test an interest group competition explanation for gridlock that complements the partisan–institutional models developed and tested by congressional specialists. It must show how differences in legislator preferences shape lobbyist conflict and, along with differences in the collective preferences of interest group memberships, influence the likelihood of gridlock.

The work in the previous chapters points the way. Since competition is a preexisting state between two or more groups, it does not directly influence legislators' choices. Lobbyists' choices to fight their competitors, however, are partially determined by their need to choose a position from which they can garner the most legislator support, as well as support from group members and other lobbyists. The greater the range of the legislator preference distribution that exists prior to advocacy, the fewer resources a lobbyist needs to commit in order to gain their support because more legislators are likely to be already pressuring the lobbyist to support positions close to his or her members' ideal position. Legislators further away will either be too expensive to lobby, or just not in the lobbyist's "access set." Polarization makes it easier for a lobbyist to balance legislator and member pressures, and it dilutes competitor counterlobbying (the indirect competitive effect) and the enticement of competitor resources toward cooperation (the direct competitive effect). Instead, after having chosen a position less likely to be amenable to compromise, the lobbyist will use group resources to help allied legislators stop bills potentially harming their members or seek to advance bills that lobbyists for competing interests will try to kill. This is what happened on the Arctic National Wildlife Refuge issue. In the aggregate, if more lobbyists choose conflict because the range of legislator preferences over an issue is large, then more will be fighting for conflicting positions; thus it is much less likely that broad majorities will form to get bills moved to the president's desk. A case study should help make this cause of gridlock clearer.

Skirting Gridlock in Dairy Politics

From 1994 to 2002 lawmakers introduced thirty bills to change the way the US Department of Agriculture (USDA) sets the floor for the price dairy farmers receive for fresh milk, not one of which became law. Of course, merely looking at whether bills on a topic actually pass or not misses the more crucial nuances of gridlock because many policy goals, especially controversial ones, find their way into other, sometimes wholly unrelated, pieces of legislation when stand-alone bills on the same topic fail to move. House and Senate conference committees, as Shepsle and Weingast (1987) note, often provide opportunities for legislators who are pushing controversial proposals to quietly insert those proposals into otherwise popular, and often "must-pass," bills that cannot be re-amended on the floor. As reported in *CQW*, forty-nine attempts were made from 1994 to 2002 to add or eliminate dairy provisions in other bills by amendment or in the reconciliation process. On four occasions they succeeded. Why?

Enacted in the 1940s, the USDA's milk marketing order system uses a complex formula to guarantee a minimum price for fresh milk to all farmers in the same region, but this floor is higher the further that region is from Eau Claire, Wisconsin. Facing competition from large California dairies (not part of the marketing order system), upper midwestern dairy farmers had for years urged for a more level playing field with eastern dairies by abolishing the regional differentials (Hosansky 1996a). Both their Republican and Democrat representatives had tried to revise the pricing equations, but for two reasons advocates thought 1996 might be the year. First, with Republicans now in control of Congress, they could align their desire to eliminate regional price supports with the majority party's desire to phase out decades-old crop and livestock support programs embedded in the Freedom-to-Farm Act. Second, the current system was expiring at year's end anyway, so something had to be done. Free-market ideology, however, has limits when it comes to dairies, and northeastern lawmakers not only opposed the elimination of the current price support system but felt that the system did not compensate their dairies enough. Their solution, which ironically they hoped might also find a home in the Freedom-to-Farm Act, was to create an interstate compact, essentially a cartel, where member states set their own regional price floor. Free-market ideology was not on their side, but Sen. Patrick Leahy (D-VT) was.

"Dairy policy has become, unfortunately, a kind of zero-sum game between regions," said Sen. Paul Wellstone (D-MN) to *CQW* (Greenblatt 1999a), and regional divisions in Congress often come hand-in-hand with similar internal divisions in the memberships of large, national, "peak" interest groups. "On a scale of one to 10, I'd give [this issue] an 11 in terms of difficulty," said John Keeling of the American Farm Bureau Federation (Hosansky 1996a). He, like lobbyists for other national groups, walked a fine line with group members and lawmakers on both sides of the debate. The National Milk Producers Federation (NMPF) lobbyist told me how his dairy cooperative members were so bitterly divided that several left the group when, under pressure from New England lawmakers and dairies, it chose to support restoring the regional price differentials after the USDA tried to eliminate them.[4] Farm Bureau and Associated Milk Producers (AMP) lobbyists told similar stories of intense pressure from lawmakers who represent regions where their members were concentrated to support positions that alienate other group members.

So, Farm Bureau and NMPF fought to defend the status quo while AMP worked to abolish it when all three would have preferred quiet compromises. The very regional diversity that normally makes groups strong was now a liability.

Regional dairy groups did not have this problem; the Upper Midwest Dairy Coalition fought tooth and nail to level the pricing system and end interstate compacts. Consumer advocates were also united in their opposition to regional price floors. "It's a pretty direct transfer from low-income families to pretty well-off farmers," said Public Voice for Food and Health Policy (now part of Consumer Federation of America) lobbyist Allen Rosenfeld about the Northeast Dairy Compact (Hosansky 1996a), which he argued would increase the average price of milk by 18 cents per gallon (Weinstein 1999). Also against price supports were free-market advocates such as Citizens Against Government Waste, which objected to the nation being "carved up into all these little fiefdoms" (Greenblatt 1999b), the National Taxpayers Union, and Americans for Tax Reform. But their problem, one lobbyist told me, was access. Only dairy lawmakers cared about the issue, and they had little interest in the views of nondairy groups.

With some Republicans wary of the Freedom-to-Farm Act (some feared the removal of decades-old price supports, whereas others wanted their immediate suspension rather than the proposed five-year phaseout), Senate Agriculture Committee chair Richard Lugar (R-IN) needed votes from Leahy, the committee's ranking member, and other Democrats.[5] Perhaps Leahy agreed with Rep. Steve Gunderson's (R-WI) claim that "there's no question that we could not [change the price support system] legislatively on the floor of the Congress" (Greenblatt 1999b), for he agreed to kick the thorny issue of restructuring the pricing system over to the USDA, but his price was congressional approval of the Northeast Dairy Compact (Hosansky 1996c).[6] For years the compact had been his priority, but even when he was Agriculture Committee chair he had not been able to move authorization legislation in the face of filibuster threats (Palmer 1994).[7] Now, in a senate where lawmakers were distributed widely on the issue, votes he controlled gave him more leverage than any filibuster.

Midwestern legislators were furious; when Freedom-to-Farm hit the Senate floor Wellstone and Herb Kohl (D-WI) stripped the compact from the bill with a filibuster threat, so Leahy took up his cause in conference committee. The night before the deadline to get a report to both houses before the Easter recess, every contentious issue in the bill except the compact was put to rest in a compromise by Rep. Gunderson; he refused to favor Vermont dairies over Wisconsin dairies. After the frustrated committee broke for the evening with House leaders threatening to drop all dairy provisions, Gunderson and Leahy continued to fight. Then they began to negotiate, and when the committee returned in the morning hoping for a miracle, they found that one had occurred. Leahy would let the USDA restructure milk prices, and Gunderson would approve the Northeast Dairy Compact for the three years it might take the USDA to do so (Hosansky 1996b). Other midwestern legislators, many of whom were majority Republicans, introduced bills to repeal the compact, and Rep. David Obey (D-MN) tried to strip funding for the compact from the USDA appropriations bill, but the deal held. It even held through 1997 when similar efforts were made to kill it.

Midwesterners did win a short-lived victory in 1998 when Agriculture Secretary Dan Glickman proposed a new milk-pricing formula that erased most regional differentials. Actually, he proposed two versions, Option 1-A that retained some financial advantages for northeastern and southeastern dairy farmers, and Option 1-B, the USDA's chosen rule, that did not. Eastern lawmakers promptly attacked Glickman's proposal and Rep. Roy Blunt (R-MO) moved legislation to suspend its implementation for six months while Congress "studied" it. Although many of their members liked the new rule, well over a hundred lawmakers were speaking against it, so Farm Bureau and NMPF reluctantly opposed Option 1-B. The NMPF lobbyist even helped Blunt write his bill. Associated Milk Producers, which had more members in the upper Midwest, worked to help Rep. Obey bring down the hand of gridlock by stripping Blunt's suspension out of the USDA appropriations bill and to try, again, to defund the Northeast Dairy Compact. Many groups lobbied with them, including every group in my survey except Farm Bureau and NMPF, but Blunt's bill (H.R. 1402) that forced the USDA to implement 1-A had 228 cosponsors.[8] Obey and his allies were overwhelmed.

The following year opened with hearings where lobbyists and lawmakers competed to tell the saddest story about dairy farmers going broke if Option 1-B was, or was not, implemented (Greenblatt 1999c). Rep. Blunt authored bills to force the USDA to permanently implement Option 1-A, to further extend the Northeast Dairy Compact, and to create a Southeast Dairy Compact (Dao 1999). Blunt's bill passed the House, but midwestern senators managed to bottle up it and the compacts with filibusters when they were offered as amendments to the USDA appropriations bill. They still lost, for Blunt and Leahy succeeded in, once again, adding their language to a conference report for a large, unrelated omnibus spending bill right before adjournment. Obey and his interest group allies again tried to stop the conference report in the House by forcing eleven votes on arcane parliamentary procedures but ultimately failed. In the Senate, Kohl and Russ Feingold (D-WI) even threatened to filibuster a continuing resolution keeping the government operational, but the weight of an entire institution trying to complete its work for the year was against them, and they gave up after they had only extracted promises from Majority Leader Trent Lott (R-MI) for dairy hearings next year (Foerstel 1999).

The northeasterner's victory proved short-lived because in 2001 it was time for a new farm bill. Opponents of regional pricing and compacts had a new ally in George W. Bush, the free-market-minded new president who was not inclined to support regional compacts and price support systems. Nor, rumor held, was he inclined to support anything desired by Vermont senator James Jeffords, whose defection from the Republican Party handed Senate control to the Democrats (Davis and Dougherty 2001; Hernandez 2001). Perhaps with this in mind, New England lawmakers changed tactics. Leahy proposed a new alternative. He would let the compact expire, and even allow the USDA to remove most regional price differentials, as long as dairy farmers were compensated when the price of milk dropped below a specified level. New Senate Agriculture Committee chair Tom Harkin (D-IA) agreed, and together they fought off efforts by some senators, upset dairy groups, and liberal and conservative citizen's groups to kill the entire dairy program during floor debate (Martinez 2001).

The big agriculture and dairy groups expressed relief in their interviews over this compromise, although the National Milk Producers Federation lobbyist was unhappy about being pressured to support a policy that his organization would have preferred to oppose (many members only supported it after a long and contentious meeting) and that still put him at odds with other dairy groups. The compromise was also not enough for Wisconsin and Minnesota dairies, so their congressional champions and interest groups such as Associated Milk Producers and Upper Midwest Dairy Coalition continued to fight, as did the consumer and free-market groups. But their dozen or so bills attacking the new dairy policy failed to move, and in 2002 no new bills were introduced. The dairy war had, at least for the moment, come to an end.

Dairy-pricing reform is the third most competitive issue of my six (see figure 4.1 in chapter 4), but it is not an example of endless gridlock. Indeed, I chose the case because it is an example of how gridlock can occur and be overcome. Here filibuster threats were sometimes effective instruments of obstruction, but sometimes they were used to force unpopular provisions into must-pass appropriations bills. It was the reconciliation process, however, that really provided opportunities for Leahy and Blunt to pass language preserving regional price differentials and compacts. These ideas were not unpopular. Recall that Blunt's bill imposing Option 1-A on the USDA had over half of the House as cosponsors, which suggests that many House members were supportive, even as the midwestern chunk was fiercely opposed. More important from the standpoint of theory, it was supported by the median House member, the majority party median member, the Agriculture committee median member, and the majority party's median member on the committee.[9] Legislator preference distributions do appear to matter when it comes to enactment or gridlock.

Many lobbyists found the dairy debate to be a thoroughly unpleasant experience. Farm Bureau and National Milk Producers Federation lobbyists had been forced to bow to pressure from powerful lawmakers such as Leahy and others, even though the debate fractured their memberships along regional lines. They told me they would have preferred to deal, but many of their own members and their legislator allies simply would not allow it. They chose conflict. Regional groups such as Associated Milk Producers and Upper Midwest Dairy Coalition also chose conflict, but their members were largely united behind a position that advocated the abolition of the regional price system; these lobbyists could more comfortably choose positions supporting Gunderson, Kohl, and Wellstone. And this conflict resulted in gridlock, each side helping their friends in Congress tear away at the other side by providing information on tactics, reasons to support or hate Option 1-A, and tear-jerking stories of dairy farms gone dry. When gridlock was overcome, it was through filibusters and conference committees. Thus, any statistical test must not only use measures of differences between median members and filibuster pivots, but a measure of lobbyist conflict, itself determined by both the positions of group members and the preference distributions of lawmakers, as well.

Conflict and Gridlock: A Statistical Analysis

My primary gridlock variable is enactment of bills into laws, but I also explore movement of bills out of their originating committees. The bills whose fates I study are drawn from my six issues, but instead of just using bills that formed my issue iterations back in chapter 3, I cast a wider net by identifying all of the major bills in the 106th and 107th Congresses that primarily addressed my issues.[10] Specifically, to be included, the bill must contain a proposal to change policy from the status quo for each of the six issues, such as a proposal to rewrite bankruptcy laws, regulate bioengineered food, or make the Arctic National Wildlife Refuge more open to oil exploration. Congress frequently lets individual bills expire but places their language in large, omnibus bills; in such cases I coded the bill as "passing," even if the bill itself died, as long as its language showed up in another that did pass. For example, Blunt's H.R. 1402 was itself never considered by the Senate, but the binary variable for it is coded 1 for "enacted" because its language was passed as part of an appropriations bill. Bills authored by minority party members sometime may be passed this way (Leahy got his dairy provisions passed this way even though Democrats were in the minority). In any case, the gridlock literature emphasizes preference distributions over partisan measures of divided government, so a bill's introduction by a majority party member is not a requirement.

Forty bills meet this criteria, thirteen (or 33 percent) of which were enacted into law, some as independent bills and others as amendments to larger pieces of legislation. The percentage on each issue is displayed in figure 7.1 and gives a rough indication of the degree of gridlock on each issue. In addition, twenty-two bills were reported by their original committees, so in order to study partial movement through the lawmaking process, I code a second dependent variable 1 if the observed bill was at least reported by committee.

I also coded a series of additional dummy variables for these bills to indicate what stages of the legislating process they made it through, such as whether they were the subjects of hearings, were passed by their original chamber of origin, or were passed by both chambers. Table 7.1 presents pair-wise correlations of all of these variables, which gives some sense of how likely it is for a bill that makes it over one hurdle to make it over the next. For the most part they reveal the pattern one might expect: Bills reported by a committee are more likely to pass that chamber, but are not guaranteed to pass the other chamber or to become law. Congressional hearings, where the importance of bills and the issues they address are highlighted, do not appear to have provided any momentum toward getting a bill through the Congress. Perhaps hearings contribute more toward setting a committee's issue agenda, even if they do not play a major role in shaping the agenda of the entire Congress that session.

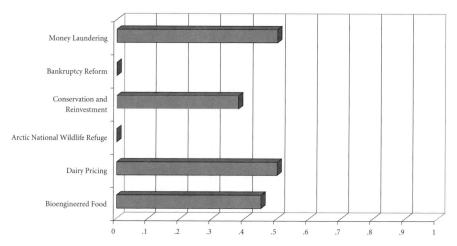

Figure 7.1. Percentage of bills enacted into law by issue

Legislator Preference Differences and Lobbyist Conflict

I consistently argue that the distribution of legislator preferences partially shapes how lobbyists choose between conflict and compromise and thus have the potential to increase the aggregate level of lobbyist conflict. I also argue here that both legislator differences and lobbyist conflict independently influence the likelihood of gridlock. Lobbyists choose positions from which they can expect the greatest legislator support based on the distribution of the latter, but then they must fight for that position against alternatives supported by their competitors. Capturing this complexity requires a two-stage analysis: the first estimates the influence of the distribution of legislator preferences on lobbyists' choices to engage in conflict, and the second estimates both influences independently on my gridlock variables. Lobbyist conflict, of course, is not a measure of interest group competition but the aggregation of the decisions of lobbyists for competing groups to fight rather than to make compromises

Table 7.1 Pairwise Correlations of Bill Movement (p-value)

	Congressional Hearing	Committee Report	Passed by Just Either House or Senate	Passed by Both Chambers
Committee Report	.29	—	—	—
	(.07)			
Passed by Just Either House or Senate	0	.70	—	—
	(1.00)	(0)		
Passed by Both Chambers	.09	.59	0.65	—
	(.58)	(0)	(0)	
Enacted into Law	−.09	.41	0.48	0.71
	(.59)	(.01)	(0)	(0)

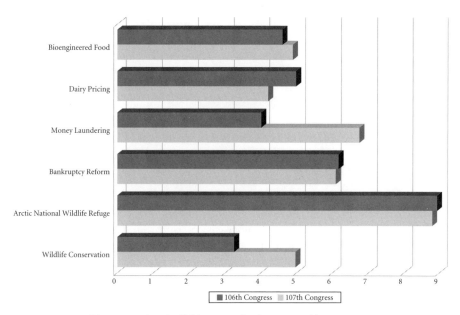

Figure 7.2. Level of lobbyist conflict by issue and by Congress

by forming coalitions. In this case it should also capture the capacity of these lobbyists to fight; greater resources allow them to persuade more legislators to support their chosen positions.

As in the previous chapter, I use the lobbying intensity scores (2, 1, −1, or −2) to find the difference between the choices made by pairs of lobbyists to support or oppose the proposals used to create the policy outcome spaces in chapter 3 (not the forty bills used to create the dependent variable here). If both support the bill, or both oppose it, regardless of the intensity (both 1 or 2 *or* both −1 or −2), I score that pair's conflict as 0. Otherwise, the absolute value of the difference is the intensity of a pair's conflict. For their capacity to fight, I again use each lobbyist's annual group budget, reduced by the proportion each lobbyist reported committing to advocacy on this issue. I subtract the adjusted budget of one group in the pair from that of the other and multiply the difference by the pair's conflict score. Some proposals occurred in the 106th Congress and others in the 107th (true for all six issues), so I summed all lobbyist-pair conflict scores for that issue in that Congress for an aggregate conflict score for each of the forty bills on that issue and in that Congress, repeating the process for the 107th Congress. Figure 7.2 shows the conflict scores.

Differences in legislator preferences should contribute to lobbyist conflict, but to meaningfully engage the gridlock literature this influence needs to be captured in ways consistent with the theoretical work on gridlock in Congress as well as Binder's empirical work. Thus, I cannot use the legislator pressure measure from chapter 4. Instead, I define partisan differences as the distance between the median Common Space score for Democrats on a committee with jurisdiction over the issue from the Republican median for the same committee, with different scores calculated for the 106th and 107th Congresses. Committee medians are used because these are the legislators most interested in these issues, the ones whose support or opposition should matter most to lobbyists and the ones who hold gate-keeping powers over bills.

I assemble the data matrix so that it includes an observation for each bill ($N = 40$), the party median difference for the committee that originated the bill, and the average lobbyist conflict scores for the appropriate issue and session of Congress. The other measure of preference difference from the theoretical literature is the difference between the majority party median and the median score of the entire committee, so I calculate this and enter the result in the matrix as well. Binder argues that the more ideological moderates there are, the more likely it is that deals will be struck to allow bills to move; thus I calculate the percentage of members of each committee whose preferences are closer to the chamber mean than to their own party's mean and enter this percentage for each committee and each Congress. This percentage is my final measure for the first stage of the analysis.

Now I regress party median differences, majority party and committee median differences, percentages of moderate legislators, and (as a control) group competition scores (displayed in figure 4.1 as the darker bars) on lobbyist conflict. The party median difference score is not statistically significant, but the difference between majority party and committee medians is ($\beta = 3.02$, S.E. $= 1.49$, $p < .05$) with a positive direction, indicating that greater differences in positions between legislators pushes lobbyists to choose conflict with each other over compromise. The percentage of moderates variable is also significant and negative ($\beta = -8.77$, S.E. $= 2.45$, $p < .005$), which indicates that the more moderating influences exist on the committee, the more likely lobbyists are to choose compromise. It is not surprising that competitive differences between the ideal positions of members is also a positive and significant contributor to lobbyist conflict ($\beta = 4.92$, S.E. $= 0.96$, $p < .005$).[11] I now use the linear prediction of the intensity of lobbyist conflict, a function of these variables, for each bill as my key estimator in the second stage, the gridlock stage, of the analysis.

Conflict and Gridlock

Now the main question: Does greater conflict between lobbyists contribute to gridlock? The conflict variable should have a straightforward negative effect on the likelihood of the dependent variable taking on a value of 1 (the observed bill was enacted), but the same legislator preferences used to estimate conflict (and through lobbyists indirectly influence gridlock) should also have a direct effect on enactment. I mentioned this endogeneity problem previously, and now I have solved it by first estimating lobbyist conflict and then using the prediction of conflict as an instrumental variable to estimate enactment along with other variables from the gridlock literature.[12]

The other explanatory variables include the difference between party committee medians, as well as the difference between a committee's median and the majority party committee median used earlier because they are emphasized in the theoretical literature. I do not include the percentage of moderates in the second stage, or gridlock stage, of the equation because not all three variables used to estimate the instrumental variable, lobbyist conflict, can be used in both stages, so I use the two capturing preference differences. I do include two other variables in the gridlock stage that Binder argues are important, differences between the House and Senate and the influence of the president (which is also emphasized in the theoretical literature by Groseclose and McCarty 2001 and Beckmann and McGann 2008). House and Senate divisions are the Common Space score differences of the median of the House or Senate committee originating the legislation from its equivalent committee in the other chamber (which may or may not have acted on the bill during my four-year study period).[13] Presidential demand is simply a binary variable coded 1 in the 106th Congress for state wildlife conservation because Bill Clinton had made it a priority issue, whereas in the 107th George Bush made drilling for oil in the Arctic and bankruptcy reform priorities of his administration.

The Senate filibuster may not have been the perfect tool for stopping legislation in the dairy debate, but Krehbiel (1998) argues that it is still important to explore the connection between the preferences of senators who are crucial, or "pivotal," because they can sustain a filibuster and the likelihood of gridlock. The filibuster pivot is the senator who is the fortieth most conservative senator when the president is liberal, or vice versa, but in this case I change the definition a little. I define it as the Common Space score difference between the fortieth most liberal senator when Republicans controlled the Senate, as was the case in the 106th Congress, from the median of the originating House or Senate committee. The fortieth most conservative senator during the 107th Congress was a Republican when Democrats held the majority for much of 2001 and all of 2002. Because the difference is between the senator and the originating committee median, this variable not only varies from bill to bill but from the 106th to the 107th Congress as well.[14]

The results of a probit estimate of the likelihood of committee passage and then enactment of a bill are presented in table 7.2. My model is better at explaining enactment of legislation than whether bills are likely to be reported from committee, although greater lobbyist conflict does make it less likely the bill in dispute will even make it out of committee. When it comes to actual enactment, it is clear that lobbyist conflict makes it less likely. In other words, interest group competition and the resulting conflict are a direct, if partial, cause of gridlock. Rep. Blunt's amendment to the 2000 Agricultural Appropriations legislation that forbids the USDA from implementing the new dairy-pricing scheme that leveled regional differentials might not have become law had producer groups such as Associated Milk Producers fought harder against the American Farm Bureau Federation and National Milk Producers Federation.

Unlike Mayhew's (1991) findings, these results appear to also provide some support for the belief that divided government hinders enactment. Greater ideological differences (measured as median differences) between the House and the Senate, a variable I can associate with divided government because the Senate was under Democratic control for most of the 107th Congress, make it less likely that one of the bills in this study would be enacted. The opposition of the pivotal senator, a partisan

Table 7.2 Estimates of Gridlock

Explanatory Variable	Committee Reported Legislation	Legislation Became Law
Level of Conflict among Interest Group Lobbyists (instrumental variable)	−.53[b] (.12)	−.99[c] (.16)
Presidential Demand	.96[a] (.55)	.87 (.56)
Difference between Originating Committee Median and Majority Party Committee Median	−.81 (1.46)	−6.87[a] (2.71)
Difference between Republican and Democratic Medians in Originating Committee	2.76 (2.22)	−.23 (2.02)
Difference between Committee Medians of Equivalent House and Senate Committees	−1.35 (1.85)	−13.12[a] (5.51)
Difference between the Filibuster Pivotal Senator and the Committee Majority Party Median	−1.53[a] (.91)	−9.03[b] (3.61)
Constant	1.55 (2.04)	11.52[c] (3.61)
Wald χ^2	33.01[c]	64.30[c]
Wald χ^2 Test of Exogeneity	4.78[b]	10.58[c]
N	40	40

Upper-cell value is maximum likelihood estimate; lower-cell value (parentheses) is robust standard error.
[a] $p < .05$; [b] $p < .01$; [c] $p < .005$.

difference as well as a preference difference, also makes both committee approval and enactment less likely. Party power within the chamber is also evident because consistent with Wiseman and Wright (2008), greater differences between the median voter and the party median also make gridlock more likely. It is interesting that a bill on the president's agenda will help get it out of committee but does not make it more likely that the president will ever actually sign it.

Calculating the first difference effects on gridlock is interesting as well, although the total observations in the model are too few to calculate them for each issue. The predicted likelihood of enactment when all explanatory variables are set at their mean or modal values is only .12, but a decrease of one standard deviation in lobbyist conflict increases the likelihood of enactment to .69. Thus, when we assume that .50 is the cut point between enactment and death, these findings show the dramatic difference that can occur when lawmakers urge lobbyists for competing groups to make compromises. Perhaps the bankruptcy reform legislation would have passed sooner than it did if citizen's group lobbyists had been pressured harder to agree to admittedly distasteful compromises with the banking industry rather than to fight. By stubbornly holding out, citizen's group lobbyists largely forfeited their input into the bill that President Bush signed in the end, which might not have happened had they negotiated with the bankers earlier.

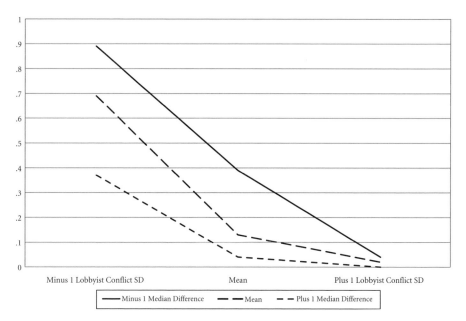

Figure 7.3. Enactment by lobbyist conflict and difference of committee and party medians

These estimates assume that other independent variables are held constant, which of course is rarely the case. Difference in preference medians is one of the core determinants in the theoretical literature on gridlock, so I explore how greater preference differences between the majority party committee median and the all-member committee median interacts with lobbyist conflict in figure 7.3. The change is substantial, which is not surprising given the importance past research has placed on differences in the preferences of members of Congress, as well as the strong results for lobbyist conflict in the statistical model. Even when lobbyist conflict is low, meaning one standard deviation below its mean value, a larger than average distance between the party and committee medians will still sink legislation, whereas even average lobbyist conflict may not be enough to prevent enactment when the distance between these medians is smaller than average. The more ideologically extreme the majority party, these results suggest, the less likely is enactment of legislation, and as our previous findings on the influence of this difference on lobbyist conflict indicate, the likelihood of conflict between lobbyists increases, which leads to further barriers to bill enactment.

I also find a few other significant effects from a first difference analysis of the difference between the filibuster pivot and lobbyist conflict variables in figure 7.4. The filibuster pivot appears exceptionally important, and it might be worthwhile in future research to learn whether this pivotal senator is lobbied more heavily than others (such as the median senator), either to change his or her preferences on an issue, or if he or she is not currently the pivot, to take that crucial position.

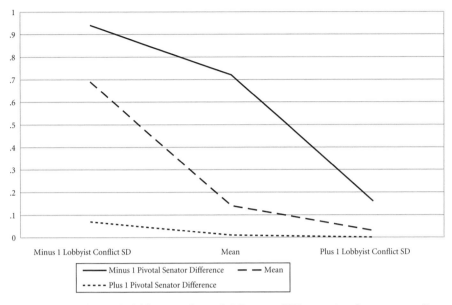

Figure 7.4. Enactment by lobbyist conflict and difference of filibuster pivot from party median

In sum, evidence shows that the more polarized members of Congress are, the more polarized are the lobbyists who represent the concerned interest groups and the less likely it is that legislation will pass. It is worth noting that although I never explored the connection between the ideal positions of interest group members and the policy preferences of legislators, there may well be one. Because of similarities in the constituencies that legislators and lobbyists both serve, legislators may initially prefer positions similar to group members, either ideologically extreme or moderate. Their preferences are determined to a significant extent by those of group members, so that constituent polarization leads to polarization in the Congress. This of course means that lobbyists are getting a double dose of ideological extremism, from the group members and legislators, that effectively nails them into their policy positions and forces them to fight each other, all of which tends to stall bills in Congress. The intense conflict with Kohl and Obey on one side (against regional milk price differentials) and Leahy and Blunt on the other (for regional pricing) is largely attributable to the need to serve angry dairy farmers in their states. Combined pressure from Leahy, Blunt, Kohl, and Obey along with their respective dairy constituents forced Associated Milk Producers and Upper Midwest Dairy Coalition to fight intensely against regional milk pricing while National Milk Producers Federation had to fight for it. It may be easy for a lobbyist to balance legislator and group member pressures when both are extreme, but it also makes it harder to actually get anything done or avoid expending tremendous resources in conflicts with rival interest groups. In these cases, lobbyists might wish to put aside competitive differences and form resource-sharing coalitions, but they dare not. Both the indirect and direct competitive effects draw lobbyists towards the ideological center, but when legislators and group members are polarized, these influences cease to exist.

Conclusion

This chapter had two primary purposes: to test an enhanced explanation of gridlock in government and to explore the implications of competition and conflict among interest groups on the dynamics of the political system. On the first front, lobbyist conflict was proposed as a means to better specify models of the failure of government to address legislative agendas that rely on partisan and institutional differences. Work by Gray and Lowery, as well as Berry, had already started down this road, but the research in this chapter makes a number of advancements. First, it grounded conflict and its impact on gridlock in a theoretical model of lobbyist behavior, namely, the competitive model. Second, it connected conflict to the larger gridlock literature through the notion of the political context that surrounds an issue by linking partisan differences within and between political institutions to the likelihood of lobbyist conflict. Third, by providing a more nuanced measure of lobbyist conflict, that is, a measure directly related to the choices of lobbyists to oppose each other's positions rather than those measures used previously, it moves beyond the simple citizen's group versus business association dichotomy.

Although the data is limited, only extending over two congresses and six issues, the results nonetheless suggest that partisan and institutional models of gridlock are underspecified as long as they do not take into account the array of private interests lobbying an issue. As long as gridlock is defined as the failure to enact legislation into law, conflict among group lobbyists had a clearly negative effect on enacting any of the bills attached to the six issues. It would be interesting to test the effects of this variable in other areas of research on gridlock and divided government. Divided government has been found to contribute to congressional delegation of authority to the bureaucracy (Epstein and O'Halloran 1996). Does lobbyist conflict, which can easily encompass agency officials, contribute to or hinder this delegation? Conflict between political officials has been found to hinder increases in government spending (Jones, True, and Baumgartner 1997; Jones, Sulkin, and Larson 2003), so can cooperation among lobbyists help break such deadlocks? Answering these questions may suggest other important new lines of future research.

The second front, arguably the more important contribution of this chapter, concerns my overall interest group competition project. Chapters 3 and 4 presented evidence in support of my hypotheses regarding the motivations of lobbyists and why they make decisions they would not make if they were solely responsive to group members and/or allied lawmakers. But what the implications of this competition or the conflict potentially emerging from it are for politics surrounding these six issues was not clear. Competition exists and is important for lobbyist decision making, but what difference does it make regarding the way issues are addressed in the political process? This chapter makes clear that competition and the resulting conflict have critical ramifications, particularly when taken in the context of the preferences and choices of other political actors in the lawmaking system such as committee and party legislators. In other words, lobbyist competition matters when it comes to the fate of legislation addressing important issues, some of which may even be desired by the public. In the larger picture of American politics, interest group competition matters.

Whether this competition is desirable or not is another matter, a normative question rather than the positive question addressed in this chapter. Interest group pluralism can facilitate the passage of legislation, but it can also lead to gridlock and stasis. Is this healthy for democratic government? The political system was designed by James Madison and his colleagues to be incremental so that change in policy only occurs after extensive deliberation and agreement among the representatives of competing factions of the public (see *Federalist No. 51* by Madison). Should interest groups be permitted to slow this process even further? Or, perhaps, is interest group competition an integral part of the way the system was designed to function and, as a result, should not only be expected but actually embraced? This normative question is the subject of chapter 8.

Notes

1. With this argument went the belief that divided government reflected a desire in the electorate for split control of government; no single party could push through its agenda, but instead would be forced to balance their proposals with input from the other side, which would result in moderate policies. However, little empirical support has been found for this kind of strategic voting (Frymer, Kim, and Bimes 1997; Sigelman, Wahlbeck, and Buell 1997).

2. In a few cases this normative belief is explicit, as in the famous (to political scientists) report of the American Political Science Association (1950) that laments the decline of effective political parties and unified government.

3. Olson argues that growing demands from trade groups and businesses to protect their own interests restrict government flexibility to the point where lawmakers become too paralyzed to cope with new developments or emergencies (Peterson 1992; Coates, Heckelman, and Wilson 2010).

4. Interestingly, the federation's two largest cooperatives, which were used to having a say in the group's policies, were in the same bind. Some of their members wanted prices leveled, whereas others preferred regional differentials.

5. In an example of how regional differences trumped partisan differences, when House Agriculture Committee chair Pat Roberts (R-KS) brought up his version of the farm bill, he suffered the indignity of having majority party Republicans defy him by voting it down. Rather than push a partisan goal of deregulation, Republicans broke almost entirely on regional lines over price subsidies and supports for dairy, sugar, and peanuts (Hosansky 1996c).

6. Section 8 of Article 1 of the Constitution requires Congress to grant formal approval to all interstate compacts.

7. Senator Kohl fought so fiercely that he even filibustered unrelated bills, such as a popular wiretapping bill, until Democratic leaders agreed to block Leahy's bill (Palmer 1994).

8. In 2001 Rep. Asa Hutchinson's (R-AR) bill, H.R. 1827, to extend the Northeast Dairy Compact and create the Southeast Dairy Compact had 164 cosponsors, and Specter's companion bill, S. 1157, had 39.

9. The median member of Congress in the 106th was Rep. Horn (R-CA), the majority Republican median was Rep. McKeon (R-CA), the Agriculture Committee median member was Rep. Simpson

(R-ID), and the majority median on the committee was Rep. Moran (R-KS). All voted for H.R. 1402 when it passed the House, roll call 436 on September 22, 1999, and all but Horn were cosponsors. It is worth noting that when calculating these scores, Rep. Virgil Goode of Virginia was counted as a Republican because only in 2000 did he become an independent.

10. For this purpose I consider only legislation that moved through Congress. Agency regulations forming a handful of the issue iterations used in chapters 3 and 4 are not used.

11. The $R^2 = .58$, the F-statistic is 14.46 ($p < .005$), and the $N = 40$.

12. In Stata, our data analysis and statistical software program, I use the "ivprobit" command.

13. Comparisons can only be made between the House and Senate medians as long as Common Space scores are used (Poole 1998).

14. Although I examine the fate of bills over a four-year period, I do not consider it time-series data. Time-series focuses on changes in the same units over different periods of time, but the bills forming my unit of analysis are not constant from year to year. Thus, traditional time-series, or fixed-effects, statistical models are unlikely to provide additional leverage. Furthermore, the primary independent variable of interest, lobbyist conflict, varies more from issue to issue than year to year, so I use a probit model.

CHAPTER 8

■

Competitive Interest Groups and Deliberative Democracy

BIG events outside of normal, everyday political maneuvering and bargaining can dramatically change the dynamics of an issue, but as McFarland (2004, 51–55) notes, such "high politics" tend not to have lasting influences on the behavior of lobbyists and lawmakers working those issues. In the previous chapters I described how gridlock over the reform of anti-money-laundering laws abruptly gave way to widespread cooperation and the quick passage of legislation immediately after the September 11, 2001, terrorist attacks. Before the attacks, lobbyists for the American Council of Life Insurers were expressing alarm over how the proposal would force their members to disclose financial data damaging their relationships with customers. America's Community Bankers argued that all that was really needed was for banks to simply police themselves better.

Then September 11 happened and these same lobbyists began tripping over themselves to make deals and pass a bill suddenly seen as crucial to national security. Negotiations were now about how to update laws to better track the movement of money linked to terrorist organizations. As I was told in several interviews, banks were now willing to risk supporting new regulatory policy because they now saw it as in their interests and in the interest of everyone else to prevent the economic chaos that would come from future attacks.[1] For a brief time the normal politics of self-interested advocacy were put aside by lobbyists and their members to support a common interest. To support, one might say, the public interest.

Deliberation over the public interest, rather than just over balancing competing special interests, is probably short-lived most of the time, and some banks came to regret the compromises their lobbyists made to pass the PatriotUSA Act. Yet this case also shows that it may be possible for competitive interest group politics to lead to something more than just conflict and bargaining over who gets what. Nobody hopes for another attack to inspire a patriotic sacrifice of interests, but could the growing pressure on lobbyists to bargain generated by a political system that pits interest groups against each other, which scholars such as McFarland (2004) and Gray and Lowery (2004) label "neopluralism," ever lead to more frequent considerations of the broader public interest, rather than just advance the self-interests of lobbyists, legislators, and group members? In this last chapter I use the competitive model to explore how lobbyists representing factions of the public with conflicting interests could find it in their interest to emphasize deliberation over the public interest because of the pressures the model identifies, pressures normal in a world of interest group competition.

Looking Back

But first I summarize what the competitive model's contributions to interest group scholarship actually are. It is significant that while the twentieth century saw decreases in voting and party membership, participation in interest groups dramatically increased. According to a recent report by the Congressional Management Foundation based on Zogby survey data, approximately 61 percent of all Americans are members of at least one organized interest group (Goldschmidt and Ochreiter 2008). More groups providing political voice for more segments of a society as heterogeneous as the United States means more diverse interests are striving to have their demands heard and met by government policymakers. It also, of course, means that it is much more likely that the demands of one interest cannot be fully satisfied without harming the interests of others. Giving regulatory protection to one interest means placing potentially severe restrictions on others' freedom to choose. Providing financial subsidies, either direct payments or tax breaks, to one interest means less for others, potentially even taking resources away from others as discretionary public budgets shrink.

Interest group scholars have documented this increase in mobilized political interests but have only begun to explore what effect it may have on how groups lobby and how policy is made. In this book I have explored competitive lobbying, how lobbyists react to challenges from other lobbyists for conflicting interests. Furthermore, I study their competitive behavior in the context of the two major pressures every lobbyist is under, the need to please the members they represent and the lawmakers on whom they depend for access to political institutions. This approach allows me to tie the collective action and legislative lobbying literatures together, which I argue is a contribution in itself, because lobbyists must try to balance these conflicting pressures as they decide how to respond to the threat posed by competing interest groups seeking to influence many of the same legislators on behalf of different group members.

The resulting model developed in chapter 2 reveals two competitive effects. By drawing off once-reliable congressional support, competitors push lobbyists into making compromises they would not have made otherwise to avoid wasting their resources on quixotic advocacy that would only end up irritating allies who have already been persuaded to support alternative policy positions. This indirect competitive effect was empirically supported in chapter 4. And as seen in chapter 6, when their legislative allies are pressured by party and committee leaders and other institutional norms to set conflict aside, lobbyists may find themselves similarly pressured to cooperate when they would have preferred to fight, at least on low-salient issues at the floor stage of the lawmaking process. But even when they are not pressured to compromise, lobbyists who find themselves confronted by resource-rich opponents may also find value in joining coalitions where resource-sharing becomes an enticement to compromise, the direct competitive effect empirically supported in chapter 5.

At least this effect can happen as long as their competitors find it in their interests to make compromises and share resources, or as long as their allies in Congress are similarly inclined to support compromises, and as long as every lobbyist's members can stomach the result. On issues of bread-and-butter importance to members, lobbyists may have to take obstinate, combative positions and expend valuable resources fighting their competitors by trying to persuade their congressional allies to fight rather than compromise, resulting in the gridlock seen in chapter 7. None of these findings suggests that the public interest is given priority in neopluralist, competitive interest group politics. But asking if there *could* be an opening for consideration of the public interest provides a way to look ahead and think more broadly about the consequences of interest group competition in a representational form of government.

Self-Interested Pluralism and Deliberation over the Public Good

Voting and party membership declined across the twentieth century while the number and ideological variety of interest groups increased (Rosenstone and Hansen 1993), which suggests that the theory of pluralism may have been dismissed a little too quickly. In his appropriately titled book, *Neopluralism* (2004), Andrew McFarland argues that American politics can be explained by pluralist theory after jettisoning Truman's (1951) assumption that new groups mobilize when citizens perceive their interests as threatened (although this does sometimes happen). I accept that this amended characterization of classic pluralism is true, and the model I developed and tested in this book contributes to the emerging theory of neopluralism. Yet I think neopluralism needs a more solid foundation that embraces group competition and the role it plays in lobbying strategy and coalition formation. It also needs to better recognize that the structures of political institutions and the preferences of the lawmakers in them can shape lobbyists' choices (explored in chapter 6). I also believe that group maintenance matters more than many neopluralists have recognized. Lobbyists must keep members convinced that they are getting a good return on their membership investment, even as they work with members of Congress and competing groups to advance new policies or defend the status quo. They must balance the needs of the faction of citizens whose interests they represent against those of lawmakers and rival factions, something they often did not have to do when the political system was characterized by subgovernments. I also believe that the lobbyist's dual role makes neopluralism, or at least my version of it, different from classic pluralism, both in terms of the motivations of lobbyists and the normative argument I hope to make regarding the role competing interest groups and their lobbyists can play in a representative democracy.

To get a better sense of how my version of neopluralism differs from classic pluralism and to set up my argument in this final chapter, I compare my model's implications regarding the behavior of lobbyists to classic pluralism's assumption that the primary role of lobbyists is simply to pressure lawmakers into exclusively serving their members' interests with policy. I also compare the implications of my model to a hypothetical scenario where deliberation, the interactive sharing of ideas and beliefs, between lobbyists and their members over the public interest is the key criterion for how policy ought to be made. These are very similar to the two poles James Madison considered in *Federalist No. 10*. One reflects his hope that political factions would resolve their differences to promote the public interest, and the other what he cynically believed would actually happen.

American politics in practice appears to justify Madison's cynicism regarding factions. Citizens' predispositions toward acting primarily in their own self-interests incline them toward organized factionalism. And the larger the electorate, the more emphasis on competition exists between factions rather than deliberations over what is best for the nation. "The smaller the society, the fewer probably will be the distinct parties and interests composing it . . . extend the sphere, and you take in a greater variety of parties and interests; you will make it less probable that a majority of the whole will have a common motive to invade the rights of other citizens," Madison wrote in *Federalist No. 10*. Since the founding, the geographic size of the United States has grown from just the eastern seaboard to encompass nearly 4 million square miles, the population has increased from not quite 4 million in 1790 to over 281 million in 2000, and the voting franchise has expanded to encompass every citizen over age 18 who has not been convicted of a felony. Consequently, the number of organized political interests has also grown and today provides voice for a much larger range of citizen demands than ever before. For better or worse, Madison's expectation of politics driven by many minority factions of citizens all pursuing their self-interest seems to have been realized.

This was not lost on mid-twentieth-century scholars. Works from Truman to Dahl embraced the idea that interest groups were the best vehicles for highly motivated citizens to pursue their self-interest. What the consequences of group competition might be for mobilized constituencies or the public interest was of little concern because they started with the premise that no individual's interest was more or less important, and thus no more or less deserving of being fought for, than anybody else's (Graziano 2001). Were citizens in these groups doing anything other than exercising their First Amendment right to assemble and petition government for a redress of grievances?

In *A Preface to Democratic Theory* (1956), Robert Dahl goes a step further, explaining how representative democracy ought to function in a pluralist political system. He argues that it was acceptable (if not actually desirable) for public factions mobilized as interest groups to dominate political decision making bodies with jurisdiction over their interests (see his chapters 3 and 4). Citizens who felt most intensely about policy were probably the ones most affected by it, so they ought to have the strongest reaction and mobilize to exert disproportionately greater influence. If the rest of the public, the great but disinterested and unmotivated majority, did not like how lawmakers served those interests, they could exercise a veto in the next election. In the meantime, government would and should get on with serving multiple minorities rather than pursue any grand notion of the public interest.

This normative edge to Dahl's work is why I choose it as the classic pluralist baseline against which I can compare the possible implications of my version of neopluralism. His belief that group members who feel most intensely about a policy ought to wield disproportionately greater influence over it means their self-interest is to be privileged, not only over other citizens who may not realize that their interests are threatened (as Bachrach and Baratz 1962 remind us) but over the public interest as well. The ability to determine who is served by public policy goes to those who feel most passionately and have the resources to press their case (giving an advantage to wealthier groups Schattschneider [1960, 34–35] reminds us, with the "heavenly chorus" singing with an "upper class accent"). Representation is minimal in the sense that legislators act primarily on behalf of these highly motivated minorities, which leaves little room for considering anything that might be called the national or public interest.

A very different view of interest groups and the role lobbyists could play is presented by Jane Mansbridge (1992). Here representative democracy is best served by enacting policy that not only benefits all citizens regardless of their group affiliations but involves members of one faction coming to believe that their interests are best served when the interests of all citizens are served. Grounded in the information-for-access theory of lobbying, she emphasizes the crucial role lobbyists play in creating deliberation in the public interest. Remember that lobbyists communicate the wants and needs of key constituencies to lawmakers who want, for electoral reasons, to serve them with policy. Only it does not need to be just a one-way flow of information. Lobbyists can also use their extensive expert knowledge of the lawmaking process and of the preferences of lawmakers and other concerned (that is, competing) interests to help their own members better understand everyone else's stake in a struggle. More important, lobbyists can engage their members in deliberation and explain to them why others feel threatened by their collective interest, why it might be beneficial to sympathize with competitor's concerns, and why all involved groups should see giving up some of their desires as advancing the collective good of society. Successful deliberation actually changes member preferences so that citizens perceive it to be in their interests to support policy benefiting every other citizen and not just themselves.

As in Dahl, a strong sense of "oughtness" prevails in Mansbridge. While respecting constitutional rights to assemble and petition, she nonetheless pushes back against the idea that citizens (through their lobbyists) should myopically pressure lawmakers into serving their interests without regard for the interests of others just because all citizens' views are equal or because those who care more ought to be advantaged. All this gets us, she argues, is an "adversary democracy" that promotes gridlock because it legitimizes and glorifies the politics of hyper self-interest and conflict. Instead, lobbyists and other elites should use what they know about the motivations of other citizens with intersecting interests to stimulate a discussion about what good policy ought to be, what outcome might make everyone better off instead of just those in mobilized groups. By striving to change member policy preferences through reasoned discussions, lobbyists could lay the building blocks of a more deliberative, less adversarial but still very much group-driven (thus pluralistic) political process finding and promoting policy in the interest of the whole public.

Deliberative Group Politics and the Competitive Model

What does this view matter? Is not Mansbridge's vision too idealistic to be realized in the rough-and-tumble world of competitive group politics? Perhaps, but I am using her vision of a deliberative group politics to help differentiate the neopluralist implications of my model from those of Dahl. Their works anchor two ends of a continuum of interaction between group leaders and members ranging from lobbyists purely fighting for member interests, with no regard for whether policy ought to just serve those interests, to extensive consideration of, and advocacy for, policy serving the public interest. The results presented in my book do not suggest that bargaining between lobbyists resembles Mansbridge's notion of deliberation, and they probably do not even come close, but I believe that my work suggests that we have an interest group system that operates a little more in line with Mansbridge's vision than Dahl's description. Given the right set of circumstances, the pressures lobbyists are trying to balance in my model may produce advocacy behavior not only different from the hyper self-interest of classic pluralism but something not dissimilar from what Mansbridge (and perhaps Madison) hoped for.

Recall the distinction I emphasized in chapter 2 that lobbyists should be considered as separate from the members they represent, just as they are separate from the lawmakers they lobby. More important, they are subject to pressure from both, and thus indirectly from lobbyists for competing groups through the legislators they all lobby (the indirect competitive effect). Each is a "pivot" deciding which audience they will turn to and whose interests they will give priority to in the potential policy outcomes they choose to support. Unfortunately (for them), the positions most members desire often fail to line up with those supported by legislative majorities and other interest groups; sometimes they do not even come close.

What are a lobbyist's options in such a circumstance? The competitive model boils it down to a choice between angering members by supporting positions more acceptable to lawmakers and competing groups or engaging in conflict by stubbornly supporting positions their members ideally prefer. I presented evidence of this choice in chapter 4, but both the theoretical model and its statistical counterpart assume that member preferences, and thus the group's collective position, are fixed and exogenous to the model. What if member preferences are not fixed? What if lobbyists could change their members' preferences? Would they, and, if so, when?

Legislators, competing group lobbyists, and even the public visibility of issues limit the positions that can be lobbied with some hope of success. I assume in the competitive model that lawmakers can be persuaded to change their positions, but an attempt at persuasion has its costs. One is retribution from these legislator allies (those in his or her access set) if pressure tactics fail, possibly even the loss of access. Another is the loss of resources by making the effort, exacerbated by greater countervailing advocacy by competing lobbyists. A less costly strategy might be to accept a compromise position advocated by other, stronger interest groups if the cost in terms of member anger and defection can be compensated. An even less costly strategy, however, would be to lessen member anger by convincing members to change their policy preferences, convincing them they want to compromise. How could this be done? Perhaps, Mansbridge suggests, through deliberation that uses the information lobbyists accumulate through constant networking in Washington, DC. They know more about issues, potential solutions, and the political environment, including why other mobilized factions perceive their interests as threatened, than most citizens. This asymmetry gives them an advantage.

Many, perhaps a majority, of interest groups involve their members when deciding what their formal policy positions will be, often through some type of committee system. During annual or biannual conventions these committees decide which issues will have priority and which positions will be advocated (Schlozman and Tierney 1986, 136). Members hash out issue complexities and their own preferences to make recommendations to the entire membership, who then vote to accept them (or not). Lobbyists are usually involved in these meetings. Not only do they help by providing information, they frequently advise members on the relative importance of issues in the first place. They lay out options and estimate the resources required to push particular positions given the amount of resistance they anticipate from lawmakers and competing interest groups. If resistance to member-ideal positions is likely to be high, lobbyists might counsel consideration of alternatives, especially if they think competitors might be willing to do likewise. More important, the information asymmetry that exists between themselves and members may make it easy for them to urge members to consider the advantages of positions that might also be acceptable to members of competing interest groups.

What a lobbyist gains from this deliberation is resolution of the conflicting pressures he or she is under. If most legislative allies prefer an outcome different from members, the lobbyist might generate considerable goodwill in Congress if he or she can convince group members to embrace positions backed by a legislative majority. They gain access, after all, because they often share constituencies, so when a lobbyist convinces members that a legislator's chosen position should also be theirs, they are turning angry constituents into enthusiastic supporters (and voters). Legislators win, group members come to believe they win, and the lobbyist, gaining everyone's gratitude, certainly wins from preference changing deliberation. Deliberation becomes a strategy, a logical choice given the conflicting pressures on lobbyists identified by the competitive model.

The balancing act is more difficult when more competition comes from other interest group lobbyists, especially when the distance on the policy outcome space dividing their members' collective preferences is large and each can bring substantial resources to a fight. But convincing members to change their preferences now has a second advantage, it saves the lobbyist from the need to expend (and ask for more) precious resources in fruitless conflict. Joining winning coalitions, Hula (1999) argues, may even give lobbyists greater credibility in their members' eyes. If they can also convince members that the coalition compromise positions are their "real" preferred positions, then lobbyists are rewarded for having convinced competing interests to join a coalition that appears to members to really be supporting their preferred position.

Achieving a win-win deliberative outcome is harder when members feel strongly about their original positions. They know more about the issue, strongly believe that their original positions are really the best, and cannot be easily pried loose from that conviction. Now the lobbyist must expend serious "political capital" to persuade members to reevaluate their preferences. The lobbyist may fail and will probably damage his or her credibility in the process (perhaps on the way out the door to look for a new job). If members are united in their preferences, so much the worse for the lobbyist who tries to persuade them that it is in their best interests to embrace an alternative. The integrity of the entire organization as a faithful advocate of member interests in that issue niche is now at risk. An advocacy conflict, even a futile one, becomes the safer bet for preserving the integrity of the organization and the lobbyist's reputation.

I summarize the choice to try deliberation with members in the following way. Lobbyists should want to try to change the preferences of interest group members to bring them into line with those of lawmakers and competing groups when at least one condition in each of these two sets is true:

SET ONE
- Legislator allies collectively prefer policy outcomes further from the lobbyist's members' collective ideal position; and/or
- More competing interest groups with greater advocacy resources collectively support policy outcomes further from the lobbyist's members' collective ideal.

SET TWO
- The lobbyist's group members do not feel strongly about how an issue concerning them is resolved with policy; and/or
- The lobbyist's group members are widely dispersed when it comes to how they would prefer to see an issue concerning them resolved with policy.

The first set gives the lobbyist a reason to want to change member preferences for a policy outcome. The second regards a lobbyist's freedom to do so.

It may be that more compromise and cooperation exist in this case than in classic pluralism, but can any of it really be considered "deliberation" as Mansbridge meant it? A process that smacks of manipulating members is a far cry from the deliberation to find the public good that she articulated. Perhaps that is too much to ask. Lobbyists, after all, are not altruistic patriots seeking to promote the public interest at the expense of their members' self-interests. They are agents employed to further those interests through the institutions of government. Considering the preferences of other factions of citizens is not a natural goal for interest groups and their lobbyists; at most it is a by-product of their need to pursue policy goals in a competitive environment. We also have no reason to assume that Madison's cynical view of individuals driven almost exclusively by uncompromising self-interest is any less true in the twenty-first century than it was in the eighteenth century. Yet the incentives identified in my model show the possibility of eliminating at least some of the "adversary" in adversary democracy.

Organizational Barriers to Deliberation

The idea that lobbyists might use information asymmetry to shape the preferences of members is hardly new. Terry Moe (1980) argues that an increase in lobbyists' influence is almost inevitable as organizations grow and not necessarily desirable. The larger an organization becomes, the more its leaders must structure the flow of communication to and among members in order to function. This is essentially Robert Michels's (1959) "iron law of oligarchy." Growth leads to more complex, top-down imposed structures that segregate members into subfactions and thus give leaders greater control over the information released to them. This structure is not necessarily the result of deliberate manipulation by the organization's leaders (although some of it very well could be) so much as the need to set in place a system for communicating information to members as part of organizational maintenance. Small, young grassroots groups can get away with loose, egalitarian structures allowing all members to frequently meet and talk, but nation-spanning interest groups simply could not operate this way even if they want to.

All of this structure arises in the name of efficiency, if not in equity, and part of this efficiency may well be the need of lobbyists to balance conflicting pressures by shaping member preferences. Keeping members informed, long considered to be a basic organizational responsibility, ceases to be informal discussions at monthly meetings and becomes e-mail alerts and twitters where leaders provide small, carefully crafted bits of information to thousands of members around the country with little opportunity for face-to-face deliberation. Consequently, leaders can probably convince members that their interests are something other than what they had believed them to be by controlling the information they receive. This type of information control is outright manipulation and is just as conceivable an outcome in the competitive model as preference-changing deliberation because the lobbyist is still balancing pressures. Whereas the previous section suggested my version of neopluralism may be like Mansbridge's, this section suggests the opposite, that is, that Michels's iron law applies to interest groups as well as the political parties he wrote about.

Higher Levels of Deliberation

If real deliberation takes place in neopluralist group politics, it might also occur at other "levels" of the political process. The information and subsidies for access theories of Milbrath (1963), Wright (1996), and Hall and Deardorff (2006) that I have drawn on so heavily assume that legislators and lobbyists often serve similar, even the same, constituencies. This leads to a portrayal of access as creating a one-way flow of information and pressure from lobbyists representing these mobilized constituencies to legislators. However, Matthews (1960), Ainsworth (1993), and I argue that information flows in two directions. I studied some of the implications of this reciprocal pressure in chapters 5 through 7 in terms of coalition formation and gridlock but not in regard to how cooperation among legislators shapes lobbyist interaction with group members. Like lobbyists, legislators are under a variety of pressures they must balance, so it may also be to their advantage to convince lobbyists to accept alternate positions and communicate the value of these positions back to their common constituents. Otherwise, constituents might doubt their elected officials' commitment to serving them.

Members of Congress must often act in concert to form majorities backing legislation or hold together as a minority party to oppose the majority, even if it means supporting positions their constituents might not approve of. Pressure to conform to norms such as logrolling may also require them to turn a blind eye toward bills their constituents might prefer them to oppose. If constituents crucial to reelection are not likely to support a position he or she must take, legislators may feel compelled to respond by doing two things. First, they and their lobbyist allies must decide how to frame their compromise position (whether supporting or opposing new policy), and one attractive possibility is to frame it as beneficial to the public interest, perhaps even striving to make it true. It will be much easier to move new legislation through Congress when there is no sign of anybody's ox being gored.

Second, legislators may then pressure lobbyists to use deliberation to convince their mutual constituents that this position actually benefits them as well. The legislator thus appears to be a faithful representative, not a duplicitous politician, and legislators, lobbyists, and constituents all see themselves as winners. Again, this pressure-driven preference change may amount to little more than manipulation of constituents, but as more and more competing interest groups take the field, the strategy of least resistance may be for legislators to encourage deliberation among them all in order to develop policy appearing to be in the public interest. It would be an easier sell.

Another opportunity for deliberation exists. In chapter 5 I showed how the competitive model can explain coalition formation, but I never explained how compromises are arrived at beyond the notions of a cooperative game theory–based bargaining process. Talk among competing lobbyists may amount to little more than threats, but it also might involve deliberation. In this case what may be termed "deliberation" is actually negotiation that leads to an understanding of each other's positions, the needs of everyone's members, and some common ground on which compromises may be built. Deliberators' positions may be backed up implicitly by threats of who will prove stronger in battle if talks fail, but bargaining could take the form of give and take and efforts to promote mutual understanding. Lobbyists must then pivot to sell the compromise to members, which again may be done with minimum anger through deliberation.

I hope that my argument here is not as naïve as it may sound. Competition helps to hold lawmakers and lobbyists a little more accountable because the extravagant claims of some can be counterbalanced by others (although perhaps with their own extravagant claims). The easiest, most politically expedient way for them to portray a new policy proposal in a competitive environment is by arguing that it is in the public interest, especially if they have genuinely tried to make it so. Arguably the Obama administration was able to get health care legislation enacted in 2009 by portraying it as a collective benefit, while its opponents portrayed it as only a benefit to some at the expense of others. Competition makes it harder to quietly serve a few special interests at public expense and makes it more likely that policy entrepreneurs will see the strategic value of portraying policy as in the public interest. Again, I am not saying that negotiation and cooperation among competing lobbyists and between lobbyists and legislators will be anything like the high-minded deliberation described by Mansbridge. I only claim that in the neopluralist world that I explore in this book, the incentives are there to produce a process of communication resolving differences that approach it.

There is, however, another problem. Even if higher-level compromises do begin occurring more frequently, Costain and Costain (1981) argue that such compromises may actually lead to another serious normative problem in a democracy where all citizen interests are considered equal. They argue that coalition formation and position compromise often results in "interest aggregation," the combining of citizen interests from multiple advocacy organizations seeking to create a united front for moving new policy. In chapter 6 I found that compromises do sometimes make it easier to move bills through Congress, and anecdotal evidence suggests that legislators often want lobbyists for competing groups to resolve their differences before initiating full-court presses. But interest aggregation also means that many policy alternatives that are desired by factions of the public, mobilized or not, are not being presented to lawmakers for consideration.

In other words, the very need to bargain and even deliberate among lobbyists, as well as with legislators, leads to interest aggregation that limits the range of alternatives presented as realistic. Many alternatives that are desired by members of interest groups, by members of groups not in coalitions, and even by citizens affected by the issue but not mobilized in any interest group are never presented to lawmakers. If they are articulated, they are likely dismissed as "unrealistic" or lacking in "common sense." Truly successful deliberation may circumvent this problem because everyone's preferences change as they come to believe that the compromise advances their interests. Anything less means compromises only create filters through which some alternatives desired by citizens pass while others are blocked.

Deliberation as an Evolving Norm

If the pressures on lobbyists highlighted by the competitive model, however, can lead to more deliberation, is it possible for it to become standard practice in neopluralist politics? The most significant barrier to regular deliberation suggested in the literature is from groups who prefer obstruction to compromise. As Baumgartner et al. (2009) remind us, interests favored by the status quo are advantaged in advocacy struggles because the American political system favors gridlock over new policy. So in the near term we would not expect lobbyists defending the status quo to be interested in deliberation or anything other than being obstinate. In the long run, however, even the most special interest–friendly policies become outdated, and interests historically benefiting from them may find they need the law updated to better serve their own changing needs. Then even lobbyists for privileged groups may have to build alliances and make compromises with competitors to move legislation. They may have to accept provisions they do not like, but now even compromise may give them a more desirable outcome than an antiquated status quo. They too would find it to their advantage to use deliberation to make it easier to form and sell new policy. Given the need for interest groups to evolve in order to remain viable, might we, then, begin to see the emergence of a norm of deliberation, even if over a long period of time?

The evolution of norms is a major theme in international relations research where scholars study the interaction of competing nations, so perhaps some of their ideas can be transferred to competitive group politics. Finnemore and Sikkink define a norm as a "standard of appropriate behavior for actors with a given identity" (1998, 891), a behavior expected by everyone in an interconnected network, who will be ridiculed and even shunned if they fail to exhibit it. Yet norms do not spring up spontaneously in a network; they are promoted by "norm entrepreneurs" who convince groups of individuals that it is to their advantage to accept and conform to them. They, in turn, spread the idea until some critical mass, some tipping point, is reached and the new norm "cascades" across the network to become generally accepted.

In neopluralist politics, who might want to be an entrepreneur for a norm of deliberation? If legislators require consensus to move legislation and know that it will be difficult to move it and sell it to constituents otherwise, then perhaps it is them. Norms have certainly emerged in Congress before, such as logrolling bills, committee property rights, and committee leadership determined by seniority. They developed because they helped lawmakers achieve goals. When they need to move bills, they might push, even expect, lobbyists to make compromises through deliberation. They would expect them to not bother lobbying until differences had been resolved and coalitions assembled around compromises that, if not exactly in the public interest, at least provide some benefit to all concerned interests. The more they need compromise, and they will as more groups mobilize to compete, the more they might expect it on a regular basis and the more accepted and expected such behavior might become. Then again, perhaps it is lobbyists who, in their need to balance pressures, have the incentive to be the entrepreneurs of a norm of deliberation.

Repeated deliberation might also lead to something else. Robert Axelrod (1984) famously demonstrated that cooperation between actors with competing interests leads to more cooperation. Defection is an irrational choice in repeated games without termination points (Axelrod and Dion 1988 show how this connects to norm emergence). In more recent research, Mark Lubell (2007) finds that trust, defined as the expectation of one actor that another will choose not to significantly harm the first's interests when making a decision, can also emerge from repeated interaction.

Examining trust through the advocacy coalition model of group conflict of Sabatier (1988) and Sabatier and Jenkins-Smith (1993), Lubell finds that trust is less likely when there is significant ideological distance between two groups. The groups find it difficult to accept each other's fundamental beliefs, but if deliberation can be prompted by lawmakers and lobbyists seeking to resolve competitive differences, then trust can be built through repeated discussion that bridges ideological chasms, even between competing coalitions of groups.

Sabatier, Lubell, and others actually find that this has occurred to some extent in regional watershed management in California, a state where the intersection of water rights and environmental interests has created a political blood sport (Sabatier et al. 2005). If deliberation and trust is possible here, then it may be possible in most domains of public policymaking. Perhaps interest group lobbyists and, with some prodding, their members can become "serial cooperators." Perhaps enough interests can come to be served by policy, so that we may approach, if not actually achieve, Mansbridge's idea of deliberation by lobbyists who serve the public interest.

Competition Remains

The pressures from interest group competition on lobbyists are almost certainly going to increase in the future, so neopluralist politics may have to evolve into a more deliberative and cooperative process just to keep the lawmaking system functioning. Thus the idea I have been exploring here of a more deliberative group politics may be more than just a flight of fancy. It may not be the deliberation envisioned by Mansbridge, but if we seriously value the public interest, then maybe something superior to the aggressive promotion of self-interest accepted in classic pluralism is achievable. Whether group-based deliberation could come to be an influential, even dominant, characteristic of neopluralism through these pressures is something I cannot prove here. A certain logic suggests it, but other, more conflictual paths may be just as likely to result. I do not know and it was not my intention in this final chapter to predict, only to contemplate. Lobbyists must want to develop deliberation as a professional norm, and Finnemore and Sikkink (1998) note that professions are an effective means of indoctrinating practitioners into accepting certain norms.

Then again, perhaps deliberation as a professional norm may not develop. It has become so much harder to pass legislation, especially legislation altering long-standing status quos when the government finds it must deal with major public problems. Partially this difficulty in enacting new policy comes from shrinking public budgets. The United States is currently under a significant debt load. Entitlement programs like Social Security and Medicare are becoming unsustainable as they slip into deficit territory as benefits paid out exceed revenues taken in. Interest groups may feel that they are better off defending what they have, the status quo, no matter how archaic it might become, rather than risk writing and promoting new legislation requiring compromise. In this case neopluralism results in competition that drives lobbyists to defend the uncompromising self-interest of members whatever the cost. Politics driven by advocacy from intense minorities may still lead to the nation-destroying stasis that Mancur Olson (1982) feared was the real consequence of greater group mobilization and competition.

However, group competition has only come about because hundreds of thousands of citizens have chosen to participate in the political process this way, even if just by writing a check to a group promoting an interest they care about. Competition exists between interest groups because divisions in American society really exist that, once latent, are now being actively expressed. Lobbyists are under great pressure to decide whose agents they really are, those of their members who pay their salary or those of the lawmakers on whom they depend for access and advancement of their careers. Perhaps they are really their own agents, balancing both pressures in whatever manner best advances their own careers. The competitive model certainly opens up room for that interpretation, but it also shows that lobbyists do have opportunities to take the lead in resolving competition into cooperation through deliberation and even have an incentive to do so. At the very least, my version of neopluralism greatly emphasizes the crucial role lobbyists play in representative politics, and it remains to be seen whose interests they will feel most pressured to serve. What is likely is that the lobbyist's crucial role as a link in the representative processes between members, lawmakers, and other interests, and the opportunities they have to choose between conflict and compromise, will only increase as group politics becomes increasingly competitive.

Note

1. In my interview with a financial institution interest group, the person I interviewed sounded utterly appalled that I would ask why they supported post–9/11 money-laundering reform legislation. A little reassurance salvaged the interview.

APPENDIX 1

Appendix to Chapter 3

Responding Interest Groups by Issue

Agriculture Policy Domain (Distributive)

LOW-SALIENCE ISSUE: DAIRY PRICING SUBSIDIES

American Farm Bureau Federation
Americans for Tax Reform
Associated Milk Producers
Citizens Against Government Waste
Consumer Federation of America
International Dairy Food Association

National Farmers Organization
National Farmers Union
National Milk Producers Federation
National Taxpayers Union
Upper Midwest Dairy Coalition

HIGH-SALIENCE ISSUE: BIOENGINEERED FOOD

Alliance for Bio-Integrity
American Corn Growers Association
American Soybean Association
American Sugarbeet Growers Association
Biotechnology Industry Organization
Center for Food Safety
Center for Science in the Public Interest

Consumers Union
Friends of the Earth
National Cotton Council
National Food Processors Association
Organic Consumers Association
Union of Concerned Scientists
USPIRG

Environmental Conservation Policy Domain

LOW-SALIENCE ISSUE: CONSERVATION AND REINVESTMENT ACT

American Land Rights Association
Americans for Our Heritage
Defenders of Wildlife
International Association of Fish and
    Wildlife Agencies
Izaak Walton League of America
League of Conservation Voters
National Wildlife Federation
Natural Resources Defense Council

Sierra Club
Southern Governors Association
Sporting Goods Manufacturers
    Association
The Nature Conservancy
US Conference of Mayors
USPIRG
Wilderness Society
Wildlife Management Institute

HIGH-SALIENCE ISSUE: DRILLING FOR OIL IN THE ARCTIC

AFL-CIO
Alaska Oil and Gas Association
American Association of Petroleum
 Geologists
American Petroleum Institute
Arctic Power
Defenders of Wildlife
Environmental Defense Fund
Friends of the Earth

Independent Petroleum Association of
 America
International Brotherhood of Teamsters
League of Conservation Voters
National Audubon Society
Natural Resources Defense Council
US Chamber of Commerce
World Wildlife Fund

Banking and Finance Policy Domain

LOW-SALIENCE ISSUE: MONEY LAUNDERING

American Civil Liberties Union
American Council of Life Insurers
America's Community Bankers

Financial Services Center of America
Financial Services Roundtable
Non-Bank Funds Transmitters Group

HIGH-SALIENCE ISSUE: BANKRUPTCY REFORM

AFL-CIO
American Bankers Association
American Bar Association
American Financial Services Association
America's Community Bankers
Commercial Law League of America
Common Cause
Consumer Bankers Association
Consumer Federation of America
Consumers Union
Credit Union National Association

Independent Community Bankers of
 America
National Association of Attorneys General
National Association of Consumer
 Bankruptcy Attorneys
National Association of Counties
National Association of Credit Managers
National Consumer Law Center
National Retail Federation
National Women's Law Center
United Auto Workers

Interest Group Lobbyist Interview Protocol

These questions are presented in two sections. The first section gives the issue iteration (specific policy proposals) questions for each of the six issues. A different set of
questions is listed for each issue. The second section is the standard battery of questions asked of all of the lobbyist respondents.

Dairy-Pricing Questions

1. In 1999 USDA issued new rules changing the way the price of Class I (fluid)
 milk is priced that reduced the regional price differential (Option 1-B before
 Congress required the Option 1-A approach).

 Did your organization support this rule?

 *Strongly opposed / reluctantly opposed / supported with reservations /
 strongly supported / did not advocate*

2. At the end of 1999 Congress enacted H.R. 3194 containing provisions suspending this new milk marketing rule (Option 1-B) and extending the life of the Northeast Dairy Compact.

Did your organization support this provision?

Strongly opposed / reluctantly opposed / supported with reservations / strongly supported / did not advocate

3. In 2001 the Senate Agriculture Committee reported S. 1731, the farm program reauthorization bill by Senator Harkin, which contained provisions setting a floor for the price of milk. If the price of milk fell below this floor (approximately $14.25 per hundredweight), processors and the government would be required to pay producers at least a portion of the difference.

Did your organization support this provision?

Strongly opposed / reluctantly opposed / supported with reservations / strongly supported / did not advocate

4. Before S. 1731 was taken up by the Senate, it was amended to remove the fee on milk processors so that only public funds were used to compensate producers. The level of funding for producers in the Northeast was also increased to compensate for the sunsetting of the Northeast Dairy Compact.

Did your organization support this provision?

Strongly opposed / reluctantly opposed / supported with reservations / strongly supported / did not advocate

Bioengineered Foods

1. How did your organization stand in regards to the US Food and Drug Administration's 1992 rules making consultation with FDA by producers voluntary and not requiring the labeling of food produced by biotechnology?

Strongly opposed / reluctantly opposed / supported with reservations / strongly supported / did not advocate

2. In 2000 Rep. Dennis Kucinich introduced H.R. 3883 requiring the FDA to conduct safety tests on all food produced by biotechnology before approval for public sale and charging producers a fee to cover the expense of the tests.

Did your organization support this bill?

Strongly opposed / reluctantly opposed / supported with reservations / strongly supported / did not advocate

3. In 2000 Sen. Barbara Boxer introduced S. 2080 requiring all food produced using genetic engineering be so labeled when sold to consumers.

Did your organization support this bill?

Strongly opposed / reluctantly opposed / supported with reservations / strongly supported / did not advocate

4. On October 4, 2001, Rep. John Tierney amended H.R. 2646 (Public Law 107-171), legislation extending funding for agriculture programs, to require the National Academy of Sciences to conduct a study on the adequacy of tests being conducted on genetically engineered food and what future regulatory process might be necessary for ensuring public safety.

   Did your organization support this amendment (it was originally H.R. 713)?

   Strongly opposed / reluctantly opposed / supported with reservations / strongly supported / did not advocate

5. On January 18, 2001, the Food and Drug Administration proposed new rules creating moderate changes in its process for approving for public sale foods produced through biotechnology and providing guidance to producers desiring to label their foods as containing, or not containing, bioengineered ingredients.

   Did your organization support these new rules?

   Strongly opposed / reluctantly opposed / supported with reservations / strongly supported / did not advocate

Bankruptcy Reform

1. House legislation H.R. 833 by Rep. Gekas, introduced in 1999, was largely the conference report from the 105th Congress version of bankruptcy reform, H.R. 3150. It had the more specific needs-testing provisions requiring debtors to file for Chapter 13 bankruptcy protection rather than for Chapter 7.

   Did your organization support this version of bankruptcy reform?

   Strongly opposed / reluctantly opposed / supported with reservations / strongly supported / did not advocate

2. The Senate bill in 1999, S. 625 by Senator Grassley, had a less stringent needs test than the House bill, partially as a concession to the Clinton administration. It also had more disclosure requirements for credit card companies and a cap on Homestead Act exemptions at $100,000. Ultimately it also contained a minimum wage increase, small business tax breaks, and the abortion clinic language.

   Did your organization support this version of bankruptcy reform?

   Strongly opposed / reluctantly opposed / supported with reservations / strongly supported / did not advocate

3. Although the House bill introduced in 2001, H.R. 333 by Rep. Gekas, largely reflected the pocket-vetoed bill from the prior Congress, the Senate new version, S. 420 by Senator Grassley, continued to have the abortion clinic language, credit card disclosure provisions, some capacity for borrowers to sue lenders under the Trust in Lending Act for unfair lending practices, and the Homestead Act cap at $125,000. It also continued to have a bit more leeway on the needs-test.

Did your organization support the Senate version of bankruptcy reform?

Strongly opposed / reluctantly opposed / supported with reservations / strongly supported / did not advocate

Money Laundering

1. In 1998 the Treasury Department and the Federal Reserve Board proposed the Know-Your-Customer rule that would have required banks and other financial institutions to monitor and report on transactions for all accounts at the institution, as well as keep general information on all customers. Customers acting in ways inconsistent with these patterns would be reported to federal authorities. The proposal was withdrawn in 1999.

   Did your organization support these new regulatory provisions?

   Strongly opposed / reluctantly opposed / supported with reservations / strongly supported / did not advocate

2. In 1999 senators Charles Schumer (D-NY) and Paul Coverdell (R-GA) introduced S. 1663 requiring domestic financial institutions to report to the government any account opened at the request of a foreign financial institution regardless of the account's size. It would also have made banks handling money from illegal foreign activities open to criminal prosecution and automatically cut off foreign banks involved from the US financial system. The bill was not acted on.

   Did your organization support this legislation?

   Strongly opposed / reluctantly opposed / supported with reservations / strongly supported / did not advocate

3. In the wake of money-laundering scandals involving the Bank of New York and Citibank, the Clinton administration proposed legislation H.R. 3886 by Rep. Jim Leach (R-IA) allowing the Treasury Department to forbid transactions between US financial institutions and foreign nations or financial institutions lacking money-laundering safeguards. It also would have required banks, brokers, and insurers to collect additional information on accounts opened by an individual or institution on behalf of another. The bill passed the House Banking Committee but died in the full chamber.

   Did your organization support this legislation?

   Strongly opposed / reluctantly opposed / supported with reservations / strongly supported / did not advocate

4. Anti-terrorism legislation enacted in late 2001, H.R. 3162, contained most of the language of H.R. 3886 in the previous Congress, although the controversial prohibition on using credit cards for Internet gambling was removed. It became Public Law 107-56 in October 2001.

   Did your organization support this legislation?

   Strongly opposed / reluctantly opposed / supported with reservations / strongly supported / did not advocate

Funding for State Wildlife Conservation from Oil Revenues

1. H.R. 701, the original Conservation and Reinvestment Act, introduced by Rep. Don Young in 1999 and approved by the House in 2000, created a number of guaranteed fifteen-year trust funds using $3 billion annually in royalties from offshore oil and gas leases for coastal conservation, the Land and Water Conservation Fund, state wildlife conservation programs, and other conservation efforts.

   Where did your organization stand on this original legislation in 1999?

   Strongly opposed / reluctantly opposed / supported with reservations / strongly supported

2. Rather than enact CARA in 2000, Congress used the FY2001 Interior and Commerce-Justice-State Appropriations bills to fund scaled-back versions of the conservation programs contained in CARA for six years. Funding for each year is at the discretion of the appropriations committees.

   Where did your organization stand on this reduced form of CARA in 2000?

   Strongly opposed / reluctantly opposed / supported with reservations / strongly supported

3. Even though the trust funds created in 2000 have a six-year life, in 2001 Representative Young reintroduced the original CARA, again numbered H.R. 701, with the fifteen-year guaranteed funding.

   Where does your organization stand on this current legislation?

   Strongly opposed / reluctantly opposed / supported with reservations / strongly supported

Drilling for Oil in the Arctic National Wildlife Refuge

1. In 1980 Congress designated the Coastal Plain of the Arctic National Wildlife Refuge as an area to study for resource development. In 1987 the Interior Department recommended opening Area 1002 for development, but Congress refused to approve any leasing of land in the refuge.

   Did your organization support the Interior Department's proposal?

   Strongly opposed / reluctantly opposed / supported with reservations / strongly supported / did not advocate

2. In 2000 and 2001 Congressional Republicans, and the Bush White House in 2001, proposed opening Area 1002 of the Refuge for leasing the rights to explore and drill to oil companies in various energy bills (e.g., S. 2557 of 2000, S. 389 and H.R. 4 of 2001).

   Did your organization support the leasing provision in these bills?

   Strongly opposed / reluctantly opposed / supported with reservations / strongly supported / did not advocate

3. In 2001 the Bush administration's FY2002 Interior budget proposal requested $2 million for studying the impact of exploration for oil in the refuge.

The proposal was denied by the House Interior Appropriations Subcommittee.

Did your organization support the proposed study?

Strongly opposed / reluctantly opposed / supported with reservations / strongly supported / did not advocate

Questions Asked of All Interest Group Lobbyists

1. What would have been the ideal resolution of this issue for your organization's members? In other words, what was their "dream" outcome? Please briefly explain.
2. Relative to other issues your organization was working on at the same time, would you say that this issue was more important or less important to your membership?

   Less important / moderately important / most important
3. Briefly describe which members of your organization are most affected by this issue, or who felt most strongly about it.

   3a. Would you describe the positions of these members as:

   Divided / moderately cohesive / very cohesive
4. In general, was it difficult or fairly easy for most of your members concerned with this issue to reach a common position?

   Very easy / moderately easy / difficult
5. As the issue progressed, did you feel that you had the flexibility to modify your organization's position on this issue in order to accommodate lawmakers and other concerned parties?

   Little flexibility / some flexibility / considerable flexibility
6. How much compromise would your members have tolerated to resolve this issue?

   Very little / some compromise / considerable compromise
7. Do you feel that most of the positions your organization took on the issue were those most preferred by your members, or were they modified to accommodate other parties?

   Ideal / modified
8. Relative to other issues your organization was working on, would you say that your organization spent more or less time and resources on this issue?

   Less / about the same / more

Spatial Positions of Interest Groups and Issue Iterations

Table A1.1 Money Laundering

Iteration	Code	Item
0	1	Status quo: Light monitoring and little regulation
1	4	Know-Your-Customer rule from banking agencies, lots of regulation (prior to 1999)
2	3	S. 1663: Also quite a bit of regulation (106th Congress)
3	2	H.R. 3886: More moderate regulation (106th Congress)
4	2	H.R. 3162: Very slightly less regulation than H.R. 3886 (107th Congress)

Code: 1 = most liberal; 4 = most conservative.

Table A1.2 Arctic National Wildlife Refuge

Iteration	Code	Item
0	1	Status quo: Complete ban
1	3	Interior Department proposes opening up Area 1002 for exploration (prior to 1999)
2	4	Opening up for oil prospecting proposed by congressional Republicans (106th Congress)
3	2	Bush administration appropriations bill desires to study the impact (107th Congress)

Code: 1 = most liberal; 4 = most conservative.

Table A1.3 Conservation and Reinvestment Act

Iteration	Code	Item
0	4	Status quo: Very little conservation money; no oil drilling
1	2	Original H.R. 701: Massive change (106th Congress)
2	3	CARA-Lite: Moderate changes (106th Congress)
3	1	New H.R. 701 (107th Congress)

Code: 1 = most liberal; 4 = most conservative.

Table A1.4 Bankruptcy Reform

Iteration	Code	Item
0	1	Status quo: Liberal debt-relief provisions
1	4	H.R. 833 in 1999: Very heavy on means testing making it hard to liquidate debt (106th Congress)
2	2	S. 625 in 1999: Much less stringent means test (106th Congress)
3	3	S. 420 in 2001: Compromise between H.R. 833 and S. 625 (107th Congress)

Code: 1 = most liberal; 4 = most conservative.

Table A1.5 Dairy Pricing

Iteration	Code	Item
0	1	Status quo: Benefits New England and Californian Dairy Farmers with high price supports; very regulatory
1	4	USDA's Option 1-B: Reduces regional price differentials; much less regulation (prior to 1999)
2	1	H.R. 3194: Returns to the status quo (106th Congress)
3	3	S. 1731: Compromise formula (107th Congress)
4	2	S. 1731 as amended: Uses more public funding than the original (107th Congress)

Code: 1 = most liberal; 4 = most conservative.

Table A1.6 Biotechnology in Food

Iteration	Code	Item
0	4	Status quo: Little oversight or regulation
1	3	FDA's 1992 rules: Propose light regulations
2	1	H.R. 3883: Lots of safety testing (106th Congress)
3	1	S. 2080: Regulations and labeling (106th Congress)
4	2	FDA's new proposal

Code: 1 = most liberal; 4 = most conservative.

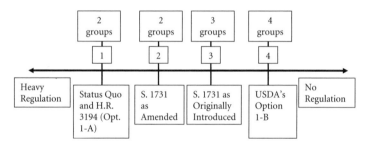

Figure A1.1. Spatial positions on dairy pricing

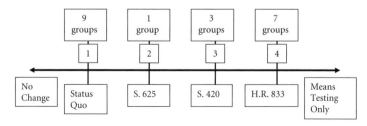

Figure A1.2. Spatial positions on bankruptcy reform

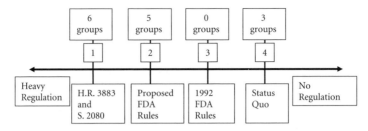

Figure A1.3. Spatial positions on bioengineered food regulation

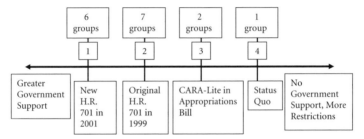

Note: This figure is based on the amount of regulation of the use of the CARA funds. Left side has less restriction on the use of government support.

Figure A1.4. Spatial positions on state wildlife conservation funding

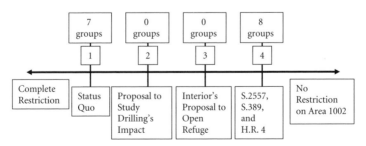

Figure A1.5. Spatial positions on drilling for oil in the Arctic National Wildlife Refuge

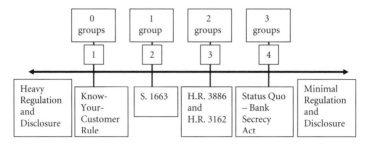

Figure A1.6. Spatial positions on money-laundering reform

Groups by Issue Positions and Annual Budgets

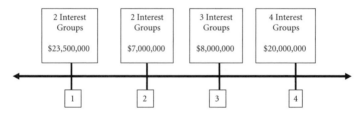

Figure A1.7. Spatial distribution of interest groups on dairy pricing by annual budgets

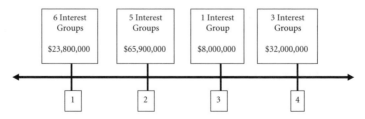

Figure A1.8. Spatial distribution of interest groups on bioengineered food regulation by annual budgets

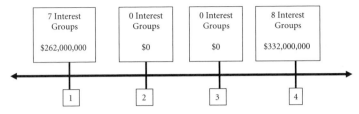

Figure A1.9. Spatial distribution of interest groups on drilling for oil in the Arctic National Wildlife Refuge by annual budgets

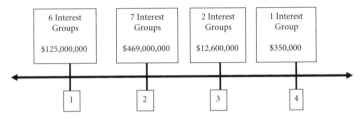

Figure A1.10. Spatial distribution of interest groups on state wildlife conservation funding by annual budgets

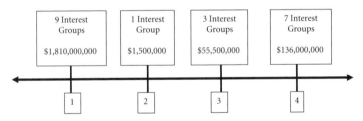

Figure A1.11. Spatial distribution of interest groups on bankruptcy reform by annual budgets

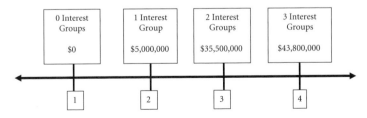

Figure A1.12. Spatial distribution of interest groups on money-laundering reform by annual budgets

Interest Group Issue Positions by Political Action Committee (PAC) Contributions

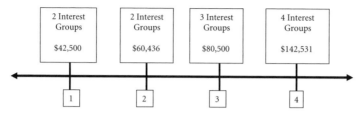

Figure A1.13. Spatial distribution of interest groups on dairy pricing by PAC contributions

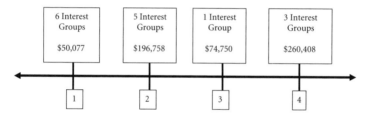

Figure A1.14. Spatial distribution of interest groups on bioengineered food regulation by PAC contributions

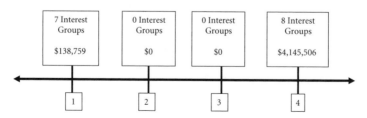

Figure A1.15. Spatial distribution of interest groups on drilling for oil in the Arctic National Wildlife Refuge by PAC contributions

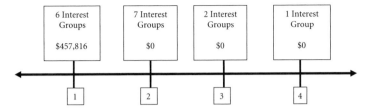

Figure A1.16. Spatial distribution of interest groups on state wildlife conservation funding by PAC contributions

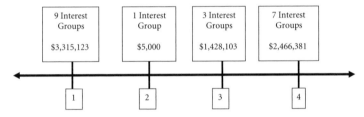

Figure A1.17. Spatial distribution of interest groups on bankruptcy reform by PAC contributions

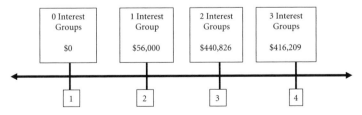

Figure A1.18. Spatial distribution of interest groups on money-laundering reform by PAC contributions

APPENDIX 2

Appendix to Chapter 4

Creating Legislator Pressure Scores

For each of the bills or regulatory proposals addressing an issue, I identified some form of legislator support. In most cases this support was sponsorship and co-sponsorship of bills, but in a few cases I used roll-call votes on amendments or the passage of legislation. In a couple of cases involving administrative rules, I could not find any indicator, and the issue histories suggested that legislators, by and large, did not care, so I entered 0 for pressure scores. Also, when possible, I used combined House and Senate scores, although in several cases only House or Senate was used.

I start by taking the Common Space scores for the 106th and 107th Congresses and dividing them into quartiles for the House, Senate, and both together (at no point do I combine both congresses).

The numbers of House members, senators, and both combined in each quartile are in the following tables.

These quartile locations are considered equivalent to the general ideological dispositions of legislators described in chapter 2, figure 2.2A, not positions they actually took on the issues. For issues I identified every legislator who supported a proposal by cosponsorship or roll call. Then I find which quartile he or she is in. In

Table A2.1 Combined 106th Congress Quartiles

Quartile	Common Space Score Range	No. of Legislators (quartile is .386)
1	−.679 to −.293	150
2	−.292 to .093	116
3	.094 to .479	217
4	.480 to .867	60

Table A2.2 Senate Quartiles in the 106th Congress

Quartile	Common Space Score Range	No. of Legislators (each quartile .322)
1	−.642 to −.320	19
2	−.319 to .002	30
3	.003 to .325	24
4	.326 to .648	29

Table A2.3 House Quartiles in the 106th Congress

Quartile	Common Space Score Range	No. of Legislators (each quartile .386)
1	−.679 to −.293	127
2	−.292 to .093	87
3	.094 to .479	175
4	.480 to .867	51

Table A2.4 Combined 107th Congress Quartiles

Quartile	Common Space Score Range	No. of Legislators (each quartile .386)
1	−.679 to −.293	152
2	−.292 to .093	118
3	.094 to .479	213
4	.480 to .867	61

Table A2.5 Senate Quartiles in the 107th Congress

Quartile	Common Space Score Range	No. of Legislators (each quartile .322)
1	−.642 to −.320	20
2	−.319 to .002	33
3	.003 to .324	21
4	.325 to .648	27

Table A2.6 House Quartiles in the 107th Congress

Quartile	Common Space Score Range	No. of Legislators (each quartile .386)
1	−.679 to −.293	128
2	−.292 to .093	86
3	.094 to .479	175
4	.480 to .867	53

tables A2.7 to A2.12 below, for each proposal that addresses each issue, I first indicate where the observed proposal is on the policy outcome space in terms of positions and quartiles in the first column. The second column is the number of legislators (House, Senate, or both combined depending on where my information is coming from) in each quartile. I am primarily interested in the number of legislators who support the observed proposal who are originally in the quartile containing the lobbyist's group member-ideal position. In other words, I am interested in those legislators who I assume can pressure the lobbyist to support the proposal at an alternative position and those who can pressure the lobbyist to support his or her members' ideal position instead (unless, of course, the proposal is at the position preferred by group members). So in the third column is the number of legislators whose general ideological scores put them in the same quartile as the observed group, but who are supporting the proposal (as identified by co-sponsorship or roll-call votes) at a different position (except in the row actually containing the proposal where all legislators are assumed to always support it).

In the fourth column is the total number of legislators who now either support the observed policy proposal (in the row with the proposal) or do not support it and so remain in their original quartiles. I am interested in the ratio of legislators who support the proposal to the number who support the lobbyist's members' ideal position, so the final score in the fifth column is obtained by dividing the number of legislators supporting the proposal by the number still in the quartile containing the lobbyist's members' ideal position. A score of less than 1 means that more legislators are pressuring the lobbyist to support the position that is desired by group members rather than the proposal, whereas a score greater than 1 means that more legislators want the lobbyist to support the proposal at a different position.

Table A2.7 Legislator Support on Bankruptcy Reform

Quartile/ Position	No. of Legislators in That Quartile	Legislators in That Quartile Supporting the Proposal	Legislators Supporting the Proposal or Their Original Quartile/ Position	Pressure Score
First Proposal. The data on legislator support comes from sponsorship and cosponsorship of H.R. 833 by members of the House of Representatives in the 106th Congress.				
1	127	10	117	1.16[a]
2	87	24	63	2.16[a]
3	175	51	124	1.10[a]
4 (proposal)	51	51	136	1[a]
Second Proposal. The data is from sponsorship or cosponsorship of S. 625 by senators in the 106th Congress.				
1	19	1	18	2[b]
2 (proposal)	30	30	36	1[b]
3	24	2	22	1.64[b]
4	29	3	26	1.38[b]

(*continued*)

Table A2.7 Legislator Support in Bankruptcy Reform (*continued*)

Quartile/ Position	No. of Legislators in That Quartile	Legislators in That Quartile Supporting the Proposal	Legislators Supporting the Proposal or Their Original Quartile/ Position	Pressure Score
Third Proposal. The data is from sponsorship and cosponsorship of S. 420 by senators in the 107th Congress.				
1	20	1	19	1.47[c]
2	33	4	29	.97[c]
3 (proposal)	21	21	28	1[c]
4	27	2	25	1.12[c]

[a] 136 divided by column 4.
[b] 36 divided by column 4.
[c] 28 divided by column 4.

Table A2.8 Legislator Support for Drilling for Oil in the Arctic National Wildlife Refuge

Quartile/ Position	No. of Legislators in That Quartile	Legislators in That Quartile Supporting the Proposal	Legislators Supporting the Proposal or Their Original Quartile/ Position	Pressure Score
First Proposal.				
1	150	0	150	1.51[a]
2	116	1	115	1.97[a]
3 (proposal)	217	217	227	1[a]
4	60	9	51	4.45[a]
Second Proposal.				
1	150	0	150	0.56[b]
2	116	1	115	0.73[b]
3	217	23	194	0.43[b]
4 (proposal)	60	60	84	1[b]
Third Proposal.				
1	150	0	150	.99[c]
2 (proposal)	116	116	148	1[c]
3	217	23	194	.76[c]
4	60	9	51	2.90[c]

For all proposals I used sponsorship and cosponsorship of the companion bills in the House and Senate as my indicator of support in the combined 106th Congress.

[a] 227 divided by column 4.
[b] 84 divided by column 4.
[c] 148 divided by column 4.

Table A2.9 Legislator Support for Dairy Pricing

Quartile/ Position	No. of Legislators in That Quartile	Legislators in That Quartile Supporting the Proposal	Legislators Supporting the Proposal or Their Original Quartile/ Position	Pressure Score
First Proposal. This data is from "nays" on Roll Call 463 on final passage of H.R. 1402. The legislation imposed Option 1-A (sustaining regional price differentials), so "nays" are taken to be expressions of support for Option 1-B (erasing differentials). This was in the House of Representatives of the 106th Congress.				
1	127	51	76	2.13[a]
2	87	20	67	2.42[a]
3	175	40	135	1.20[a]
4 (proposal)	51	51	162	1[a]
Second Proposal. This is House and Senate sponsorship and cosponsorship of H.R. 1604 (extending dairy compacts), H.R. 1402 (imposing Option 1-A), and S. 1265 (imposing Option 1-A) in the 106th Congress.				
1 (proposal)	150	150	354	1[b]
2	116	63	53	6.68[b]
3	217	113	104	3.40[b]
4	60	28	32	11.06[b]
Third Proposal. Roll Call vote to lay Senate Amendments 2473 and 2851 to S. 1731 on the table for the 107th Congress. These amendments would have largely eliminated the new milk pricing programs so voting to lay them on the table means protecting the program as laid out in S. 1731.				
1	20	17	3	22[c]
2	33	28	5	13.20[c]
3 (proposal)	21	21	66	1[c]
4	27	0	27	2.44[c]
Fourth Proposal. Same as for the third proposal.				
1	20	17	3	18.33 [d]
2 (proposal)	33	33	55	1[d]
3	21	5	16	3.44[d]
4	27	0	27	2.04[d]

[a] 162 divided by column 4.
[b] 354 divided by column 4.
[c] 66 divided by column 4.
[d] 55 divided by column 4.

Table A2.10 Legislator Support for Bioengineered Food

Quartile	Pressure Score

First Proposal. The proposal is USDA's action to impose minor regulations on genetically modified foods. Congress never specifically acted on it, so the pressure score is simply the percentage of legislators in each quartile for combined House and Senate.

Quartile	Pressure Score
1	0.28
2	0.21
3	0.40 (proposal)
4	0.11

Quartile/ Position	No. of Legislators in That Quartile	Legislators in That Quartile Supporting the Proposal	Legislators Supporting the Proposal or Their Original Quartile/ Position	Pressure Score

Second Proposal. Data comes from sponsorship and cosponsorship of H.R. 3377 and H.R. 3883 to impose labeling and testing requirements on genetically modified foods. This was for the House of Representatives in the 106th Congress.

Quartile/ Position	No. of Legislators in That Quartile	Legislators in That Quartile Supporting the Proposal	Legislators Supporting the Proposal or Their Original Quartile/ Position	Pressure Score
1 (proposal)	127	127	139	1[a]
2	87	7	80	1.74[a]
3	175	5	170	.82[a]
4	51	0	51	2.73[a]

Third Proposal. Data comes from sponsorship and cosponsorship of S. 2080 and S. 2315 imposing labeling and testing of genetically modified foods. This was for the Senate in the 106th Congress.

Quartile/ Position	No. of Legislators in That Quartile	Legislators in That Quartile Supporting the Proposal	Legislators Supporting the Proposal or Their Original Quartile/ Position	Pressure Score
1 (proposal)	19	19	20	1[b]
2	30	1	29	.69[b]
3	24	0	24	.83[b]
4	29	0	29	.69[b]

Fourth Proposal. From legislation in the House and Senate to overturn FDA's somewhat more stringent rules regarding bioengineered food for the 107th Congress.

Quartile/ Position	No. of Legislators in That Quartile	Legislators in That Quartile Supporting the Proposal	Legislators Supporting the Proposal or Their Original Quartile/ Position	Pressure Score
1	152	5	147	1.15[c]
2 (proposal)	118	118	169	1[c]
3	213	41	172	.98[c]
4	61	5	56	3.02[c]

[a] 139 divided by column 4.
[b] 20 divided by column 4.
[c] 169 divided by column 4.

Table A2.11 Legislator Support for State Wildlife Conservation

Quartile/ Position	No. of Legislators in That Quartile	Legislators in That Quartile Supporting the Proposal	Legislators Supporting the Proposal or Their Original Quartile/ Position	Pressure Score
First Proposal. Data is from sponsorship and cosponsorship of H.R. 701, the original CARA, in the House of Representatives in the 106th Congress.				
1	127	122	5	64.4[a]
2 (proposal)	87	87	322	1[a]
3	175	98	77	4.18[a]
4	51	15	36	8.94[a]
Second Proposal. Data is from the roll call vote, the "ayes," for the so-called CARA-Lite provisions in the Interior Appropriations Bill in the House of Representatives for the 106th Congress.				
1	127	113	14	21[b]
2	87	48	39	7.54[b]
3 (proposal)	175	175	294	1[b]
4	51	5	46	6.39[b]
Third Proposal. Data comes from sponsorship and cosponsorship of H.R. 701 in the House of Representatives in the 107th Congress.				
1 (proposal)	128	128	253	1[c]
2	86	58	28	9.04[c]
3	175	59	116	2.18[c]
4	53	8	45	5.62[c]

[a] 322 divided by column 4.
[b] 294 divided by column 4.
[c] 2534 divided by column 4.

Table A2.12 Legislator Support for Money-Laundering Reform

Quartile	Pressure Score

First Proposal. Although many members of Congress spoke out against the Federal Reserve's Know-Your-Customer rule, there was not any legislation specifically overturning it or any vote cast to overturn it. Pressure scores are just the percentage of legislators in each quartile for the combined 106th Congress.

1	.28
2	.21
3	.40
4	.11 (proposal)

Quartile/ Position	No. of Legislators in That Quartile	Legislators in That Quartile Supporting the Proposal	Legislators Supporting the Proposal or Their Original Quartile/ Position	Pressure Score

Second Proposal. Data comes from sponsorship and cosponsorship of S. 1663 and H.R. 2896 in the 106th Congress.

1	150	4	146	.90[a]
2 (proposal)	116	116	131	1[a]
3	217	11	206	.64[a]
4	60	0	60	2.18[a]

Third Proposal. Data comes from sponsorship and cosponsorship of H.R. 3886 in the House of Representatives in the 106th Congress.

1	127	2	125	1.42[b]
2	87	0	87	2.03[b]
3 (proposal)	175	175	177	1[b]
4	51	0	51	3.47[b]

Fourth Proposal. Data is from sponsorship and cosponsorship of H.R. 3004 in the House of Representatives in the 107th Congress.

1	128	3	125	1.46[c]
2	86	5	81	2.26[c]
3 (proposal)	175	175	183	1[c]
4	53	0	53	3.45[c]

[a] 131 divided by column 4.
[b] 177 divided by column 4.
[c] 183 divided by column 4.

Interest Group Membership Pressure Variable

Table A2.13 provides additional information on the survey questions used to construct the measure for interest group member pressure from a confirmatory factor analysis.

Table A2.13 Factor Analysis of Group Member Pressure

Variable	Factor Loading Variance
Importance of the Issue to Group Members (Q. 2-2)	.36
Cohesion of Group Members' Preferences (Q. 2-3a)	.64
Ease of Finding a Common Member Position (Q. 2-4)	.60
Lack of Flexibility to Support an Alternative (Q. 2-5)	.78
Lack of Member Tolerance for a Compromise (Q. 2-6)	.74

Interest Group Competition Scores

This measure of interest group competition is issue, proposal, and position specific. On each issue, and for each proposal, I calculated the spatial distance between group-ideal positions at one position, say position 1, and those every other position, given that the observed proposal in question at that iteration is also in that direction. If the observed group is at position 2, and the proposal is at position 3, then I identified all other groups lobbying that issue with ideal positions at 3 and 4, but not at 1. Adding position 1 would create a counterpressure away from the bill and potentially result in indeterminate results in an analysis where the dependent variable is whether the group's lobbyist supported the bill (position 1 would be in the opposite direction from 2 if the bill is at 3). Since position 4 is in the same direction, this pull is still valid for the observation. In the case of groups at positions 1 or 4, all groups at positions left or right of them were counted, so this qualification only applies to groups with ideal positions at 2 or 3.

I then calculated the absolute value of the ideological distance between the observed group's ideal position and the ideal position of the identified competing group, and multiplied that absolute value by the natural logarithm of the competing group's annual budget because the competing group's level of resources is supposed to increase the competitors' capacity to counterpressure legislators. I then sum the product for all groups at the positions in the proposal-ward direction away from the observed group and then calculated the average. This creates the observed group's competition pressure score. Every group at the same ideal position in the same iteration has the same competition score. The final scores for each position for each issue are displayed in tables A2.14 through A2.19.

Table A2.14 Interest Group Competition on State Wildlife Conservation

First Proposal		Second Proposal	
Position	Competition Score	Position	Competition Score
1	20.99	1	20.99
2	0	2	18.87
3	23.21	3	0
4	35.90	4	35.90

Third Proposal

Position	Competition Score
1	0
2	16.03
3	23.21
4	35.90

Table A2.15 Interest Group Competition on Drilling for Oil in the Arctic National Wildlife Refuge

First Proposal		Second Proposal	
Position	Competition Score	Position	Competition Score
1	50.35	1	50.35
2	no groups	2	no groups
3	no groups	3	no groups
4	50.08	4	0

Third Proposal

Position	Competition Score
1	50.35
2	no groups
3	no groups
4	50.08

Table A2.16 Interest Group Competition on Bankruptcy Reform

First Proposal		Second Proposal	
Position	*Competition Score*	*Position*	*Competition Score*
1	41.36	1	41.36
2	27.75	2	0
3	16.32	3	31.61
4	0	4	40.79

Third Proposal	
Position	*Competition Score*
1	41.36
2	27.75
3	0
4	40.79

Table A2.17 Interest Group Competition on Money-Laundering Reform

First Proposal		Second Proposal	
Position	*Competition Score*	*Position*	*Competition Score*
1	no groups	1	no groups
2	0	2	0
3	15.42	3	15.42
4	20.45	4	20.45

Third Proposal		Fourth Proposal	
Position	*Competition Score*	*Position*	*Competition Score*
1	no groups	1	no groups
2	25.28	2	25.28
3	0	3	0
4	20.45	4	20.45

Table A2.18 Interest Group Competition on Dairy Pricing

First Proposal

Position	Competition Score
1	33.65
2	23.88
3	15.40
4	0

Second Proposal

Position	Competition Score
1	0
2	15.94
3	23.48
4	28.55

Third Proposal

Position	Competition Score
1	33.65
2	23.88
3	0
4	28.55

Fourth Proposal

Position	Competition Score
1	33.65
2	0
3	23.48
4	28.55

Table A2.19 Interest Group Competition on Bioengineered Food Regulation

First Proposal

Position	Competition Score
1	28.25
2	28.13
3	0
4	35.79

Second Proposal

Position	Competition Score
1	0
2	14.37
3	22.72
4	35.79

Third Proposal

Position	Competition Score
1	0
2	14.37
3	22.72
4	35.79

Fourth Proposal

Position	Competition Score
1	28.25
2	0
3	22.72
4	35.79

REFERENCES

Adams, Rebecca. 2001. "Conservation Bill's Backers Court Bush." *CQ Weekly,* January 27, p. 234.

Ainsworth, Scott H. 1993. "Regulating Lobbyists and Interest Group Influence." *Journal of Politics* 55 (February): 41–56.

———. 1997. "The Role of Legislators in the Determination of Interest Group Influence." *Legislative Studies Quarterly* 22 (November): 517–33.

Ainsworth, Scott H., and Itai Sened. 1993. "The Role of Lobbyists: Entrepreneurs with Two Audiences." *American Journal of Political Science* 37 (August): 834–66.

Alvarez, Lizette. 2001. "House Committee Approves Bush's Plan for Drilling Alaskan Refuge." *New York Times,* July 18.

Alvarez, Lizette, and Joseph Kahn. 2001. "House Republicans Gather Support for Alaska Drilling." *New York Times,* August 1.

Ando, Amy Whritenour. 2003. "Do Interest Groups Compete? An Application to Endangered Species." *Public Choice* 114 (January): 137–59.

Arnold, R. Douglas. 1990. *The Logic of Congressional Action.* New Haven, CT: Yale University Press.

Atlas, Riva D. 2001. "Bill to Alter Bankruptcy Seems to Stall." *New York Times,* October 19.

Austen-Smith, David. 1993. "Information and Influence: Lobbying for Agendas and Votes." *American Journal of Political Science* 37 (August): 799–833.

Austen-Smith, David, and John R. Wright. 1992. "Competitive Lobbying for a Legislator's Vote." *Social Choice and Welfare* 9 (Spring/Summer): 229–57.

———. 1994. "Counteractive Lobbying." *American Journal of Political Science* 38 (February): 25–44.

Axelrod, Robert. 1967. "Conflict of Interest: An Axiomatic Approach." *Journal of Conflict Resolution* 11 (March): 87–99.

———. 1970. *Conflict of Interest.* Chicago: Markham.

———. 1984. *The Evolution of Cooperation.* New York: Basic Books.

Axelrod, Robert, and Douglas Dion. 1988. "The Further Evolution of Cooperation." *Science* 242 (December): 1385–90.

Bacheller, John M. 1977. "Lobbyists and the Legislative Process: The Impact of Environmental Constraints." *American Political Science Review* 71 (March): 252–63.

Bachrach, Peter, and Morton S. Baratz. 1962. "Two Faces of Power." *American Political Science Review* 56 (December): 947–52.

Barboza, David. 1999a. "Biotech Companies Take On Critics of Gene-Altered Foods." *New York Times*, November 12.

———. 1999b. "Is the Sun Setting on Farmers?" *New York Times,* November 28.

Bauer, Raymond A., Ithiel de Sola Pool, and Lewis Anthony Dexter. 1963. *American Business and Public Policy.* New York: Atherton Press.

Baumgartner, Frank R., Jeffrey M. Berry, Marie Hojnacki, David C. Kimball, and Beth L. Leech. 2009. *Lobbying and Policy Change.* Chicago: University of Chicago Press.

Baumgartner, Frank R., and Beth L. Leech. 1996. "The Multiple Ambiguities of 'Counteractive Lobbying.'" *American Journal of Political Science* 40 (May): 521–42.

———. 1998. *Basic Interests.* Princeton, NJ: Princeton University Press.

———. 2001. "Interest Niches and Policy Bandwagons: Patterns of Interest Group Involvement in National Politics." *Journal of Politics* 63 (November): 1191–213.

Beckmann, Matthew N., and Anthony J. McGann. 2008. "Navigating the Legislative Divide." *Journal of Theoretical Politics* 20 (April): 201–20.

Benson, Bruce L. 1981. "Why Are Congressional Committees Dominated by 'High Demand' Legislators? A Comment on Niskanen's View of Bureaucrats and Politicians." *Southern Economic Journal* 48 (July): 68–77.

Bentley, Arthur F. 1908. *The Process of Government.* Chicago: University of Chicago Press.

Berkman, Michael B. 2001. "Legislative Professionalism and the Demand for Groups: The Institutional Context of Interest Population Density." *Legislative Studies Quarterly* 26 (November): 661–79.

Bernstein, Marver. 1955. *Regulating Business by Independent Commission.* Princeton, NJ: Princeton University Press.

Berry, Jeffrey M. 1999. *The New Liberalism: The Rising Power of Citizen Groups.* Washington, DC: Brookings Institution Press.

———. 2002. "Interest Groups and Gridlock." In *Interest Group Politics*, 6th ed., edited by Allan J. Cigler and Burdett A. Loomis. Washington, DC: Congressional Quarterly Press.

Bettelheim, Adriel. 2000. "Reluctant Congress Drafted into Bioengineering Battle." *CQ Weekly*, April 22, p. 938.

Binder, Sarah A. 1999. "The Dynamics of Legislative Gridlock, 1947–96." *American Political Science Review* 93 (September): 519–33.

Binder, Sarah A., Eric D. Lawrence, and Forrest Maltzman. 1999. "Uncovering the Hidden Effect of Party." *Journal of Politics* 61 (August): 815–31.

Binmore, Ken, Ariel Rubinstein, and Asher Wolinsky. 1986. "The Nash Bargaining Solution in Economic Modeling." *RAND Journal of Economics* 17 (Summer): 176–88.

Birnbaum, Jeffrey H. 1992. *The Lobbyists: How Influence Peddlers Work Their Way in Washington.* New York: Random House.

Birnbaum, Jeffrey H., and Alan S. Murray. 1987. *Showdown at Gucci Gulch.* New York: Vintage Books.

Black, Duncan. 1958. *The Theory of Committees and Elections.* Cambridge: Cambridge University Press.

Blackwell, Rob, and Michele Heller. 2001. "Senate Democrats Put Up Fight against Bankruptcy Bill." *New York Times*, February 28.

Botelho, David, and Hilda Kurtz. 2008. "The Introduction of Genetically Modified Food in the United States and the United Kingdom." *Social Science Journal* 45 (March): 13–27.

Bowler, Shaun, and Robert Hanneman. 2006. "Just How Pluralist Is Direct Democracy? The Structure of Interest Group Participation in Ballot Proposition Elections." *Political Research Quarterly* 59 (December): 557–68.

Bowling, Cynthia J., and Margaret R. Ferguson. 2001. "Divided Government, Interest Representation, and Policy Differences: Competing Explanations of Gridlock in the Fifty States." *Journal of Politics* 63 (February): 182–206.

Brady, David, and Craig Volden. 1998. *Revolving Gridlock*. Boulder, CO: Westview Press.

Brody, Jane E. 2000. "Gene Altered Foods: A Case against Panic." *New York Times,* December 5.

Browne, William P. 1988. *Private Interests, Public Policy, and American Agriculture*. Lawrence: University of Kansas Press.

———. 1990. "Organized Interests and Their Issue Niches: A Search for Pluralism in a Policy Domain." *Journal of Politics* 52 (May): 477–509.

———. 2001. *The Failure of National Rural Policy*. Washington, DC: Georgetown University Press.

Burns, James MacGregor. 1963. *The Deadlock of Democracy: Four-Party Politics in America*. Englewood Cliffs, NJ: Prentice Hall.

Carpenter, Daniel P., Kevin M. Esterling, and David M. J. Lazer. 2004. "Friends, Brokers, and Transitivity: Who Informs Whom in Washington Politics?" *Journal of Politics* 66 (February): 224–46.

Cater, Douglass. 1964. *Power in Washington*. New York: Random House.

Church, Thomas W., and Robert T. Nakamura. 1993. *Cleaning Up the Mess: Implementation Strategies in Superfund*. Washington, DC: Brookings Institution Press.

Clark, Peter B., and James Q. Wilson. 1961. "Incentive Systems: A Theory of Organizations." *Administrative Science Quarterly* 6 (September): 129–66.

Clausen, Aage R. 1973. *How Congressmen Decide: A Policy Focus*. New York: St. Martin's Press.

Clemens, Elisabeth S. 1997. *The People's Lobby: Organizational Innovation and the Rise of Interest Group Politics in the United States, 1890–1925*. Chicago: University of Chicago Press.

Coates, Dennis, Jac C. Heckelman, and Bonnie Wilson. 2010. "Special Interest Groups and Growth." *Public Choice*, in press.

Costain, Anne N. 1981. "Representing Women: The Transition from Social Movement to Interest Group." *Western Political Quarterly* 34 (March): 100–113.

Costain, W. Douglas, and Anne N. Costain. 1981. "Interest Groups as Policy Aggregators in the Legislative Process." *Polity* 14 (Winter): 249–72.

Cox, Gary W., and Mathew D. McCubbins. 1993. *Legislative Leviathan: Party Government in the House*. Berkeley: University of California Press.

———. 2002. "Agenda Power in the U.S. House of Representatives." In *Party, Process, and Political Change in Congress*, edited by David W. Brady and Mathew D. McCubbins. Stanford, CA: Stanford University Press.

Cushman, John H. 1994. "Environmental Lobby Beats Tactical Retreat." *New York Times,* March 25.

Cutler, Lloyd N. 1988. "Some Reflections about Divided Government." *Presidential Studies Quarterly* 18 (Summer): 485–92.

Dahl, Robert A. 1956. *A Preface to Democratic Theory*. Chicago: University of Chicago Press.

———. 1961. *Who Governs?* New Haven, CT: Yale University Press.

Danielian, Lucig H., and Benjamin I. Page. 1994. "The Heavenly Chorus: Interest Group Voices on TV News." *American Journal of Political Science* 38 (November): 1056–78.

Dao, James. 1999. "Congress Weighs Bill to Expand the Cartel Letting Northeast Dairy Farmers Set Prices." *New York Times*, May 2.

Davidson, Roger H. 1981. "Subcommittee Government: New Channels for Policymaking." In *The New Congress*, edited by Thomas E. Mann and Norman J. Ornstein. Washington, DC: American Enterprise Institute.

———. 1990. "The Advent of the Modern Congress: The Legislative Reorganization Act of 1946." *Legislative Studies Quarterly* 15 (August): 357–73.

Davis, Julie Hirschfield, and Suzanne Dougherty. 2001. "Spilled Milk in Vermont." *CQ Weekly,* May 26, p. 1247.

Deering, Christopher J., and Steven S. Smith. 1997. *Committees in Congress.* 3rd ed. Washington, DC: Congressional Quarterly Press.

Dodd, Lawrence C. 1977. "Congress and the Quest for Power." In *Congress Reconsidered*, edited by Lawrence C. Dodd and Bruce I. Oppenheimer. New York: Praeger.

Domhoff, William G. 1967. *Who Rules America?* Englewood Cliffs, NJ: Prentice Hall.

———. 1978. *Who Really Rules?* Santa Monica, CA: Goodyear Publishing.

Dougherty, John. 2009. "Audubon Feathers Fly in Arizona: Huge Mine Proposal Deepens Schism between State's Green Groups." *High Country News* 12 (October): 7, 25.

Downs, Anthony. 1957. *An Economic Theory of Democracy.* New York: Harper & Row.

Drew, Elizabeth. 1999. *The Corruption of American Politics: What Went Wrong and Why.* Secaucus, NJ: Birch Lane Press.

Edelman, Murray. 1964. *The Symbolic Uses of Politics.* Urbana: University of Illinois Press.

Epstein, David, and Sharyn O'Halloran. 1996. "Divided Government and the Design of Administrative Procedures: A Formal Model and Empirical Test." *Journal of Politics* 58 (May): 373–97.

Fenno, Richard F., Jr. 1973. *Congressmen in Committees.* Boston: Little, Brown.

Finnemore, Martha, and Kathryn Sikkink. 1998. "International Norm Dynamics and Political Change." *International Organization* 52 (Autumn): 887–917.

Fiorina, Morris. 1996. *Divided Government.* 2nd ed. Boston: Allyn & Bacon.

Foerstel, Karen. 1999. "Accepting the Inevitable, Foes of New Milk Price Policy Drop Effort to Tie Up Senate." *CQ Weekly*, November 20, p. 2785.

Fowler, James H. 2006. "Connecting the Congress: A Study of Cosponsorship Networks." *Political Analysis* 14 (Autumn): 456–87.

Friedman, Milton, and Rose Friedman. 1979. *Free to Choose.* San Diego, CA: Harcourt.

Frymer, Paul, Thomas P. Kim, and Terri L. Bimes. 1997. "Party Elites, Ideological Voters, and Divided Party Government." *Legislative Studies Quarterly* 22 (May): 195–216.

Gais, Thomas L., Mark A. Peterson, and Jack L. Walker Jr. 1984. "Interest Groups, Iron Triangles, and Representative Institutions in American National Government." *British Journal of Political Science* 14 (April): 161–85.

Gaskell, G., Bauer, M., Durant, J., and Allum, N. 1999. "Worlds Apart? The Reception of Genetically Modified Foods in Europe and the U.S." *Science* 285 (July 5426): 384–88.

Goldschmidt, Kathy, and Leslie Ochreiter. 2008. *Communicating with Congress: How the Internet Has Changed Citizen Engagement.* Washington, DC: Congressional Management Foundation.

Gray, Virginia, and David Lowery. 1995. "Interest Representation and Democratic Gridlock." *Legislative Studies Quarterly* 20 (November): 531–52.

———. 1996. *The Population Ecology of Interest Representation.* Ann Arbor: University of Michigan Press.

———. 1997. "Life in a Niche: Mortality Anxiety among Organized Interests in the American States." *Political Research Quarterly* 50 (March): 25–47.

———. 2004. "A Neopluralist Perspective on Research on Organized Interests." *Political Research Quarterly* 57 (March): 163–75.

Graziano, Luigi. 2001. *Lobbying, Pluralism, and Democracy.* New York: Palgrave Macmillan.

Greenblatt, Alan. 1998. "Agriculture Spending Bill Gets Fast Committee Approval, but Floor Fights Are Likely." *CQ Weekly,* June 13, p. 1618.

———. 1999a. "Dairy States See Pricing Plan as a Glass Half-Empty." *CQ Weekly,* April 24, p. 947.

———. 1999b. "Lawmakers Jostle for Advantage in Dairy Policy Debate." *CQ Weekly,* June 26, p. 1533.

———. 1999c. "Senate Prepares for Struggles over Farm Aid, Dairy Policy as Agriculture Bill Heads to Floor." *CQ Weekly,* June 19, p. 1471.

Greenwald, Carol S. 1977. *Group Power: Lobbying and Public Policy.* New York: Praeger.

Groseclose, Tim, and Nolan McCarty. 2001. "The Politics of Blame: Bargaining before an Audience." *American Journal of Political Science* 45 (January): 100–119.

Grossman, Gene M., and Elhanan Helpman. 2001. *Special Interest Politics.* Cambridge, MA: MIT Press.

Hall, Richard L., and Alan V. Deardorff. 2006. "Lobbying as Legislative Subsidy." *American Political Science Review* 100 (February): 69–84.

Hall, Richard L., and Frank W. Wayman. 1990. "Buying Time: Moneyed Interests and the Mobilization of Bias in Congressional Committees." *American Political Science Review* 84 (September): 797–820.

Hansen, John Mark. 1991. *Gaining Access: Congress and the Farm Lobby, 1919–1981.* Chicago: University of Chicago Press.

Healey, Jon. 1993. "Energy Taxes Offer Clinton a Choice of Enemies." *CQ Weekly,* January 30, p. 214.

Heaney, Michael T. 2004. "Outside the Issue Niche: The Multidimensionality of Interest Group Identity." *American Politics Research* 32 (November): 611–51.

———. 2006. "Brokering Health Policy: Coalitions, Parties, and Interest Group Influence." *Journal of Health Politics, Policy, and Law* 31 (October): 887–944.

Hebert, H. Josef. 2002. "Oil Companies Largely Silent on Alaska." Associated Press. Available from Arctic Power at www.anwr.org/features/oil-silent.htm.

Heclo, Hugh. 1978. "Issue Networks and the Executive Establishment." In *The New American Political System,* edited by Anthony King. Washington, DC: American Enterprise Institute.

Heinz, John P., Edward O. Laumann, Robert L. Nelson, and Robert H. Salisbury. 1993. *The Hollow Core: Private Interests in National Policymaking.* Cambridge, MA: Harvard University Press.

Heitshusen, Valerie. 2000. "Interest Group Lobbying and U.S. House Decentralization: Linking Informational Focus to Committee Hearing Appearances." *Political Research Quarterly* 53 (March): 151–76.

Hernandez, Raymond. 2001. "Senator's Defection May Doom Milk Bill." *New York Times,* May 16.

Herring, E. Pendleton. 1929. *Group Representation before Congress.* Washington, DC: Brookings Institution Press.

Herrnson, Paul S. 2009. "The Role of Party Organizations, Party-Connected Committees, and Party Allies in Elections." *Journal of Politics* 71 (October): 1207–24.

Hinich, Melvin J., and Michael C. Munger. 1997. *Analytical Politics*. New York: Cambridge University Press.

Hirschman, Albert O. 1970. *Exit, Voice, and Loyalty*. Cambridge, MA: Harvard University Press.

Hojnacki, Marie. 1997. "Interest Groups' Decisions to Join Alliances or Work Alone." *American Journal of Political Science* 41 (January): 61–87.

———. 1998. "Organized Interests' Advocacy Behavior in Alliances." *Political Research Quarterly* 51 (June): 437–59.

Hojnacki, Marie, and David C. Kimball. 1998. "Organized Interests and the Decision of Whom to Lobby in Congress." *American Political Science Review* 92 (December): 775–90.

Holyoke, Thomas T. 2003. "Choosing Battlegrounds: Interest Group Lobbying across Multiple Venues." *Political Research Quarterly* 56 (September): 325–36.

———. 2004. "Community Mobilization and Credit: The Impact of Nonprofits and Social Capital on Community Reinvestment Act Lending." *Social Science Quarterly* 85 (March): 187–205.

———. 2008. "Interest Group Competition and Cooperation at Legislative Hearings." *Congress and the Presidency* 35 (Autumn): 17–38.

———. 2009. "Interest Group Competition and Coalition Formation." *American Journal of Political Science* 53 (April): 360–75.

Hosansky, David. 1996a. "Agriculture: Snare of Competing Interests Entangles Dairy Debate." *CQ Weekly*, March 16, p. 691.

———. 1996b. "Farm Policy on the Brink of a New Direction." *CQ Weekly*, March 23, p. 786.

———. 1996c. "House and Senate Assembly Conflicting Farm Bills." *CQ Weekly*, February 3, p. 295.

———. 1997a. "Potent Forces Brace for Battle on Bankruptcy Law Overhaul." *CQ Weekly*, October 18, p. 2534.

———. 1997b. "Senate Bill Would Require More Debtor Repayment." *CQ Weekly*, October 25, p. 2589.

———. 2001. "Cultivating Confidence." *CQ Weekly*, April 28, p. 17.

Hosansky, David, and Lori Nitschke. 1998. "Bankruptcy Law Rewrite Hangs in the Balance as Senate Democrats Balk." *CQ Weekly*, October 10, p. 2746.

Hotelling, Harold. 1929. "Stability in Competition." *Economic Journal* 39 (March): 41–57.

Howell, William, Scott Adler, Charles Cameron, and Charles Riemann. 2000. "Divided Government and the Legislative Productivity of Congress, 1945–94." *Legislative Studies Quarterly* 25 (May): 285–312.

Huitt, Ralph K. 1954. "The Congressional Committee: A Case Study." *American Political Science Review* 48 (June): 340–65.

Hula, Kevin W. 1999. *Lobbying Together: Interest Group Coalitions in Legislative Politics*. Washington, DC: Georgetown University Press.

Hundley, Norris. 2001. *The Great Thirst: Californians and Water, a History*. Berkeley: University of California Press.

Hurwitz, Mark S., Roger J. Moiles, and David W. Rohde. 2001. "Distributive and Partisan Issues in Agriculture Policy in the 104th House." *American Political Science Review* 95 (December): 911–22.

Jewell, Malcolm E., and Chu Chi-Hung. 1974. "Membership Movement and Committee Attractiveness in the U.S. House of Representatives, 1963–1971." *American Journal of Political Science* 18 (May): 433–41.

Jones, Bryan D. 2001. *Politics and the Architecture of Choice.* Chicago: University of Chicago Press.

Jones, Bryan D., Tracy Sulkin, and Heather A. Larson. 2003. "Policy Punctuations in American Political Institutions." *American Political Science Review* 97 (February): 151–70.

Jones, Bryan D., James L. True, and Frank R. Baumgartner. 1997. "Does Incrementalism Stem from Political Consensus or from Institutional Gridlock?" *American Journal of Political Science* 41 (October): 1319–39.

Kelly, Sean Q. 1993. "Divided We Govern? A Reassessment." *Polity* 25 (Spring): 475–84.

Key, V. O., Jr. 1942. *Politics, Parties, and Pressure Groups.* New York: Crowell.

Kingdon, John W. 1973. *Congressmen's Voting Decisions.* Ann Arbor: University of Michigan Press.

———. 1984. *Agendas, Alternatives, and Public Policies.* Boston: Little, Brown.

Kirchhoff, Sue. 1999. "WTO's Changes Too Slow for Troubled U.S. Farmers." *CQ Weekly,* December 4, p. 2921.

Knoke, David. 1986. "Associations and Interest Groups." *Annual Review of Sociology* 12: 1–21.

Kollman, Ken. 1997. "Inviting Friends to Lobby: Interest Groups, Ideological Bias, and Congressional Committees." *American Journal of Political Science* 41 (April): 519–44.

———. 1998. *Outside Lobbying.* Princeton, NJ: Princeton University Press.

Kollman, Ken, John Miller, and Scott Page. 2000. "Decentralization and the Search for Policy Solutions." *Journal of Law, Economics, and Organization* 16 (April): 102–28.

Krehbiel, Keith. 1990. "Are Congressional Committees Composed of Preference Outliers?" *American Political Science Review* 84 (March): 149–63.

———. 1991. *Information and Legislative Organization.* Ann Arbor: University of Michigan Press.

———. 1993. "Where's the Party?" *British Journal of Political Science* 23 (April): 235–66.

———. 1998. *Pivotal Politics: A Theory of U.S. Lawmaking.* Chicago: University of Chicago Press.

Lacireno-Paquet, Natalie, and Thomas T. Holyoke. 2006. "Moving Forward or Sliding Backward? The Evolution of Charter School Policies in Michigan and the District of Columbia." *Educational Policy* 21 (January): 185–214.

Lasswell, Harold D. 1936. *Politics: Who Gets What, When, How?* New York: Meridian.

Latham, Earl. 1952. "The Group Basis of Politics: Notes for a Theory." *American Political Science Review* 46 (June): 376–97.

Laumann, Edward O., and David Knoke. 1987. *The Organizational State.* Madison: University of Wisconsin Press.

Leech, Beth L., and Frank R. Baumgartner. 1998. "Lobbying Friends and Foes in Washington." In *Interest Group Politics,* 5th ed., edited by Allan J. Cigler and Burdett A. Loomis. Washington, DC: Congressional Quarterly Press.

Leech, Beth L., Frank R. Baumgartner, Timothy M. La Pira, and Nicholas A. Semanko. 2005. "Drawing Lobbyists to Washington: Government Activity and the Demand for Advocacy." *Political Research Quarterly* 58 (March): 19–30.

Leyden, Kevin W. 1995. "Interest Group Resources and Testimony at Congressional Hearings." *Legislative Studies Quarterly* 20 (August): 431–39.

Lohmann, Susanne. 2003. "Representative Government and Special Interest Politics." *Journal of Theoretical Politics* 15 (July): 299–319.

Lowery, David, and Virginia Gray. 1994. "The Nationalization of State Interest Group System Density and Diversity." *Social Science Quarterly* 75 (March): 369–77.

Lowery, David, Virginia Gray, Jennifer Wolak, Erik Godwin, and Whitt Kilburn. 2005. "Reconsidering the Counter-Mobilization Hypothesis: Health Policy Lobbying in the American States." *Political Behavior* 27 (June): 99–132.

Lowi, Theodore J. 1964. "American Business, Public Policy, Case-Studies, and Political Theory." *World Politics* 16 (July): 677–715.

———. 1969. *The End of Liberalism*. New York: W. W. Norton.

———. 1972. "Four Systems of Policy, Politics, and Choice." *Public Administration Review* 32 (July): 298–310.

Lubell, Mark. 2007. "Familiarity Breeds Trust: Collective Action in a Policy Domain." *Journal of Politics* 69 (February): 237–50.

Luttbeg, Norman R., and Harmon Zeigler. 1966. "Attitude Consensus and Conflict in an Interest Group: An Assessment of Cohesion." *American Political Science Review* 60 (September): 655–66.

Madison, James. 1961. *Federalist No. 10*. In *The Federalist Papers* by Alexander Hamilton, James Madison, and John Jay, pp. 77–84. Ed. Clinton Rossiter. New York: Mentor.

———. 1961. *Federalist No. 51*. In *The Federalist Papers* by Alexander Hamilton, James Madison, and John Jay, pp. 320–25. Ed. Clinton Rossiter. New York: Mentor.

Maltzman, Forrest, James F. Spriggs II, and Paul J. Wahlbeck. 1999. *Crafting Law on the Supreme Court*. New York: Cambridge University Press.

Mansbridge, Jane J. 1992. "A Deliberative Theory of Interest Representation." In *The Politics of Interests*, edited by Mark P. Petracca. Boulder, CO: Westview Press.

Martinez, Gebe. 2001. "Vermont's Dairy Compact Fallback Plan Generates Broad Opposition." *CQ Weekly*, December 1, p. 2842.

Matthews, Donald R. 1960. *U.S. Senators and Their World*. New York: Vintage Books.

May, Peter J., Joshua Sapotichne, and Samuel Workman. 2006. "Policy Coherence and Policy Domains." *Policy Studies Journal* 34 (August): 381–403.

Mayhew, David R. 1974. *Congress: The Electoral Connection*. New Haven, CT: Yale University Press.

———. 1991. *Divided We Govern*. New Haven, CT: Yale University Press.

McConnell, Grant. 1966. *Private Power and American Democracy*. New York: Random House.

McCool, Daniel. 1990. "Subgovernments as Determinants of Political Viability." *Political Science Quarterly* 105 (Summer): 269–93.

McFarland, Andrew S. 1984. *Common Cause*. Chatham, NJ: Chatham House.

———. 1993. *Cooperative Pluralism: The National Coal Policy Experiment*. Lawrence: University of Kansas Press.

———. 2004. *Neopluralism: The Evolution of Political Process Theory*. Lawrence: University of Kansas Press.

McKay, Amy. 2008. "A Simple Way of Estimating Interest Group Ideology." *Public Choice* 136 (July): 69–86.

McKay, Amy, and Susan Webb Yackee. 2007. "Interest Group Competition on Federal Agency Rules." *American Politics Research* 35 (May): 336–57.

Meyer, David S. 2004. "Protest and Political Opportunities." *Annual Review of Sociology* 30: 125–45.

Michaelis, Laura. 1994. "Senate Makes a Breakthrough in Bankruptcy Overhaul." *CQ Weekly*, April 23, p. 993.

Michels, Robert. 1959. *Political Parties*. New York: Dover.

Milbrath, Lester W. 1960. "Lobbying as a Communication Process." *Public Opinion Quarterly* 24 (Spring): 32–53.

———. 1963. *The Washington Lobbyists*. Chicago: Rand McNally.

Mills, C. Wright. 1956. *The Power Elite*. New York: Oxford University Press.

Moe, Terry M. 1980. *The Organization of Interests*. Chicago: University of Chicago Press.

Monoson, Ted. 2000. "Swollen Conservation Bill Faces Real Fight in Senate." *CQ Weekly*, May 13, p. 1095.

Moss, Alan L. 2008. *Selling Out America's Democracy: How Lobbyists, Special Interest Groups, and Campaign Finance Undermine the Will of the People*. New York: Praeger.

Nash, John F., Jr. 1953. "Two-Person Cooperative Games." *Econometrica* 21 (January): 128–40.

Nitschke, Lori. 1998. "Bankruptcy Overhaul Bill Faces House Democratic Blockade; Senate Takes Up Narrower Measures." *CQ Weekly*, April 25, p. 107.

———. 1999. "House Passes Bankruptcy Overhaul Bill." *CQ Weekly*, May 8, p. 1082.

Nownes, Anthony J. 2000. "Policy Conflict and the Structure of Interest Communities: A Comparative State Analysis." *American Politics Quarterly* 28 (July): 309–27.

Odegard, Peter H. 1928. *Pressure Politics: The Story of the Anti-Saloon League*. New York: Columbia University Press.

Olson, Mancur, Jr. 1965. *The Logic of Collective Action*. Cambridge, MA: Harvard University Press.

———. 1982. *The Rise and Decline of Nations*. New Haven, CT: Yale University Press.

Ota, Alan K. 2000a. "Deal on Democrats' Amendments Clears Way for Senate to Vote on Bankruptcy Overhaul Bill." *CQ Weekly*, January 29, p. 189.

———. 2000b. "Leaders Work behind Scenes to Settle Differences on Bankruptcy Overhaul Bill." *CQ Weekly*, May 27, p. 1268.

———. 2000c. "Revived Bankruptcy Bill Clears Senate by Strong Margin." *CQ Weekly*, December 9, p. 2811.

Page, Benjamin I., and Robert Y. Shapiro. 1983. "Effects of Public Opinion on Policy." *American Political Science Review* 77 (March): 175–90.

Page, Scott E. 2008. "Uncertainty, Difficulty, and Complexity." *Journal of Theoretical Politics* 20 (April): 115–49.

Palmer, Elizabeth A. 1994. "Agriculture: Bill to Alter Milk Pricing Advances in House." *CQ Weekly*, October 8, p. 2879.

Parks, Daniel J., and Pherabe Kolb. 1999. "Bankruptcy Bills Move in Partisan Fits and Starts." *CQ Weekly*, April 24, p. 961.

Peltzman, Samuel. 1976. "Towards a More General Theory of Regulation." *Journal of Law and Economics* 19 (April): 211–40.

Peterson, Paul. 1992. "The Rise and Fall of Special Interest Politics." *Political Science Quarterly* 105 (Winter): 539–56.

Petracca, Mark P., ed. 1992. *The Politics of Interests: Interest Groups Transformed*. Boulder, CO: Westview Press.

Plott, Charles R. 1991. "Will Economics Become an Experimental Science?" *Southern Economic Journal* 57 (April): 901–19.

Plungis, Jeff. 2000. "GOP Lashes Clinton Energy Policy as OPEC Eases Quotas Modestly."*CQ Weekly*, April 1, p. 761.

Poole, Keith T. 1998. "Recovering Basic Space from a Set of Issue Scales." *American Journal of Political Science* 42 (July): 954–93.

Poole, Keith T., and Howard Rosenthal. 1997. *Congress: A Political Economic History of Roll Call Voting*. New York: Oxford University Press.

Pope, Charles. 1999. "Bills to Conserve Open Land Take Tentative Root on Hill." *CQ Weekly* June 19, p. 1435.

———. 2000a. "Consumer Worries Force Farmers to Rethink Engineered Seed." *CQ Weekly*, April 22, p. 938.

———. 2000b. "Tapping Fears about Fuel Supply, Senate Votes to Allow Drilling for Oil in Alaskan Wilderness." *CQ Weekly*, April 8, p. 836.

Price, David E. 1978. "Policy Making in Congressional Committees: The Impact of 'Environmental Factors.'" *American Political Science Review* 72 (June): 569–71.

Rauch, Jonathan. 1995. *Demosclerosis*. New York: Times Books.

Ripley, Randall B., and Grace A. Franklin. 1980. *Congress, the Bureaucracy, and Public Policy*. Homewood, IL: Dorsey.

Rosenstone, Steven J., and John Mark Hansen. 1993. *Mobilization, Participation, and Democracy in America*. New York: Macmillan.

Ross, Robert L. 1970. "Relations among National Interest Groups." *Journal of Politics* 32 (February): 96–114.

Rothenberg, Lawrence S. 1992. *Linking Citizens to Government: Interest Group Politics at Common Cause*. New York: Cambridge University Press.

Rubinstein, Ariel. 1982. "Perfect Equilibrium in a Bargaining Model." *Econometrica* 50 (January): 97–100.

Sabatier, Paul A. 1988. "An Advocacy Coalition Framework of Policy Change and the Role of Policy-Oriented Learning Therein." *Policy Sciences* 21(2): 129–68.

———. 1992. "Interest Group Membership and Organization: Multiple Theories." In *The Politics of Interests*, edited by Mark Petracca. Boulder, CO: Westview Press.

Sabatier, Paul A., Will Focht, Mark Lubell, and Zev Trachtenberg. 2005. *Swimming Upstream: Collaborative Approaches to Watershed Management*. Cambridge, MA: MIT Press.

Sabatier, Paul A., and Hank C. Jenkins-Smith. 1993. *Policy Change and Learning: An Advocacy Coalition Approach*. Boulder, CO: Westview Press.

Sabatier, Paul A., and Susan M. McLaughlin. 1990. "Belief Congruence between Interest-Group Leaders and Members: An Empirical Analysis of Three Theories and a Suggested Synthesis." *Journal of Politics* 52 (August): 914–35.

Salisbury, Robert H. 1969. "An Exchange Theory of Interest Groups." *Midwest Journal of Political Science* 13 (February): 1–32.

———. 1984. "Interest Representation: The Dominance of Institutions." *American Political Science Review* 78 (March): 64–76.

———. 1990. "The Paradox of Interest Groups in Washington: More Groups, Less Clout." In *The New American Political System*, 2nd ed., edited by Anthony J. King. Washington, DC: American Enterprise Institute.

———. 2000. "Bentley Was Right?" Paper presented at the Annual Meeting of the American Political Science Association. Chicago, IL.

Santiago, Nellie R., Thomas T. Holyoke, and Ross D. Levi. 1998. "Turning David and Goliath into the Odd Couple: The Community Reinvest Act and Community Development Financial Institutions." *Journal of Law and Policy* 6 (Fall): 571–651.

Schattschneider, E. E. 1942. *Party Government*. New York: Holt, Rinehart, and Winston.

———. 1960. *The Semisovereign People*. New York: Holt, Rinehart, and Winston.

Schlozman, Kay Lehman, and John T. Tierney. 1986. *Organized Interests and American Democracy*. New York: Harper & Row.

Schneider, Keith. 1993. "U.S. Approves Use of Drug to Raise Milk Production." *New York Times*, November 6.

———. 1994. "Grocers Challenge Use of New Drug for Milk Output." *New York Times*, February 4.

Seelye, Katharine Q. 1998. "Senate Votes to Curb Bankruptcy Abuse by Consumers." *New York Times*, September 24.

Seiberg, Jaret. 1997. "Lenders Coalition Urges Congress to Deep-Six Bankruptcy Proposals." *New York Times*, July 15.

———. 1999. "Rush to Pass Bankruptcy Reform Runs into Trouble." *New York Times*, March 12.

Shepsle, Kenneth A. 1979. "Institutional Arrangements and Equilibrium in Multidimensional Voting Models." *American Journal of Political Science* 23 (February): 27–59.

Shepsle, Kenneth A., and Barry R. Weingast. 1987. "The Institutional Foundations of Committee Power." *American Political Science Review* 81 (March): 85–104.

———. 1994. "Positive Theories of Congressional Institutions." *Legislative Studies Quarterly* 19 (May): 149–79.

Sigelman, Lee, Paul J. Wahlbeck, and Emmet H. Buell Jr. 1997. "Vote Choice and the Preference for Divided Government: Lessons of 1992." *American Journal of Political Science* 41 (July): 879–94.

Smith, Richard A. 1984. "Advocacy, Interpretation, and Influence in the U.S. Congress." *American Political Science Review* 78 (March): 44–63.

———. 1995. "Interest Group Influence in the U.S. Congress." *Legislative Studies Quarterly* 20 (February): 89–139.

Solowiej, Lisa A., and Paul M. Collins Jr. 2009. "Counteractive Lobbying in the U.S. Supreme Court." *American Politics Research* 37 (July): 670–99.

Stanley, Harold W. and Richard G. Niemi. 2010. *Vital Statistics on American Politics, 2009–2010*. Washington, DC: Congressional Quarterly Press.

Stigler, George J. 1971. "The Economic Theory of Regulation." *Bell Journal of Economics and Management Science* 2 (Spring): 3–21.

———. 1972. "Economic Competition and Political Competition." *Public Choice* 13 (Fall): 91–106.

Sundquist, James L. 1988. "Needed: A Political Theory for the New Era of Coalition Government in the United States." *Political Science Quarterly* 103 (Winter): 613–35.

Thomas, Clive S., and Ronald J. Hrebenar. 1992. "Changing Patterns of Interest Group Activity: A Regional Perspective." In *The Politics of Interests*, edited by Mark P. Petracca. Boulder, CO: Westview Press.

Thompson, Margaret Susan. 1986. *The Spider Web: Lobbying in the Age of Grant*. Ithaca, NY: Cornell University Press.

Tichenor, Daniel J., and Richard A. Harris. 2002. "Organized Interests and American Political Development." *Political Science Quarterly* 117 (Winter): 587–612.

Truman, David B. 1951. *The Governmental Process*. New York: Alfred A. Knopf.

Victor, Jennifer Nicoll. 2007. "Strategic Lobbying: Demonstrating How Legislative Context Affects Interest Groups' Lobbying Tactics." *American Politics Research* 35 (November): 826–45.

Walker, Jack L., Jr. 1983. "The Origin and Maintenance of Interest Groups in America." *American Political Science Review* 77 (June): 390–406.

Weinstein, Michael M. 1999. "Bringing Markets to Milk." *New York Times*, April 11.

Weiss, Rick. 2006. "Americans Still Uncomfortable with Biotech Foods." *Washington Post*, December 6.

Wiegand, Steve. 2009. "Water Package: Sealing the Deal." *Sacramento Bee*, November 29.

Wilson, James Q. 1973. *Political Organizations*. Princeton, NJ: Princeton University Press.

Wiseman, Alan E., and John R. Wright. 2008. "The Legislative Median and Partisan Policy."*Journal of Theoretical Politics* 20 (January): 5–29.

Wright, John R. 1996. *Interest Groups and Congress*. Boston: Allyn & Bacon.

INDEX

AARP, 28, 56
access, information theory of, 29,
    142–43
"access set," 29–32
"adversary democracy," 138–39, 142
AFL-CIO, 55, 56
agriculture policy domain. *See also*
    bioengineered food regulation; dairy
    pricing subsidies
  coalitions and, 79–80, 87–92, 96
  distributive policy and, 42
  gridlock and, 118–23
  interest group competition on, 176t
  interest group lobbyist interview questions
    on, 150–52
  issue salience in, 46
  legislator support on, 169–70t
  lobbyist conflict and, 97–99
  responding interest groups in, 149
  spatial distribution of interest groups on,
    by annual budgets, 160f
    by PAC contributions, 161–62f
  spatial positions of interest groups and issue
    iterations, 157–58t
  special interests in, 10
Alaska Oil and Gas Association, 65–66
Alliance for Better Foods, 90
"alternate set," 34, 83–84, 85
American Audubon Society, 15, 53, 66
American Bankers Association, 49,
    106
American Council of Life Insurers,
    134

American Farm Bureau Federation, 14, 49, 55,
    119–22, 127
American Land Rights Association,
    65
American Petroleum Institute, 49, 59,
    65–66
America's Community Bankers, 83, 108,
    134
Arctic National Wildlife Refuge,
    oil drilling in
  committee lobbying and, 105–6
  contributions and, 56
  interest group competition on, 174t
  interest group lobbyist interview questions
    on, 154
  legislator support on, 168t
  lobbyist conflict and, 62–63, 65–67
  overview of, 46
  polarization on, 53
  responding interest groups in, 150
  spatial distribution of interest groups on, by
    annual budgets, 161f
    PAC contributions, 162f
  spatial positions of interest groups and issue
    iterations, 156t, 159f
Arctic Power, 55, 65, 66
Aspinall, Wayne, 101
Associated Milk Producers, 119–20, 121, 122,
    127, 130
attention, public. *See* salience
Audubon Society, 15, 53, 66
Audubon Society of Arizona, 24
Axelrod, Robert, 86, 145